STRUCTURAL
HUMAN
ECOLOGY

STRUCTURAL HUMAN ECOLOGY

New Essays in Risk, Energy, and Sustainability

EDITED BY
THOMAS DIETZ AND ANDREW JORGENSON

Washington State University Press
Pullman, Washington

Washington State University Press
PO Box 645910
Pullman, Washington 99164-5910
Phone: 800-354-7360
Fax: 509-335-8568
Email: wsupress@wsu.edu
Website: wsupress.wsu.edu

Library of Congress Cataloging-in-Publication Data available from the publisher.

Fine Quality Books from the Pacific Northwest

Table of Contents

Section IV
Directions for the Future

Preface

A PERSONAL THANKS TO GENE

Paul Ehrlich

I HAVE BEEN A FAN OF GENE ROSA since he became one of a team (along with Tom Dietz and Richard York) who were among the pioneers in the social sciences taking a serious look at the environmental dimensions of the human predicament. This was especially important for humanity, since it is clear that while environmental scientists have long been aware that humanity is on a course potentially fatal to civilization, we don't understand enough about human behavior. In short, the ball is now in the court of the social sciences, and Gene was one of the first to pick it up. His work, I must admit,

Gene Rosa

has pleased me personally because he was one of the first to pay attention to the I=PAT formulation that John Holdren, Anne Ehrlich, and I developed in the 1970s, and extend it with his colleagues into the STIRPAT analyses. Gene and his colleagues were among the first social scientists to realize that the old social science model—human societies acting on an essentially constant physical-chemical environmental stage—was totally flawed as the world entered the Anthropocene. They saw that the human socio-economic-political complex adaptive system (CAS) was interacting strongly with the biosphere CAS, with potentially catastrophic results induced in the biosphere system by the human system.

Gene's group realized that social science and environmental science could no longer remain separate if a successful evidence-based system of inquiry was to be developed to deal with the growing human population-resource-environment-equity predicament. That led the group to press their STIRPAT work, actually measuring such things as the impacts of growing populations and expanding consumption on environmental variables, and refuting a variety of claims that those impacts will be handily reduced by economic factors and technological innovation. Gene was also involved in work to improve global risk governance, finding ways to bring science to bear on risk-related decision making, especially in connection with risky technologies and how society should deal with the risks related to future natural disasters. His careful analyses of the difference between the ontology and epistemology of risk, and of cultural differences in approach to risk, have been a major factor in clarifying thought in the area.

The importance of Gene's concerns and approaches has been underlined recently by the mounting problem of climate disruption. The science of climate change has been studied intensively by international groups of scholars, and a broad consensus reached within the scientific community that the risks could include a dissolution of society as we know it—a "quite possible-infinity" problem—one where the chances of occurrence are far above zero, but if it does happen the results are utterly catastrophic (near infinitely bad). That consensus has been as widely broadcast by scientists as possible, but ignorance and distorted coverage by the media have prevented the magnitude of the problem from reaching most of the public and decision makers. That failure, linked with a determined disinformation campaign financed by, among others, the oil and coal industries, has, especially in the United States, resulted in essentially no preparation for likely coming disasters.

In the face of such developments, Gene became a central figure in the MAHB (the *Millennium Alliance for Humanity and the Biosphere*—mahb. stanford.edu). The MAHB has been dedicated to focusing the attention of the academic community (especially the social sciences) on solving the human predicament and to attempting to unite the efforts of the extremely diverse but uncoordinated elements of civil society trying to deal with various aspects of the colossal risks we face. Gene worked tirelessly in this cause, even while struggling with an extremely serious disease. This book is a small indication of the debt I, and his other colleagues, owe him. He was a great scientist and a great friend.

I. Theoretical and Conceptual Issues

CHAPTER 1

Introduction to
Structural Human Ecology

Thomas Dietz, Michigan State University
Andrew K. Jorgenson, University of Utah

THE TERM "HUMAN ECOLOGY" has seen myriad uses. But the most straightforward approach is simply to define human ecology as the study of the inter-relations between humans and their biophysical environment. In sociology, the term human ecology is most closely associated with earlier "Chicago School" scholars who emphasized the importance of spatial patterning in social structure and borrowed concepts like succession from the ecology current at the time the Chicago School emerged in the early twentieth century. Later, key thinkers in the Chicago School, notably Amos Hawley, distanced themselves from the ecological/evolutionary thinking that had inspired earlier scholars (e.g. Hawley 1986) although Otis Dudley Duncan long emphasized the importance of such links (Duncan 1964).

The emphasis in the Chicago School on the biophysical environment is something of an exception in sociology. The disjunction between mainstream sociology and concerns with human interaction with the biophysical world is well documented (Catton and Dunlap 1978, 1980; Dunlap 1980; Dunlap 1997). But independent of the Chicago School tradition, a number of scholars within sociology and in the larger social and ecological science community have continued to engage with the image of the "cultural evolutionary play in the human ecological theater"—a metaphor inspired by G. Evelyn Hutchinson's classic essays (Hutchinson 1965). Much of environmental sociology is concerned with what might be called human ecology and a tradition of evolutionary theory has continued (Dietz, Burns, and Buttel 1990; Lenski 2005; Burns and Dietz 1992; McLaughlin 2001). Meanwhile, work on human/environment relations have flourished in a variety of other

3

disciplines (overviews include Moran 2006; Rosa, Diekmann, et al. 2010; Moran 2010b; Stern 1993; Richerson 1977; U.S. National Research Council 1992).

Recently, a confluence of several streams of environmental research in sociology and kindred disciplines has yielded what might be thought of as, if not a "school" at least a community of researchers with overlapping interests and approaches. Eugene Rosa was the first to refer to this approach as "structural human ecology" (Rosa 2004b; Knight 2009). While not all members of this emerging community share the same intellectual interests, three themes serve as links between many of them. The first is an interest in meta-theory—in careful thought about ontology, epistemology, normative and positive aspects of theory, and in developing coherent overarching concepts to guide research. A second theme is attention to issues of risk and uncertainty. Risk analysis became a dominant mode of environmental and technological policy analysis starting in the 1980s, and has flourished both as a practical tool and as a topic for social science investigation (Dietz, Frey, and Rosa 2002; Rosa, McCormick, and Frey 2007; Rosa, McCright, and Renn in press). The structural human ecology community is informed by research on how humans handle uncertainty and has contributed to social science analysis of risk since that literature first emerged in the 1980s. The third theme is a flourishing body of quantitative macro-comparative research on how humans place stress on the environment but also on the factors, including the environment, that influence human well-being.

It is important to note that there is no dominant paradigm or overarching theoretical program that constitutes structural human ecology, save perhaps three points frequently made by Gene Rosa: 1–Context matters; 2–Theory must be disciplined with data; 3–Progress requires careful thought about concepts and basic premises. Some scholars work on all three themes: meta-theory, risk analysis, and quantitative analysis of drivers. Some work in only one or two areas. But overall a strong network of collaboration and co-citation has produced an intellectual community that moves rapidly by sharing ideas and by respectful and supportive debate.

Eugene Rosa was a central figure and leader in this network. He contributed germinal research in all three areas and pioneered the ongoing work of building the connections between them. So when Gene was awarded the Boeing Professorship of Environmental Sociology at Washington State University in 2011, it seemed an ideal time to bring together structural human ecology scholars to reflect on the state of the science and where we might move in the future. Because of his contributions, the Symposium on Structural Human Ecology also would naturally serve as an engagement with Gene's work at the start of his Boeing Professorship.

The Symposium was held on 24 September 2011 at Washington State University with the generous support of the Thomas S. Foley Institute for Public Policy and Public Service and the Department of Sociology, Gene's academic homes for decades. Ten scholarly presentations and concluding remarks by Gene made for a very exciting intellectual engagement. The participants were eager to see the papers collected into a volume that would assess the state of the emerging field of Structural Human Ecology.[1] This book is the result.

The opening section contains papers by Richard York and Thomas Dietz that are reflections of Gene's contributions to meta-theory, and in particular the issues of ontology and epistemology that he raised in his germinal paper "Metatheoretical Foundations for Post-Normal Risk" (Rosa 1998a) and in related work. "Meta" as York and Dietz refer to this body of work, is about the appropriate ways to think about ontology and epistemology in the context of risk decisions. Gene, drawing on ideas of Funtowicz and Ravitz (1993), identified a two-dimensional space defined by the degree to which our knowledge is based on phenomena that are ostensible and by the degree to which observations are repeatable. From this he argues for a HEROic approach to using science—Hierarchical Epistemology applied with a Realist Ontology.[2] In the areas of science most important for environmental decision making, ostensibility and/or repeatability may be limited. Unlike many sociologists of science, Gene promoted a realist ontology—there is a reality we are trying to observe rather than simply a set of social constructions. Interestingly, he also argued that most of the public engaged in risk disputes hold a realist ontology (Rosa 1998b). But because of problems of ostensibility and repeatability we must avoid hubris about our understanding of reality. In some cases it is reasonable to believe our understanding is a close match to reality, in other cases, including for many things important for structural human ecology, we have to acknowledge that our understanding involves substantial uncertainty. Thus he called for a hierarchical epistemology, open to questions for which our understanding can be asserted with great confidence and to circumstances where we must acknowledge great uncertainty and the potential for social processes to shape substantially scientific understanding.

Richard York, in his chapter, expands on the idea of HERO by noting that much of science, and nearly all of science used for policy, is about predicting the future. That means that uncertainty is inherent. He argues that there are multiple sources of uncertainty and several ways to interpret statistical analyses. In work on relatively simple systems, such as those of classical physics, uncertainty is handled by statistical procedures based on an idea of measurement error that stretches back at least to Galileo (Bennett 1998; Salsburg 2001; Bernstein 1998; Stigler 1986). This approach to uncertainty makes sense for many kinds of risk analysis deployed in engineering. In contrast, the "standard model" of contemporary physics that incorporates quantum mechanics allows for uncertainty "all the way down." Richard offers a key insight for structural human ecology: when we are dealing with complex ecosystems, social systems, or coupled human and natural systems (Rosa and Dietz 2010; Liu et al. 2007), we have not only measurement error but also specification error—our models are almost certainly wrong.[3] This has implications not only for risk analysis, the subject of Section II of this volume, but also for how we interpret the statistical results in macro-comparative analyses that are the theme of Section III. As Richard notes, realizing the several sources of error in our models and thus the limits of our ability to make predictions does not lead us to a post-modern rejection of the scientific enterprise. Rather it encourages a more nuanced understanding of what we know and of how to work with the limits of our knowledge—an enterprise where Gene's work stands as an exemplar.

Tom Dietz's arguments follow a parallel logic to Richard's analysis. Logically, all decisions have to take into account both facts and values. Gene's work has given us clarity about the problem of "getting the facts right" in circumstances when there is scientific uncertainty, and Richard has shown us how broadly Gene's logic applies to science. But in many environmental and sustainability decisions, there can also be value uncertainty (Dietz 2003, 2013). When confronted with a decision about the environment, about emerging technology, about any aspect of sustainability, the implications for things we value may not be obvious to most individuals. And it may not be obvious how we should aggregate individual value considerations into a societal decision. Tom argues that Gene's insights apply to this problem as well as to factual uncertainty. The problem of ostensibility and repeatability apply not only to our understanding of the facts but also to our ability to assess the value implications of courses of action. Many of the issues addressed by structural human ecology, and many decisions about risk, require us to develop positions about novel phenomena. That the value implications of these problems are not obvious can be thought of as another example of low ostensibility. When the phenomena are novel it is hard to draw on past experience to make value judgments and that can be thought of as a problem of low repeatability. Tom considers the implications of Gene's work for linking scientific analysis to public deliberation, an approach Gene long advocated.

Section II of the book addresses problems of risk directly, with each paper focusing on risk associated with technologies of emerging importance as a testbed. This approach follows Gene's long history of honing his ideas around the decades-long controversies about nuclear power. Ortwin Renn, Nadine Bratchatzek, Sylvia Hiller, and Dirk Scheer take on a major technological challenge of the twenty-first century: climate engineering. Roger Kasperson considers the broad array of technological choices we must make. Paul Stern examines a third technology that may have huge impacts on climate change: hydrofracking. Like Gene's work on nuclear power, each of these three chapters makes a contribution to our understanding of an important set of technological risks. And like Gene's work, they use these examples to probe deeply into how best to think about and develop reasoned societal approaches for dealing with risk.

Climate engineering, sometimes called geo-engineering, is an emerging set of methods for limiting the magnitude of climate change (U.S. National Research Council 2010, Chapter 15). One major approach is to pull greenhouse gases, especially carbon dioxide, from the atmosphere. The other is to reduce the amount of solar radiation warming the earth's surface. There are a number of specific technologies proposed within each of these two categories. As emissions of greenhouse gases have continued to increase, interest in climate engineering as a mechanism for reducing harm from climate change has grown. From the earliest discussions of geo-engineering, the importance of social science analysis has been clear. Most major reports on the technology note the importance of effective governance mechanisms and of anticipating public acceptance or rejection of it (Royal Society 2009; U.S. National Research Council 2010, Chapter 15). While the research on public acceptance is still in its early stages, Ortwin and his collaborators provide a commanding overview of the work that has been done to assess public views of technologies that have not yet received much attention in the media. An important feature of their review is that it examines work on multiple countries—we know from the history of nuclear power and genetically modified organisms that there can be substantial differences across nations in how technologies are perceived (Rosa, Matsuda, and Kleinhesselink 2000; Kleinhesselink and Rosa 1991). As Gene often noted in his work comparing risk perceptions across cultures, context matters. Ortwin and colleagues also report results from an expert workshop intended to identify appropriate analogies in recent technological controversies to various aspects of climate engineering, a comparative approach Gene favored (e.g. Rosa and Clark 1999). Nearly all the existing literature on climate engineering calls for early public deliberation linked to ongoing scientific analysis—a theme that crosses many chapters in this volume. Given the initial social science work on climate engineering, Ortwin and his collaborators offer clear suggestions about how to implement that dialogue.

Roger Kasperson shows the utility of distinguishing three types of uncertainty: aleatory uncertainty (situations where further data and analysis could, at least in principle, reduce uncertainty); model-parameter uncertainty (where more data alone won't help but more research to build a better understanding and better models and parameter estimates might); and deep uncertainty (where not enough is known to use data to model). It is this last category that is most troubling for decision making and often encourages delays and continuing "business as usual." The parallels across types of technology is something Gene also addressed (Rosa and Clark 1999). Roger suggests two strategies for this situation: adaptive management and resilience building. Adaptive management starts with best available knowledge but makes provisions for corrections as we learn and as the situation changes. It is based on social learning (Henry 2009). Resilience building takes steps so that society is better able to cope with whatever stresses the future holds, even though we cannot predict them with much accuracy. Roger then identifies a series of institutional properties that facilitate adaptive management and resilience. However, if deploying adaptive management, building resilience, and coping with deep uncertainty were easy, we would probably have done it already. Roger notes six dilemmas, each worthy of detailed consideration, that challenge our abilities to build the institutions we need. He posits that while the challenges are substantial, there are ways to move forward, and much to be learned.

Paul Stern examines the factors that influence public acceptance or rejection of new technologies, drawing on an extensive review of the literature by a National Research Council committee on which Gene served. Paul summarizes work on nuclear power and radioactive waste management. These are topics on which Gene wrote extensively for more than three decades (Rosa and Freudenburg 1984; Rosa 1988; Rosa and Dunlap 1994; Rosa and Clark 1999; Rosa 2004a, 2007; Freudenburg and Rosa 1984; Dunlap, Kraft, and Rosa 1993), including an engagement with the recent Presidential Blue Ribbon Commission on America's Nuclear Future (Rosa, Tuler, et al. 2010). Paul also examines the history of public concern with DNA manipulation and a variety of other public controversies over risk assessment and management and environmental assessment and decision making. In addition to these extended case studies, some insights about technological controversies can be derived inductively from social science research that is not directed at technological controversies per se. He summarizes what has been learned from work on science communication and the use of science, international policy networks and governance of common-pool resources—all extensive and robust literatures. Moving beyond this summary of what we know, Paul develops a set of design principles for governing emerging technologies. He examines the way Elinor Ostrom (Ostrom 1990, 2010a, 2010b; Dietz, Ostrom, and Stern 2003) synthesized principles for the management of common pool resources, acknowledging the differences between the local to regional institutions most extensively examined in the commons literature (Ostrom et al. 2002) and some emerging technologies. From these lessons, and drawing on the insights from the literature on technological controversies and other social science literature, he proposes seven design principles for managing emerging technologies.

The third section of the volume focuses on macro-comparative analyses of the stress humans place on the environment, human well-being, and the tradeoffs between them. It is to describe this body of research that the term Structural Human Ecology was coined. In the 1990s Gene, Thomas Dietz, and Richard York (who was Gene's PhD student) developed a line of analysis that is given the acronym STIRPAT. Scholars since Malthus, and even earlier, had offered arguments about the effects of population, affluence, choice of technology, and other factors on the environment (Dietz and Rosa 1994). In a series of papers centered around the Presidential Commission on Population Growth and the American Future (1972)—also known as the Rockefeller Commission—Barry Commoner and colleagues debated the relative importance of drivers of environmental change with Paul Ehrlich and John Holdren (Ehrlich and Holdren 1972; Commoner 1972). From that debate emerged the "IPAT equation": **I**mpact = **P**opulation x **A**ffluence x **T**echnology (Dietz and Rosa 1994; Chertow 2001) which is also known as the Kaya identity (Kaya 1990a; Kaya and Yokobori 1997; Kaya 1990b). STIRPAT acknowledges that as an accounting equation IPAT cannot be used to test hypotheses. But it can be converted into a stochastic form and then becomes a vehicle for empirical research. Gene coined the term STIRPAT based both on the acronym STochastic Impacts by Regression on Population, Affluence and Technology and on the stirp (descendent) of IPAT. This formulation has helped a community of sociologists, economists, geographers, political scientists, and others engage in macro-comparative analysis of human stress on the environment. STIRPAT forms a bridge between the social and the physical and biological sciences—where IPAT originated and remains popular. But it also connects with the venerable tradition of quantitative macro-comparative work in the social sciences that has long been used to explore issues of development, economic growth, inequality and human well-being. The STIRPAT research program and Gene's formative influence on it are described in more detail in Chapters 8 and 10.

It is hardly surprising that Gene would be an innovator in macro-comparative analysis. One of his earliest publications was a pioneering examination of the relationship between human standards of living and energy consumption using cross-national data (Mazur and Rosa 1974; see also Rosa 1997). His dissertation advisor, Allan Mazur, has continued this line of work. The first part of his chapter in this collection updates our understanding of the links between energy consumption and quality of life, finding that the general conclusion of the original paper—that energy consumption decouples from quality of life at high levels of consumption—continues to stand. He then considers what drives energy consumption, focusing in particular on the variable that has been subject to debate at least since Malthus—population. He finds that for total energy supply, while population has a modest effect compared to other factors, growth in population always leads to increased energy use while other drivers vary in their impact over time. But population growth is largely decoupled from electricity use. This distinction is especially important because, as he notes, most future growth in energy use is likely to be in the form of electricity, including the demands associated with increased use of electric vehicles.

Andrew Jorgenson begins his contribution with a comprehensive review of the STIRPAT approach, including both its logic and the literature that has applied it to the political economy of environmental change. He notes in particular the methodological progress in this line of work and especially the move towards considering the stability of the effects of population and the environment over time and across space, an approach he and collaborators initiated. Andrew then brings the concern with temporal stability and regional differences together in a new empirical analysis. He examines the effects of population, affluence (gross domestic product per capita), urbanization (often proposed as a driver of environmental stress), and international trade, looking in particular at how the effects of population and affluence may have changed over time and across regions. Population and affluence remain key drivers of stress on the environment in all analyses. However, there are important regional differences in the effects of both population and affluence over time. In the mostly developed nations of Europe, North America, and Oceania, the effects of population are stable over the time period studied (1960–2005). But in other regions the effects of population or affluence or both change over time. Again, "context matters."

Sandra Marquart-Pyatt addresses another key issue for structural human ecology—the need to work across multiple levels of social organization. Structural human ecology acknowledges that individual humans operate within a hierarchy of emergent forms—households, social networks, communities, organizations, nations, and global society are examples of the social forms, while ecosystems, landscapes, airsheds and watersheds, biomes, and the biosphere are examples of the ecological forms (Dietz, Rosa, and York 2010). But the lack of data that span these levels has meant that most research has been able to work only at a single level, typically the individual or the nation-state. Research in the land use / land cover change tradition (e.g. Moran 2010a; Turner, Lambin, and Reenberg 2007) and on commons (e.g.McCay and Svein 2010; Ostrom et al. 2002) frequently examines individuals and households in a regional context. But efforts to look across many local studies to understand how context influences individuals and households are still in early stages (e.g. the International Forestry Resources and Institutions Network: http://www.ifriresearch.net/). Gene's views on integrating across levels of analysis are discussed in Chapter 10. In Chapter 9, Sandra makes use of an approach pioneered by the World Fertility Survey (Cleland, Scott, and Whitelegge 1987) and supported by Gene: using comparable survey data from individuals in multiple countries to allow assessment of both individual level and country level effects. This approach allows a much desired link between individual level social psychology and the political economy of nation states, with the national context potentially influencing individuals' environmental concerns directly and also shaping how individual characteristics (age/cohort, gender, income, education) influence those concerns. Sandra reviews existing theories and evidence that characterize the links between micro and macro influences on environmental concern. She expands on current theory by incorporating results from the STIRPAT research program and related studies that have dealt extensively with the macro-level drivers of human stress on the environment. Her argument is that the findings of these programs should inform the macro-level of multi-level models of environmental concern.

To test this approach, she uses data from the International Social Survey Program (ISSP) on representative samples of individuals in 25 countries, mostly but not exclusively countries that are industrialized and affluent. Using multi-level regression modeling, she finds that characteristics of nation-states do influence individual concerns, including factors prominent in the STIRPAT tradition that have not been much considered in the cross-national literature on environmental concern. In particular, she finds that population density and age structure have influences at the individual level. The effects are complex, so analyses that do not deploy a multi-level approach may miss some important influences on environmental concern. One notable finding is that neither economics nor objective measures of environmental conditions have much effect on individual level concern. This suggests, within the limits of the data set, that the feedback on concern from environmental conditions or economic conditions do not provide much basis for social learning about sustainability (Henry 2009). These interesting findings that span the micro and the macro also make it clear that the structural human ecology research community is poised to conduct analyses linking the micro and macro in effective ways, and is being held back primarily by the lack of data that allow for such important analyses.

In the final chapter of the volume Thomas Dietz looks across Gene's contributions to these multiple themes that constitute structural human ecology. He situates Gene's work in the larger literature. But he also examines the general lessons to be learned from how he conducted research over a career that spanned four decades, including extensive engagement throughout North America and Europe, and with disciplines spanning the social, physical, and biological sciences, engineering, and the arts and humanities. It shows Gene's contributions not only to scientific understanding but also as a role model for scholars.

Conclusion

The papers collected in this volume show the breadth of work in structural human ecology that has developed, in large part, from Gene's germinal work. The metaphor of a rhizome may be useful here.[4] A strong network of researchers is emerging who frequently collaborate and otherwise build on each other's work. This network spans multiple generations of scholars and at least three areas: meta-theory, risk, and macro-comparative analysis. The connections between these three "aboveground" and visible clusters of research may not be evident. Rather, the connections are "underground" in that they are not based on a "school" or explicit program of work. They are connected at the root level—ongoing collaborations, mutual engagement with the same ideas, cross-citations that build on emergent ideas.

In reading across the chapters in this volume, it is clear that the emergent structural human ecology community is at the leading edge of research on issues that are critical to both understanding coupled human and natural systems and to guiding adaptive management of the risks we face as a planetary species. In much of the twentieth century, social sciences could progress while mostly ignoring the ecosystems in which we live. Ecological sciences could do meaningful work by focusing on systems that could be presumed relatively isolated from human pressures. Policy could be developed based on an assumption of "stationarity"—that what had gone on over the century or so before was a sound guide to the future. Now, assuming stationarity and isolated systems almost ensures miscalibrated research and policy failure.

The goal of structural human ecology is to provide solid theoretical, conceptual, and methodological approaches to study coupled human and natural systems. It hopes to occupy Pasteur's Quadrant—like Pasteur, producing research that contributes to fundamental knowledge but also research that is useful for societal decision making (Stokes 1997). Work on meta-theory and risk are driven in large part by policy questions. Recent macro-comparative work is starting to engage directly with policy issues (York 2012; Jorgenson 2012). The longer tradition of examining the influence of population, affluence, and many other factors on anthropogenic environmental stress provides an essential background for discussions about the desirability of growth and the factors that mediate its adverse effects. In particular, a number of studies are beginning to address the tradeoff between human well-being and stress placed on the environment, moving from local studies and conceptual frameworks such as those that provide the basis of the Millennium Ecosystem Assessment (Reid et al. 2005) to quantitative estimates of tradeoffs and trajectories.

The scholarly discourse around structural human ecology at the Symposium to celebrate Gene's Boeing Professorship was one of the richest we have experienced. We thank the participants for preparing the excellent analyses that follow. We think they capture in a snapshot much of the excitement that emerges when engaging with structural human ecology and in particular with Gene's work. He has given us a great deal to think about and build upon.

Notes

1. Rachael Shwom and Steve Fuller also presented papers but the press of deadlines prevented them from contributing to this volume.

    At the time of the event, Gene was in good health. Sadly, in late December of 2012 he was diagnosed with stage four lung cancer. With the support of family and friends from around the globe, he battled strongly against the cancer while maintaining the best of spirits and engaging in important intellectual work, including ongoing discussions of this volume. He died on 21 February 2013, just a little more than a year after the initial diagnosis.

2. Gene has always shown great talent at developing acronyms that facilitate scientific communication including HERO, STIRPAT, and, to describe global change, PaSSAGE (Pace, Scale, Spread, Autocatalysis, Globalization and Ecological interdependence) (Rosa and Dietz 2010).

3. Gene has emphasized the work of Richard Levins on the limits of model building in some of his recent writing on risk (Levins 1966, 1993; Orzack and Sober 1993; Rosa et al. 2012).

4. I thank Linda Kalof for this idea.

References

Bennett, Deborah J. 1998. *Randomness*. Cambridge, Massachusetts: Harvard University Press.

Bernstein, Peter L. 1998. *Against the Gods: The Remarkable Story of Risk*. New York: John Wiley & Sons.

Burns, Tom R., and Thomas Dietz. 1992. "Socio-cultural Evolution: Social Rule Systems, Selection and Agency." *International Sociology* 7:259-283.

Catton, William R. Jr, and Riley E. Dunlap. 1978. "Environmental Sociology: A New Paradigm." *The American Sociologist* 13:41-49.

———. 1980. "A New Ecological Paradigm for Post-Exuberant Sociology." *American Behavioral Scientist* 24:14-57.

Chertow, Marion. 2001. "The IPAT Equation and Its Variants: Changing Views of Technology and Environmental Impact." *Journal of Industrial Ecology* 4 (4):13-29.

Cleland, J. G., C. Scott, and D. Whitelegge. 1987. *The World Fertility Survey: An Assessment*. Oxford: Oxford University Press.

Commission on Population Growth and the American Future. 1972. *Population and the American Future*. Washington, DC: Signet.

Commoner, Barry. 1972. "The Environmental Cost of Economic Growth." In *Population, Resources and the Environment*, edited by Ronald G. Ridker, 339-363. Washington, DC: Government Printing Office.

Dietz, Thomas. 2003. "What is a Good Decision? Criteria for Environmental Decision Making." *Human Ecology Review* 10 (1):60-67.

———. 2013. "Bringing Values and Deliberation to Science Communication." *Proceedings of the National Academy of Sciences* 110(10):14081-87.

Dietz, Thomas, Tom R. Burns, and Frederick H. Buttel. 1990. "Evolutionary Theory in Sociology: An Examination of Current Thinking." *Sociological Forum* 5:155-171.

Dietz, Thomas, R. Scott Frey, and Eugene Rosa. 2002. "Risk, Technology and Society." In *Handbook of Environmental Sociology*, edited by Riley E. Dunlap and William Michelson, 562-629. Westport, Connecticut: Greenwood Press.

Dietz, Thomas, Elinor Ostrom, and Paul C. Stern. 2003. "The Struggle to Govern the Commons." *Science* 301 (5652):1907-1912.

Dietz, Thomas, Eugene A. Rosa, and Richard York. 2007. "Driving the Human Ecological Footprint." *Frontiers in Ecology and Environment* 5 (1):13-18.

————. 2009. "Environmentally Efficient Well-Being: Rethinking Sustainability as the Relationship between Human Well-being and Environmental Impacts." *Human Ecology Review* 16 (1):113-122.

————. 2010. "Human Driving Forces of Global Change: Examining Current Theories." In *Threats to Sustainability: Understanding Human Footprints on the Global Environment*, edited by Eugene A. Rosa, Andreas Diekmann, Thomas Dietz, and Carlo Jaeger, 83-132. Cambridge, Massachusetts: MIT Press.

————. 2012. "Environmentally Efficient Well-Being: Is There a Kuznets Curve?" *Journal of Applied Geography* 32:21-28.

Dietz, Thomas, and Eugene A. Rosa. 1994. "Rethinking the Environmental Impacts of Population, Affluence and Technology." *Human Ecology Review* 1:277-300.

Duncan, Otis Dudley. 1964. "From Social System to Ecosystem." *Sociological Inquiry* 31:140-149.

Dunlap, Riley E. 1997. "The Evolution of Environmental Sociology: A Brief History and Assessment of the American Experience." In *The International Handbook of Environmental Sociology*, edited by Michael R Redclift and Graham Woodgate, 21-39. Cheltanham, United Kingdom: Edward Elgar Publishing.

————. 1980. "Paradigmatic Change in Social Science: From Human Exceptionalism to an Ecological Paradigm." *American Behavioral Scientist* 24:5-14.

Dunlap, Riley E., Michael E. Kraft, and Eugene A. Rosa. 1993. *The Public and Nuclear Waste: Citizen's Views of Repository Siting*. Durham, North Carolina: Duke University Press.

Ehrlich, Paul R., and John P. Holdren. 1972. "Impact of Population Growth." In *Population, Resources and the Environment*, edited by Ronald G. Ridker, 365-377. Washington, DC: U.S. Government Printing Office.

Freudenburg, William F., and Eugene A. Rosa. 1984. *Public Reactions to Nuclear Power: Are There Critical Masses?* Boulder, Colorado: Westview Press/American Association for the Advancement of Science.

Funtowicz, S., and J. Ravetz. 1993. "Science in the Postnormal Age." *Futures* 25 (7):739-755.

Hawley, Amos H. 1986. *Human Ecology: A Theoretical Essay*. Chicago, Illinois: University of Chicago Press.

Henry, Adam Douglas. 2009. "The Challenge of Learning for Sustainability: A Prolegomenon to Theory." *Human Ecology Review* 16 (2):131-140.

Hutchinson, G. Evelyn. 1965. *The Ecological Theater and the Evolutionary Play*. New Haven, Connecticut: Yale University Press.

Jorgenson, Andrew K. 2012. "Energy: Analyzing Fossil Fuel Displacement." *Nature Climate Change* 2:398-399.

Jorgenson, Andrew K., and Ryan Birkholz. 2010. "Assessing the Causes of Anthropogenic Methane Emissions in Comparative Perspective, 1990-2005." *Ecological Economics* 69 (2634-2643).

Jorgenson, Andrew K., and Brett Clark. 2010. "Assessing the Temporal Stability of the Population / Environment Relationship in Comparative Perspective: A Cross-national Panel Study of Carbon Dioxide Emissions, 1960–2005." *Population and Environment* 32 (1):27-41.

————. 2012. "Are the Economy and the Environment Decoupling? A Comparative International Study, 1960-2005." *American Journal of Sociology*. In press.

Kaya, Y. 1990a. *Impact of Carbon Dioxide Emission Control on GNP Growth: Interpretation of Proposed Scenarios*. Paris: IPCC Energy and Industry Subgroup, Response Strategies Working Group.

Kaya, Yoichi. 1990b. Impact of Carbon Dioxide Emission Control GNP Growth: Interpretation of Proposed Scenarios. In *IPCC Energy and Industry Subgroup, Response Strategies Working Group*. Paris.

Kaya, Yoichi, and Keiichi Yokobori. 1997. *Environment, Energy, and Economy: Strategies for Sustainability*. Tokyo & New York: United Nations University Press.

Kleinhesselink, Randall R., and Eugene A. Rosa. 1991. "Cognitive Representation of Risk Perceptions: A Comparison of Japan and the United States." *Journal of Cross-Cultural Psychology* 22:11-28.

Knight, Kyle, and Eugene Rosa. 2009. "The Environmental Costs of Life Satisfaction: A Cross-National Empirical Test." In *Workshop of the Sustainable Research and Action Network (SCORAI)*. Worcester, Massachusetts: Clark University.

Knight, Kyle, and Eugene A. Rosa. 2010. "The Environmental Efficiency of Well-Being: A Cross-National Analysis." *Social Science Research* 40:931-949.

Knight, Kyle W. 2009. "Structural Human Ecology and STIRPAT: Theory and Method." In *Panel Contribution to the Population-Environment Research Network's Cyberseminar on Theoretical and Methodological Issues in the Analysis of Population Dynamics and the Environment*. New York: Population-Environment Research Network.

Lenski, Gerhard. 2005. *Ecological-Evolutionary Theory: Principles and Applications*. Boulder, Colorado: Paradigm Publishers.

Levins, Richard. 1966. "The Strategy of Model Building in Population Biology." *American Scientist* 54:421-431.

———. 1993. "A Response to Orzack and Sober: Formal Analysis and Fluidity of Science." *Quarterly Review of Biology* 68 (547-555).

Liu, Jianguo, Thomas Dietz, Stephen R. Carpenter, Marina Alberti, Carl Folke, Emilio Moran, Alice N. Pell, Peter Deadman, Timothy Kratz, Jane Lubchencko, Elinor Ostrom, Zhiyun Ouyang, William Provencher, Charles L. Redman, Stephen H. Schneider, and William W. Taylor. 2007. "Complexity of Coupled Human and Natural Systems." *Science* 317 (5844):1513-1516.

Mazur, Allan, and Eugene Rosa. 1974. "Energy and Life-Style: Massive Energy Consumption May Not Be Necessary to Maintain Current Living Standards in America." *Science* 186:607-610.

McCay, Bonnie J., and Jentoft Svein. 2010. "Uncommon Ground: Critical Perspectives on Common Property." In *Human Footprints on the Global Environment: Threats to Sustainability*, edited by Eugene A. Rosa, Andreas Diekmann, Thomas Dietz, and Carlo Jaeger, 203-230. Cambridge, Massachusetts: MIT Press.

McLaughlin, Paul. 2001. "Towards an Ecology of Social Action: Merging the Ecological and Constructivist Traditions." *Human Ecology Review* 8 (2):12-28.

Moran, Emilio F. 2006. *People and Nature: An Introduction to Human Ecological Relations*. London: Blackwell Publishers.

Moran, Emilio. 2010a. "Progress in the Last Ten Years in the Study of Land Use/Cover Change and the Outlook for the Next Decade." In *Human Footprints on the Global*

Environment: Threats to Sustainability, edited by Eugene A. Rosa, Andreas Diekmann, Thomas Dietz, and Carlo C. Jaeger, 135-164. Cambridge, Massachusetts: MIT Press.

———. 2010b. *Environmental Social Science: Human Environment Interactions and Sustainability*. Chicester, United Kingdom: Wiley-Blackwell.

Orzack, Steven Hecht, and Elliott Sober. 1993. "A Critical Assessment of Levins's *The Strategy of Model Building* (1966)." *Quarterly Review of Biology* 68 (534-546).

Ostrom, Elinor. 1990. *Governing the Commons: The Evolution of Institutions for Collective Action*. New York: Cambridge University Press.

———. 2010a. "A Multi-Scale Approach to Coping with Climate Change and Other Collective Action Problems." *Solutions* 1 (2):27-36.

———. 2010b. "Polycentric Systems for Coping with Collective Action and Global Environmental Change." *Global Environmental Change* 20:550-557.

Ostrom, Elinor, Thomas Dietz, Nives Dolsak, Paul C. Stern, Susan Stonich, and Elke Weber. 2002. *The Drama of the Commons*. Washington, DC: National Academy Press.

Reid, Walter V., Harold A. Mooney, Angela Cropper, Doris Capistrano, Stephen R. Carpenter, Kanchan Chopra, Partha Dasgupta, Thomas Dietz, Anantha Kumar Duraiappah, Rashid Hassan, Roger Kasperson, Rik Leemans, Robert M. May, Tony (A. J.) McMichael, Prabhu Pingali, Cristián Samper, Robert Sholes, Robert T. Watson, A. H. Zakri, Zhao Shidong, Neville J. Ash, Elena Bennett, Pushpam Kumar, Marcus J. Lee, Ciara Raudsepp-Hearne, Henk Simons, Jillian Thonell, and Monica B. Zurek. 2005. *Ecosystems and Human Well-Being: Synthesis*. Washington, DC: Island Press.

Richerson, Peter J. 1977. "Ecology and Human Ecology: A Comparison of Theories in the Biological and Social Sciences." *American Ethnologist* 4:1-26.

Rosa, Eugene A. 1988. ""NAMBY PAMBY and NIMBY PIMBY: Public Issues in the Siting of Hazardous Waste Facilities." *Forum for Applied Research and Public Policy* 3 (114-123).

———. 1997. "Cross National Trends in Fossil Fuel Consumption, Societal Well-Being and Carbon Releases." In *Environmentally Significant Consumption: Research Directions*, edited by Paul C. Stern, Thomas Dietz, Vernon W. Ruttan, Robert H. Socolow and James L. Sweeney, 100-109. Washington, DC: National Academy Press.

———. 1998a. "Metatheoretical Foundations for Post-Normal Risk." *Journal of Risk Research* 1:15-44.

———. 1998b. "Comments on Commentary by Ravetz and Funtowicz: 'Old fashioned hypertext'." *Journal of Risk Research* 1 (2):111-115.

———. 2004a. *The Future Acceptability of Nuclear Power in the United States*. Paris: Institute Francais des Relations Internationales.

———. 2004b. "Tracking the Human Sources of Ecological Footprints: The STIRPAT Research Program." In *Presentation at Center for Environmental Policy, The Institute for International Studies, Stanford University*. Stanford, California.

———. 2007. "Long-Term Stewardship and Risk Management: Analytic and Policy Challenges." In *Long-Term Management of Contaminated Sites*, edited by Thomas Leschine, 227-255. Amsterdam: Elsevier.

Rosa, Eugene A., Andreas Diekmann, Thomas Dietz, and Carlo Jaeger. 2010. *Human Footprints on the Global Environment: Threats to Sustainability*. Cambridge, Massachusetts: The MIT Press.

Rosa, Eugene A., and Thomas Dietz. 2010. "Global Transformations: PaSSAGE to a New Ecological Era." In *Human Footprints on the Global Environment: Threats to Sustainability*, edited by Eugene A. Rosa, Andreas Diekmann, Thomas Dietz, and Carlo C. Jaeger, 1-45. Cambridge, Massachusetts: MIT Press.

Rosa, Eugene A., Thomas Dietz, Richard H Moss, Scott Atran, and Susanne Moser. 2012. "Managing the Risks of Climate Change and Terrorism." *Solutions* 3 (2):59-65.

Rosa, Eugene A., and Riley E. Dunlap. 1994. "The Polls-Poll Trends: Nuclear Energy: Three Decades of Public Opinion." *Public Opinion Quarterly* 58:295-325.

Rosa, Eugene A., and William R. Freudenburg. 1984. "Nuclear Power at the Crossroads." In *Public Reactions to Nuclear Power: Are There Critical Masses?*, edited by William R. Freudenburg and Eugene A. Rosa, 3-37. Boulder, Colorado: Westview/AAAS.

Rosa, Eugene A., Noriyuki Matsuda, and Randall R. Kleinhesselink. 2000. "The Cognitive Architecture of Risk: Pancultural Unity or Cultural Shaping?" In *Comparative Risk Perception*, edited by Ortwin Renn and Bernd Rohrmann, 185-210. Dordrecth, The Netherlands: Kluwer.

Rosa, Eugene A., Sabrina McCormick, and R. Scott Frey. 2007. "The Sociology of Risk." In *21st Century Sociology: A Reference Handbook*, edited by Clifton D. Bryant and Dennis L. Peck, 81-87. Thousand Oak, California: Sage.

Rosa, Eugene A., Aaron McCright, and Ortwin Renn. In press. *The Risk Society: Social Theory and Governance*. Philadelphia: Temple University Press.

Rosa, Eugene A., Seth P. Tuler, Baruch Fischhoff, Thomas Webler, Sharon M. Friedman, Richard E. Sclove, Kristin Shrader-Frachette, Mary R. English, Roger E. Kasperson, Robert L. Goble, Thomas M. Leschine, William Freudenburg, Caron Chess, Charles Perrow, Kai Erikson, and James F. Short. 2010. "Nuclear Waste: Knowledge Waste?" *Science* 329:762-763.

Rosa, Eugene A., and Donald L. Clark Jr. 1999. "Historical Routes to Technological Gridlock: Nuclear Technology as Prototypical Vehicle." *Research in Social Problems and Public Policy* 7 (21-57).

Royal Society. 2009. *Geoengineering the Climate: Science, Governance and Uncertainty*. London: The Royal Society.

Salsburg, David. 2001. *The Lady Tasting Tea: How Statistics Revolutionized Science in the Twentieth Century*. New York: W.H. Freeman and Company.

Stern, Paul C. 1993. "A Second Environmental Science: Human-Environment Interactions." *Science* 260:1897-1899.

Stigler, Stephen M. 1986. *The History of Statistics: The Measurement of Uncertainty Before 1900*. Cambridge, Massachusetts: Belknap.

Stokes, Donald E. 1997. *Pasteur's Quadrant: Basic Science and Technological Innovation*. Washington, DC: Brookings Institution.

Turner, B. L. III, Eric F. Lambin, and Annette Reenberg. 2007. "The Emergence of Land Change Science for Global Environmental Change and Sustainability." *Proceedings of the National Academy of Sciences, USA* 104 (52):20666-20671.

U.S. National Research Council. 1992. *Global Environmental Change: Understanding the Human Dimensions*. Washington, DC: National Academy Press.

———. 2010. *Advancing the Science of Climate Change*. Washington, DC: National Academies Press.

York, Richard. 2012. "Do Alternative Energy Sources Displace Fossil Fuels?" *Nature Climate Change* 2:441-443.

CHAPTER 2

Metatheoretical Foundations of Post-Normal Prediction

Richard York, University of Oregon

O NE OF THE MOST DISTINCTIVE FEATURES of Gene Rosa's thinking is his concern not only with developing rigorous analyses of matters of substantive importance, particularly the anthropogenic forces behind the global environmental crisis in the midst of which we currently struggle, but also with understanding the philosophical, historical, and sociological aspects of how we gain knowledge about the world. These interests are intimately connected to one another in his work on risk assessment. Here, I aim to engage with one of Gene's most influential papers, "Metatheoretical Foundations for Post-normal Risk" (Rosa 1998), or "Meta," as Gene refers to it for short, to develop its implications for our understanding of the nature of prediction-making in the natural and social sciences. This chapter is consciously written in a Rosaian fashion, whereby I address the philosophical issues behind scientific endeavors, drawing on scholarship from a diversity of intellectual perspectives. In fact, in certain ways, this chapter is a microcosm of the macrocosm that is this volume: an exploration of the diverse and interconnected facets of Gene's work. I begin my assessment by summarizing some of the central points Gene developed in Meta. Then, I present some of the philosophical and historical aspects of risk, probability, and uncertainty that inform my utilization of his work to develop further insights about the nature of prediction. Finally, I will present a view of "post-normal prediction," which broadens the implications of post-normal risk.

Metatheory and Uncertainty

While it covers a great deal of intellectual territory, one of Meta's major objectives is to develop metatheoretical foundations for risk analysis that allow us to move beyond tensions among contrasting perspectives, particularly the tensions between realism and social constructionism and between positivism and cultural theory, by incorporating the best features of these various perspectives into a new framework, Reconstructed Realism. This framework is based on *ontological realism* (OR) and *epistemological hierarchicalism* (EH), which together Meta refers to with the acronym OREH, but which Gene subsequently renamed to the more pleasing HERO for hierarchical epistemology and realist ontology. Ontological realism is the philosophical stance that a real world exists independent of human perception of it. Epistemological hierarchicalism is a philosophical orientation toward knowledge which recognizes that, while human perceptions of the world are unavoidably filtered through our physical and mental apparatus and our interpretation of these perceptions mediated by our social context, humans can gain genuine, if imperfect, knowledge of the world and that some epistemological approaches do better at generating this knowledge than do others.

Meta is, of course, focused on understanding risk, which is defined as "a situation or event where something of human value (including humans themselves) has been put at stake and where the outcome is uncertain" (Rosa 1998, 28). The consideration of risk brings to the fore an issue of central substantive and philosophical interest: uncertainty. The concern with uncertainty is the issue on which the metatheoretical concerns of Meta pivot, and it is my primary interest here. There are at least a couple of layers of uncertainty in risk analysis. First, there can be a known *probability* of an event occurring, but there is uncertainty about whether or not the event actually will occur in a particular instance or within a particular time frame. For example, when rolling a fair six-sided die, the probability of rolling a one is known as one in six,[1] but the actual outcome of a particular roll is unknown. Second, there can be uncertainty about what the actual probability is itself for a particular event or phenomenon, such as whether or not the global average temperature will rise four or more degrees Celsius over the next 100 years.

The value of epistemological hierarchicalism can be best understood in the context of risk assessment. A key argument laid out in Meta is that scientific approaches to explanation will do better than other approaches when studying phenomena with high ostensibility and repeatability. Ostensibility refers to the extent to which one can point to examples of the phenomenon in question, and repeatability refers to the degree to which such examples recur. In cases where there is a high level of ostensibility and repeatability, traditional risk calculation procedures work well, because probabilities can be reasonably estimated. For example, there is much car driving in many different types of circumstances and many car accidents in the world. Therefore, it is quite easy to calculate reasonably sound risk estimates for how likely it is to get in a car accident in particular circumstances—e.g., how likely a person is to get in a car accident if they drive 20,000 miles a year in a particular setting (e.g., rural vs. urban) for the next five years. Thus, in these types of circumstances, there is a clear hierarchy of epistemological methods, where rational, scientific calculation will do much better than other approaches.

In contrast, when ostensibility and repeatability are low, the hierarchy becomes compressed and scientific approaches may do little better than others. After all, a central feature of scientific analysis is its reliance on empirical evidence on which to base its assessments. If empirical evidence is lacking (low ostensibility and repeatability), scientists are forced to speculate. For example, before a new potential medicine is tested on subjects, it is difficult to know with confidence what its effects will be, especially if it is not closely related to other medicines that have been tested previously. We are commonly in a situation like this when new technologies are introduced, since it is hard to know what their social and environmental consequences will be before they are widely used. Since many of the potential risks of the twenty-first century, such as concerns over nanotechnology and genetic engineering, are unprecedented in human history, we are faced with trying to assess risks where we lack data and face high uncertainty—i.e., where we cannot estimate accurately the probability of a particular hazard occurring.

To help us address this type of risk landscape, Meta draws on Funtowicz and Ravetz's (1992) "post-normal science." Due to the novel and often complex nature of many of our challenges, and the intrinsic value-laden nature of them, Meta (Rosa 1998, 37) notes that "science is an essential but incomplete knowledge system for many of the environmental and other risk problems facing the world." Meta then notes, citing Funtowicz and Ravetz's (1992, 253) own words, that this core idea "has been motivated by the realization that the new problems facing our industrial civilization, although requiring scientific inputs for their resolution, involve a problem-solving activity that is different in character from the kind that we have previously taken for granted." Circumstances like many of the ones we face, where there are issues of high stakes about which we are highly uncertain of how the systems that influence them operate, such as the geopolitical forces that affect the likelihood of nuclear war, are "post-normal," and are where the traditional tools of science and expert analysis are inadequate for the task. Post-normal science, then, is the approach to studying these types of issues, where a variety of techniques, both scientific and non-scientific, must be used and certain results cannot be achieved. Post-normal risk is the application of this type of approach to risk analysis, where scientists and other experts do not have valid claim to substantially superior judgment, and a variety of stakeholders have equal claim to representation in decision-making.

Post-Normal Prediction

Risk assessment is, to a large extent, about prediction-making, in that it aims to assess the likelihood of various events occurring in the future and the likely consequences of those events. Now, of course, risk assessments typically do not presume to predict which actual events will occur, but rather to assess the relative likelihood of various events over certain time horizons. Risk assessment is an essential part of any type of planning, since planning is by its nature about preparing for the future, and having some sense of what is likely and what is unlikely to occur in the future allows for setting priorities for resource allocation. Whether or not we classify the potential types of events that may occur as "hazards" is not particularly relevant from an analytic point of view. Thus, in my consideration of the broader implications of Meta, I focus on the issue of uncertainty around assessing the likelihood of various outcomes, not the stakes per se, which are obviously of central importance in risk assessment (of course, there could also be uncertainty about the stakes themselves, adding a second problematic layer to risk assessment).

So, risk analysis is in many respects a subset of efforts to make predictions, and it is only the classification of the types of events to be studied as "hazards" that marks risk analysis as distinct from other forms of prediction-making. For example, the U.S. government needs to make some sort of prediction about the size and age structure of the population in the future if it is to manage the Social Security system, since how much will need to be paid out and how much will be paid in revolves around these demographic factors. While we do not typically refer to having a certain age-dependency ratio as a "hazard," and therefore do not typically classify demographic projections under the category of "risk assessment," analytically speaking, estimating the likelihood of various demographic scenarios is little different from estimating the likelihood of various degrees of global warming, disease epidemics, or economic crashes. It is for this reason that I consider Meta to be not only important to the field of risk analysis but to the much wider realm of questions about how we can go about prediction-making and, especially, the pitfalls inherent in the whole endeavor of prediction-making.

My thinking about the nature of prediction in the social and natural sciences has been influenced by Meta and other of Gene's works (e.g., Jaeger et al. 2001). My colleague, Brett Clark, and I have engaged with some of the challenges of prediction-making (York and Clark 2006, 2007), and I draw on that work here. A prominent concern of this work is the model of science that sociology should use. Lieberson and Lynn (2002) note that a lot of work in sociology uses classical physics as its model science, but argue that this is largely inappropriate, and that the methods and conceptualizations used in biology are a better fit with the social sciences. The diversity of views within the sciences in many ways is connected with how different perspectives see the importance of developing a body of knowledge that allows for prediction-making.

The ability to make accurate predictions has clearly been a hallmark of some of the most successful and powerful scientific programs. Newtonian physics are at the pinnacle of predictive sciences, which, for example, can make accurate and precise predictions of the locations of celestial objects far into the future. Theories that can reliably predict future observations are without doubt held in the highest esteem in the scientific community. However, other well-established scientific theories do not make precise predictions of the same type as can be made in physics.

Historical sciences, such as evolutionary biology and geology, which are based on rational principles and are supported by voluminous empirical evidence, do not allow for reliable predictions of the future, although they can explain past events well and can provide some of the most general contours of how things will likely unfold in the future. For example, geologists understand a lot about the processes that lead to earthquakes, can identify regions where earthquakes are more likely compared to other regions, and, based on historical data, can make fairly reasonable predictions of the likelihood of an earthquake of a specified magnitude over a given timeframe in a particular region, but they cannot reliably predict exactly when and where an earthquake will occur. Likewise, evolutionary biologists understand much about the basic processes behind evolutionary change, most notably the forces of natural and sexual selection, but they cannot predict the course any particular lineage will take over long stretches of time. This inability to make precise predictions does not indicate that these sciences are less mature or less rigorous than physics. Rather, the inability to make precise predictions is a reflection of the nature of the phenomena that are studied. The revolution of the planets around the sun is governed by the basic physical laws of gravitation and motion, in a system largely isolated from outside disturbances or multiple, interacting causal processes. In contrast, the evolution of life on earth and the geologic history of the planet, while controlled by natural laws, develop based on innumerable particular historical events and emergent processes, which combine to make precise prediction-making impossible.

The social sciences are akin to the historical natural sciences, since, while all social phenomena occur in the physical world and are constrained by its natural laws, they are not the result of one simple process played out in isolation. Rather, social phenomena develop out of many interacting layers of causal processes, from physical laws, to biological processes, to emergent psychological characteristics, to social structures that stem from the complex intersection of all of these. Due to the emergent nature of social phenomena, they do not yield to simple predictive laws, which is not to say they are unintelligible or inaccessible to scientific inquiry. Social phenomena can indeed be understood in a scientific fashion, but this does not mean that the social sciences will allow for accurate predictions of social phenomena into the future.

One way of understanding the challenge of prediction-making is to consider the nature of statistical models, particularly the sources of error in these models. Newtonian physics can make predictions of things such as the orbits of the planets based on a deterministic mathematical model. Similarly, there are mathematical models for many types of phenomena, but when processes are not deterministic, including stochastic error (roughly speaking, random noise), then statistical models are used, which are designed to deal with this type of error. In fact, statistics is a field that is fundamentally about measuring uncertainty (Stigler 1986). Statistical models became increasingly used over the past century and are now the basis of a large share of scientific analyses, in disciplines ranging from economics to medicine to ecology (Salsburg 2002). Since many processes in the real world are disturbed by "noise"—e.g., many other processes with small effects that are uncorrelated with the main effects under study—deterministic models fail to make perfect predictions in any one case. Statistical models allowing for stochastic error recognize this fact and do not aim to predict each observation, but rather aim to characterize the overall pattern of observations, and specify the character of the stochastic process so that probabilistic statements can be made based on the model.

One of the conceptual revolutions that occurred in physics in the early twentieth century was the shift from deterministic to stochastic thinking when considering phenomena occurring at the subatomic level. Note that most common interpretations of quantum mechanical processes posit an unavoidable *ontological* source of stochastic variance. That is to say, the source of stochastic error in models of quantum processes is believed not to stem from our ignorance of the full set of factors influencing these processes, but rather the fundamentally probabilistic nature of the processes themselves (Kumar 2010; Lindley 2007). It is important to note that, while the Standard Model, which reflects our current best understanding of quantum processes, cannot predict the position or velocity of a specific particle reliably, it can predict with remarkable precision the *probability* of the characteristics of particles. In this sense, quantum mechanics is a very *certain* science.

Stochastic statistical models are ideal for analyses of "normal" risks, where the processes being studied are well understood, there is a large amount of data from which to estimate the probabilities of various outcomes, and the basic context has not changed from the period during which the data were collected. It is important to note that if there is only stochastic error and there is sufficient data to reasonably estimate its nature, then probability estimates for an event or the confidence intervals for an estimated variable (e.g., the average win/loss at a roulette wheel) are entirely valid, since these estimates are explicitly designed to deal with stochastic error. However, when the forces underlying the generation of a phenomena are not well understood, and therefore the statistical models used to estimate risks do not accurately represent the processes being analyzed, there is not only stochastic error, but also *specification* error in the models. Specification error refers to whether the structure of a model fits the phenomenon it is modeling, and misspecification can arise from many sources, including an omitted independent variable or an inappropriate functional form, such as using a linear model for a non-linear phenomenon. Models of complex phenomena, such as the global economy, are almost certainly misspecified, since it will typically be impractical to fully account for the many relevant factors involved and the interactions among them. In a sense, then, post-normal risk and post-normal prediction are about making assessments when we are dealing with misspecified models and have little or no hope of achieving properly specified ones.

Even apparently fairly straightforward social phenomena can be surprisingly post-normal in terms of our ability to reliably predict them. Consider the field of demography, which draws on a large body of data, and many of the phenomena it models are seemingly simple. For example, changes in total population size of a nation are a deterministic function of births, deaths, in-migration, and out-migration. However, births, deaths, and migration are influenced by many factors. So, while there are many patterns in data on these factors, population projections are notoriously unreliable.

Distinguished population scientist Joel Cohen (1995) notes that many demographic projections turned out to be widely off the mark, even shortly after they were made. His analyses of projection making led him to develop the "Law of Prediction," which states: "The more confidence someone places in an unconditional prediction of what will happen in human affairs, the less confidence you should place in that prediction. If a prediction comes with an estimated range of error, then the narrower that range, the less you should believe it" (Cohen 1995, 134).

Displaying his ability for clarity and parsimony, Gene once, for my edification, summed up the field of sociology as centering on the insight that "context matters." This insight led me to see that one of the fundamental problems that arises in prediction making has to do with the dynamic nature of historical context. All of the data we collect comes from a certain context, and that context is prone to change as history has demonstrated many times. Brett Clark and I (York and Clark 2006) referred to the context—including economic, political, cultural, and ecological factors—particular to a time and place as "historical background conditions." We noted that relationships established among variables via empirical analysis may be dependent on the historical background conditions in which the data were collected—in a statistical sense, arising from interaction-effects with one or more of the structural factors that characterize these background conditions—and may not hold in other historical contexts. Thus, even well-established models that are based on rigorous empirical analysis may not be valid in novel circumstances. Given the inevitability of historical change, circumstances may change more frequently that we often think.

A prime example of how changing historical background conditions can invalidate models that made reliable predictions during a limited span of time comes from financial markets and the global economic crisis that began to unfold in 2007. One of the factors that led to the crisis was the widespread reliance among Wall Street banks, bond investors, regulators, ratings agencies, and other actors in the financial sector on the Gaussian copula function developed by David X. Li to estimate complex risks (Salmon 2009). This model for making risk assessments was based on estimated correlations that were derived from data spanning less than a decade, a period during which housing prices grew rapidly. The broad application of this model was based on the Herculean assumption that those correlations would hold generally across changing context. Of course, that assumption was profoundly wrong, and the relationships among financial quantities assumed in the model changed dramatically when housing prices began to decline. Thus, many investments proved to be vastly more risky than the model estimated, as was proven by the widespread financial collapse. Rather than this being an anomalous case, it is almost surely true that most models in the social sciences are based on assumptions that are only valid in a specific context, and those models are unlikely to hold in changing circumstances.

Due to the changing nature of historical background conditions, many regularities in societies that are identified by researchers may not persist into the future, making prediction problematic. In this sense, the social sciences are by their nature post-normal, in that a substantial level of uncertainty is inherent in the phenomena under study. This does not mean that the social sciences do not contribute to our understanding of social phenomena; they surely do. However, central to our understanding of social phenomena is the recognition that social structures are imbedded in historical contexts, and these contexts inevitably change, and this change, while not insensible, is dependent on many contingent events. So, social sciences can explain things sensibly after the fact, but cannot typically make reliable predictions. As noted above, this does not mean that the social sciences are less "scientific" than the natural sciences. For example, there is clear continuity between the social sciences and Darwinian evolutionary theory, which has identified sensible natural laws (e.g., natural selection), but these laws do not allow for certain predictions of the course of evolution (Dietz and Burns 1992; McLaughlin 2001; York and Clark 2011).

The social sciences are often called on to make predictions about a wide variety of matters—demographic, economic, political—and any planning process requires some form of prediction making, if only implicitly. However, due to the inherent challenges involved in making such predictions, as explained here, the predictions cannot be made in a "normal" manner. Thus, the social sciences are in many regards deeply "post-normal." This realization points to the importance and broad relevance of Gene's Meta paper, since the insights contained therein do not, then, only apply to risk assessment, but to the very nature of applying social science to understanding our world.

Post-Normal Rosa

As I hope I have shown here, Meta, which made a highly important contribution to risk research, also has important implications about the philosophical underpinnings of and the practice of social (as well as natural) scientific research. A central feature of Meta, which is made abundantly clear by its title, is that it takes metatheory seriously. While most scientists rarely think about metatheoretical issues explicitly, Gene clearly recognizes the importance of considering the broader assumptions that underlie scientific research and practical action. He knows that part of being a good scientist is recognizing the limits of science to answer some questions. This does not involve giving in to unclear, postmodernist-style thinking, but, rather, reflects a rational understanding of the limits imposed on us by available information. In this, Gene is a model of a reflexive scientist, one who understands the importance of thinking about the constraints on our knowledge, some of which stem from the availability of evidence and some from paradigmatic strictures, without giving in to intellectual nihilism. In some respects, Gene's perspective represents a shift away from "normal" science and its commitment to work within a given paradigm. Therefore, his perspective is in a sense "post-normal," but it maintains a strong commitment to rational, scientific inquiry. In fact, Gene is in many regards post-normal, in all of the best senses of that term.

Note

1. I am not ignorant of the complicated philosophical problems around the concept of probability. In one sense, we don't truly know the probability with certainty of even something as simple as rolling a one on a six-sided die. We can estimate this empirically by rolling it many times and examining the frequency distribution of each number. But for the purpose of this discussion I rely on the intuitive and common sense recognition that there is a one in six chance of rolling a one on a six-sided die, which is implicit in the assumption that the die is "fair."

References

Dietz, Thomas, and Tom R. Burns. 1992. "Human Agency and the Evolutionary Dynamics of Culture." *Acta Sociologica* 35:187-200.

Funtowicz, Silvio O., and Jerome R. Ravetz. 1992. "The Good, the True and the Post-Modern." *Futures* 24: 963-976.

Goldstein, Rebecca. 2005. *Incompleteness: The Proof and Paradox of Kurt Gödel.* New York: W.W. Norton.

Jaeger, Carlo C., Ortwin Renn, Eugene A. Rosa, and Thomas Webler. 2001. *Risk, Uncertainty, and Rational Action.* London: Earthscan.

Kumar, Manjit. 2010. *Quantum: Einstein, Bohr, and the Great Debate about the Nature of Reality.* New York: W.W. Norton.

Lindley, David. 2007. *Uncertainty: Einstein, Heisenberg, Bohr, and the Struggle for the Soul of Science.* New York: Doubleday.

McLaughlin, Paul. 2001. "Towards an Ecology of Social Action: Merging the Ecological and Constructivist Traditions." *Human Ecology Review* 8:12-28.

Rosa, Eugene A. 1998. "Metatheoretical Foundations for Post-Normal Risk." *Journal of Risk Research* 1(1): 15-44.

Salmon, Felix. 2009. "Recipe for Disaster: The Formula that Killed Wall Street." *Wired Magazine* 17(3). http://www.wired.com/techbiz/it/magazine/17-03/wp_quant?currentPage=all.

Salsburg, David. 2002. *The Lady Tasting Tea: How Statistics Revolutionized Science in the Twentieth Century.* New York: Owl Books.

Stigler, Stephen M. 1986. *The History of Statistics: The Measurement of Uncertainty before 1900.* Cambridge: Harvard University Press.

York, Richard, and Brett Clark. 2011. *The Science and Humanism of Stephen Jay Gould.* New York: Monthly Review Press.

———. 2007. "The Problem with Prediction: Contingency, Emergence, and the Reification of Projections." *The Sociological Quarterly* 48: 713-743.

———. 2006. "Marxism, Positivism, and Scientific Sociology: Social Gravity and Historicity." *The Sociological Quarterly* 47(3): 425-450.

CHAPTER 3

Epistemology, Ontology, and the Practice of Structural Human Ecology

Thomas Dietz, Michigan State University

O NE OF THE KEY FEATURES of structural human ecology is its concern with foundational theoretical issues, what some refer to as meta-theory. While engagement with conceptual issues is evident in the work of, for example, Andrew Vayda (Vayda 1988; Vayda 2009) or Paul McLaughlin (McLaughlin 2012; McLaughlin and Dietz 2008), it is generally absent from most threads of human ecological work. The high quality of research in such traditions as coupled human and natural systems (Liu et al. 2007a; Liu et al. 2007b), land change science (Turner et al. 2007), resilience (Folke 2006; Turner 2010), and sustainability science (Clark and Dickson 2003; Kates et al. 2001) demonstrate that inattention to theoretical fundamentals is not a fatal flaw. But Gene Rosa's work also shows how much can be gained, and how much confusion can be avoided, by careful thought about the meta-theoretical underpinnings of our efforts.[1] Equally important, attention to foundational issues clarifies the relationship between science and decision making, a topic too much neglected in traditional human ecology (Dietz 1988; Dietz 1994).

Gene's most noted contribution to the meta-theoretical underpinnings of structural human ecology is "Meta-Theoretical Underpinnings of Post-Normal Risk" (Rosa 1998b), which Richard York (Chapter 2) and I refer to as Meta.[2] Richard shows that Gene's arguments about uncertainty apply to all scientific contexts in which we must make predictions, that is, to virtually all science applied to problems of decision making. I want to focus on a related but slightly different aspect of Meta—the implications of Gene's arguments for how we think about expertise for decision making. In a sense, Gene provides a much needed epistemological basis for analytic deliberative processes that have become a common approach to linking science and values.

The literature on linked scientific analysis and public deliberation has only engaged the issue of knowledge formation informally. Rather than address epistemology, much of the deliberative literature is grounded in practical and ethical considerations, so examination of ontological and epistemological issues seems warranted.[3]

The Meta Framework

Risk analysis has some features that are quite different from those of science conducted for its own sake—"pure" science. In "pure" science the goal is simply advancing knowledge. In contrast, risk analysis is nearly always done to advance knowledge in ways that inform policy. In pure science, the stance towards uncertainty is largely a matter of "wait and see."[4] Being unable to choose among several or even myriad possible outcomes of an event or action is seen as an interesting challenge. The appropriate response is to develop better theory and methods. Reducing uncertainty may be of tremendous scientific importance, but uncertainty does not present any critical epistemological or ethical concerns. For example, high energy physics or paleontology can usually claim substantial distance from normative or ethical considerations.[5] Risk analysis, and, by strong analogy, most environmental and sustainability science, cannot maintain this distance. Risk analysis is at the doorstep of, or even in the conference room with, ethical discussions about what decision to make. Thus, relationships between the positive and the ethical require elaboration. The Meta framework provides a way to conduct that elaboration. Richard has discussed the implications of uncertainty for predictions. I will focus on the ethical or value implications of Meta.

There is an aspect of risk analysis where we would like positive science to prevail. Risk analysis requires assessing the facts of things such as the toxicity of a compound, the transport mechanisms that move pollutants through soil, water, air and other media, or the sensitivity of climate to human actions. Most of us adopt, *a la* Meta, a realist ontology (there are facts independent of our thoughts about them) and a "reconstructed realist" or hierarchical epistemology (our understanding of the facts may be imperfect and influenced by social and psychological forces) when dealing with these sorts of knowledge claims. For example, we believe that there is a real process that links increased greenhouse gas concentrations in the atmosphere to climate change. We also acknowledge that our understanding of this process is uncertain and can be influenced, at least over the short term, by social forces.

A hierarchical epistemology acknowledges that at levels ranging from the individual scientist to the global scientific community, there are many biasing forces that drive our perception of reality away from reality. As individuals we are certainly biased toward seeing results that we hope or expect to see. Stephen Gould eloquently documented the tragedy of these biases in the study of human difference (Gould 1965). The tradition of laboratory studies in the sociology of science shows the influence of social construction processes on the results reported from the labs studied (Knorr-Cetina 1981; Knorr-Cetina 2005; Latour and Woolgar 1986). At least since Kuhn we have been attentive to the pressures within scientific communities to favor results consistent with dominant paradigms and ignore or question results that challenge the paradigm (Kuhn 1962). Around issues with substantial political charge, including decisions about risk, campaigns attempt to emphasize uncertainty in science and favor results that question evidence of environmental and health problems (McCright 2000; McCright and Dunlap 2010; Michaels and Monforton 2005; Michaels 2006, 2008).

Reconstructed realists argue that these intended and unintended biases in factual understanding are usually countered, at least in the long term, by an evolutionary epistemology (Campbell 1960; Campbell 1987; Radnitzky and Bartley 1987). Strong norms of science favor accepting ideas that seem to match empirical observations and that are theoretically coherent. Thus there is selective pressure in the scientific community to favor ideas that line up with empirical reality. This selection process leads to increasing coherence between scientific knowledge and reality. Because the selective pressure comes from norms that must be interpreted to be applied to a particular problem, and the process is one of selective retention acting over time, it can take a considerable period of time for new ideas to replace old ones. Nor is the process innocent of power and unconscious bias. But reconstructed realists argue that these selective pressures are usually fairly strong because the norms of science are an important part of the identity of scientists. So over time, scientific knowledge becomes a better match to reality. It is this kind of process that underpins Gene's argument that: "The important points are that knowledge does not result from all social processes and that some knowledge seems to accord better with the world or is, at least, more reliable than other knowledge" (Rosa 1998b 23).

Meta then noted that the place where evolutionary epistemology works best is in situations where we have high ostensibility and repeatability. Of course, ostensibility has to be determined in a context-sensitive way. "In essence, the ostensibility criterion asks the question: 'Do you see what I see?'" (Rosa 1998b 35). Much of the elaboration of science across the late nineteenth and twentieth centuries was via the development of ever more subtle observational technologies and methods of handling data (Bennett 1998; Galison 1997; Salsburg 2001; Stigler 1986). The result is that in the early twenty-first century, some of the science that is seen as highly ostensible is based on a long chain of inference linking measurement of subtle phenomena to statistical analysis of what is observed. "Seeing what I see" in these fields of research depends on belonging to the same epistemic community and thus sharing in the same understanding of measurement processes.[6] Work in high energy physics, observational aspects of cosmology, much of molecular biology, and many other areas involve well accepted observations that no one detects directly with human senses but rather a long chain of instrumentation and data processing. This has not proven troubling given that each step in the process is well established. These are also areas of science where repeatability is very strong. A new finding is firmly established when either the experiment or observation is repeated by other research teams or when other lines of evidence provide confirmation.[7] At a more detailed level, many measurements involve data from millions or billions of instances of the phenomena being studied.

The use of invariance principles makes progress in many areas of the physical and biological sciences much easier than in the more historical and evolutionary sciences, including most of the social sciences.[8] With strong invariance principles, a measurement conducted at one time and place should yield the same results if it were conducted in other places at other times. For these fields of study we can confidently apply principles and even measurements developed in contemporary laboratories on earth to phenomena billions of years distant in time and comparably remote in space. In many other fields of inquiry it would be naïve to make such heroic assumptions. As Richard notes, Gene has made the point that the major lesson of sociology (and kindred disciplines) is that "context matters." Invariance principles must be applied with great caution. So in that sense, sociology and the other evolutionary/historical disciplines are the "hard"—in the sense of difficult—sciences.

The science we must deploy in risk analysis varies considerably with regard to invariance. Key physical properties used in some aspects of risk analysis are invariant for all practical purposes. The half-life of Iodine-131 can always be assumed to be about eight days.[9] But ecological and social dynamics can be very context dependent. So repeatability can be high when strong invariance principles apply but low when they do not. In many cases the new context we must address in risk analysis is the future, and given climate change and other global environmental changes, the future will entrain environmental stresses that are not part of the recent historical record.

Ostensibility also varies. Some forms of air and water pollution are manifestly evident to our senses, as are some changes in ecosystems. But other phenomena are harder to observe because they are not directly detectable to our senses, e.g. radiation and many pollutants, or because the effects are cumulative changes to complex systems over time, e.g. climate change. Perhaps the largest problem for ostensibility, one Richard discusses in detail in Chapter 2, is that most risk analysis requires projections into the future, usually conditional projections about what would happen if we pursue one course of action over another. Projecting conditional futures nearly always requires modeling, and with modeling we cannot expect much ostensibility.[10] The models involved are often complex so they can capture the interactions being considered (else we would not need models), and most humans require substantial training to understand even relatively simple mathematics and systems dynamics (Sterman 2008; Sterman and Sweeney 2007).

Gene made clear that the variation in ostensibility and repeatability across the scientific analyses used in risk and environmental science preclude a simple neo-positivist epistemology. Rather he suggested a space defined by the degree to which an understanding is based on ostensible and on repeatable phenomena, and noted that we often must occupy areas within that space where the underpinnings of standard realist epistemology are not well justified. These are places where evolutionary epistemology will be slow to lead to concordance between scientific understanding and reality because selective pressures against incorrect understandings will not be as strong as would be the case when we are in the area of high ostensibility and repeatability.[11]

The challenge of risk analysis, and of most decisions with regard to environment and sustainability, is that we must either apply general understandings to specific contexts or make predictions about the future or both. So while we may draw substantially on knowledge that comes from a "normal science" region of high ostensibility and repeatability, that knowledge by itself is usually not sufficient to draw conclusions useful for making decisions. Nor can we wait in the hope that such knowledge will emerge from the evolutionary process that improves our understanding. As Collins and Evans put it: "Science, if it can deliver truth, cannot deliver it at the speed of politics (Collins and Evans 2007: 1)."[12]

Gene wrote extensively on technological controversies and especially the conflict around nuclear power (Freudenburg and Rosa 1984; Rosa 1988; Rosa 2007; Rosa and Dunlap 1994; Rosa et al. 2010; Rosa and Clark 1999).[13]

In these situations, as in most other collective decisions, trust is crucial. As Gene noted in his response to the comments of Ravetz and Funtowicz on Meta (Ravetz and Funtowicz 1998; Rosa 1998a: 113), "The typical objections of laypersons, then, is not to science per se—nor with the ontological assumption of realism upon which it builds—but to institutions that attempt to maintain a monopoly on knowledge claims and which sometimes misapply abstract science to the peculiarities of local settings." This is a situation where trust can be shattered. Trust in conclusions that might be warranted in an area of high ostensibility and repeatability should not be granted in contexts where there is a lack of ostensibility and repeatability. Sharp conflicts can arise when it is necessary to generalize to a context that has not been much studied. General findings may lead risk analysts to believe that risks are minimal. Members of the public understandably want to know how their community and their children will be affected, not about generalities. Such circumstances, common in risk analysis, warrant considerable humility about the validity and reliability of our conclusions. They also require recognition of multiple forms of expertise.

A long line of scholarship, to which Gene contributed, argues that the proper way to bring science to bear in risk analysis is through linking public deliberation with scientific analysis, and acknowledging multiple forms of expertise, including the knowledge of local context that can come from life experience.[14] The idea is that dialogue between scientific analysts and the interested and affected public will build trust in the science and help the scientific community understand the local context. It also can clarify the concerns of those who will bear the costs, benefits, and risks that follow from a decision.

The Problem of Values

Early in Meta, Gene made the point that "the field of risk is a topic involving scientific investigation where the long venerated philosophical dictum of separating facts from values, of separating the categorical from the normative ('Don't mix is with ought'), is relentlessly blurred..." (Rosa 1998b: 16). In the forthcoming *The Risk Society: Social Theory and Governance* he and his co-authors emphasized this point: "This is not to deny the importance of normative considerations, since they are important requisites for the decision-making and governance features of risk characterization and management, but not of risk per se" (Rosa et al. 2013: 65). I interpret this to mean that one can and must draw a distinction between factual and ethical considerations but that this is difficult to do in risk decision making and often is not done adequately.

I will take a lesson from Gene's continual emphasis on conceptual clarity. It is useful to make several points about the relationship between ethical considerations and scientific analysis in the context of risk. First, I suggest that it is possible to distinguish between facts and values, between what is and what one ought to do, in a way that is useful in making decisions about risk. But that is not to say that there is not slippage between the two in practice.

Thus my second point is that values—what people care about—should influence what topics are considered in scientific research but not the outcomes of that research. The analytic deliberation literature follows up on Dewey's definition of the public (Dewey 1923): all those interested in or affected by a decision. Scientific analysis in support of decision making should examine both issues that the scientific community thinks are important and issues that the public, à la Dewey, considers important. Such items should be given attention in the research agenda even if they would not be on the list of priorities generated by the scientific community acting alone. This is one way in which it is legitimate for values and ethical considerations to influence factual analysis.

Of course, we know from long and difficult experience that it is all too easy for powerful actors to influence science so that conclusions they prefer are more likely to be reached. This happens even if elite influence violates the norms of science. The influence of the powerful will be more problematic when we are in areas of low ostensibility and repeatability. Concern with these political pressures has informed some major statements calling for use of analytic deliberative processes in risk and policy analysis. These statements emphasize that care must be taken to avoid political influence on the outcomes of research, even while allowing the public to influence the questions asked by the research (e.g. U.S. National Research Council 2010). Of course, given finite time and scientific resources, adding items to the research agenda has an influence on what we understand and what we don't understand. As a result the content of scientific understanding is never free of the influence of values.[15] But we can produce science that is reasonably trustworthy for decision making if we keep such influences transparent and minimize them. The norms of science can help us to guard against values influencing conclusions while allowing values to influence the research topics we give priority.[16]

Linking deliberation to analysis can aid in this, especially if we acknowledge that there are multiple forms of expertise needed in understanding context and assessing values in making a decision. Paul Stern (Stern 2005, Chapter 6, personal communication) had noted that bringing people with different values to a discussion can make it easier to see value-laden assumptions hidden in seemingly objective analysis. Over time, this can help avoid such assumptions or compensate for them. In domains of knowledge with high ostensibility and repeatability it can be relatively easy to purge value-based biases. Relatively few people today have value-based positions on existence of earth-like planets outside the solar system or on whether or not the Higgs boson could be detected.[17] But when we lack ostensibility and repeatability, we have to find additional ways to identify and control value biases that may creep into factual conclusions. As Paul argues, having multiple value standpoints in the discussion can aid substantially with this.[18]

My final point is that, as Gene and his collaborators have eloquently noted, there can be a strong tendency to move from assumptions about how humans behave, in particular the rational actor model, to ethical positions about how to decide what policy is best (see also Dietz 1994; Jaeger et al. 2001). Those who assume that humans make decisions via a utility maximization rational actor process often assume that it is appropriate to use a utilitarian logic (the greatest good to the greatest number) for making collective decisions. But the rational actor model is a description of how humans make decisions. Even if one accepts it as true—and many of us question it (Dietz and Stern 1995; Kahneman 2011)—that does not provide justification for using a utility maximization calculus to make collective decisions. When a decision-making process assumes that the rational actor model implies benefit-cost ratios as a basis for decisions, then there is an inappropriate slippage between positive scientific analysis (which might or might not support the rational actor model) and value-based ethical analysis of how we ought to make decisions.[19]

Ostensibility and Repeatability in the Realm of Values

Gene's contributions have clarified what we can expect of science, drawing on the insights of constructivism while embracing both a realist ontology and a reconstructed realist or evolutionary epistemology. This not only helps clarify conflicts over risks and other sustainability challenges but also suggests the importance of linked scientific analysis and public deliberation when we are in areas with low ostensibility and repeatability.

These arguments may also provide considerable clarification to the problem of uncertain values, which I have argued is a major cause of conflict over risk, environmental, technology, and sustainability decisions (Dietz 2001; Dietz 2003). Many of these decisions require us to think about phenomena that are new to us. Often we have to consider things that have not yet happened or at least not happened in the context about which a decision must be made. On routine issues we can deploy our values with relative ease and use them as guides to what options we prefer (Dewey 1888/1969). But for decisions about new problems and decisions in new contexts we must construct our preferences by consulting our values. We often do this with great speed. We construct preferences by looking for clues about how the new decision relates to our existing preferences, including trying to decide what social role—parent, citizen, consumer, etc.—is the most appropriate one for making a particular decision. We attempt to assess the decision before us in relationship to issues on which we already have views (Dietz and Stern 1995). Once an initial judgment is in place, processes of biased assimilation of new information and homophily in personal association can reinforce the casually formed initial position. All this is troubling if we hope for reasoned ethical discourse on complex issues such as climate change, biodiversity loss, direct interfaces between the human brain and machines, the role of intelligent robots in society, and a myriad of other issues.

Perhaps when novel ethical problems are ostensible and repeatable, it may be relatively easy to move away from quickly formed and then reinforced initial views and toward more reasoned processes of thinking through the ethics of new and complex issues. Most of human existence has been spent in food foraging societies. There the implications of individual and group decisions on things people valued were reasonably ostensible and repeatable. Of course interactions of coupled human and natural systems are often subtle and some aspects of them were always beyond the detection limits of folk ecologies based on sensory observation and verbal transmission of information. But for the most part, cause and effect links would have been fairly visible and most decisions were of a character that they would be often repeated, if not by the same individual, then at least by other members of the community and across generations.

In the twenty-first century the impacts of our actions on things we value are much harder to observe. Of course, some decisions, such as how to interact face to face with others, are in many ways similar to the same kinds of decisions made by food foraging ancestors tens of millennia ago.[20] However many of the issues for which we deploy risk analysis raise the same difficulties in deciding what ethical stance we wish to take as they do in understanding what the facts are. This is especially true, as Richard emphasizes, when we must consider the future outcomes of our actions. Should we allow parents to manipulate the genome of their offspring? Should we allow an individual to clone him or herself? We have a strong tendency to say "no" on ethical grounds. But how do we come to this judgment? It a bit strained to argue that shaping the genome of a child or altering the global climate has ostensible consequences for our values, or that it is just one more repetition of a class of ethical problems we have considered frequently before. Some of the risks we face, such as terrorism, are perhaps just modern versions of the threats of unexpected violence (e.g. invaders from across the steppes) that we have faced for millennia. But decisions about nuclear power make commitments for millennia to come. The consequences of burning fossil fuel effects everyone on the globe and will continue to unfold for one or two millennia. We are reminded "Extinction is forever."[21] For each of these issues we have to think about the implications over long time periods as the dynamics of complex adaptive systems unfold. And I mean this not just in terms of determining the facts: will storing radioactive waste at Yucca Mountain contaminate groundwater?; will the global mean temperatures increase by 5°C or more? The Meta perspective draws attention to the difficulties we face in thinking through what these changes will mean for the things we value.

Are There Ways to Enhance Ostensibility and Visibility?

The Meta approach urges us to be reflective regarding where we sit in the space of ostensibility and repeatability, and to be properly humble about claims regarding factual knowledge when we sit far from the high ostensibility and repeatability "sweet spot" for traditional science. By analogy, I would suggest humility is warranted in asserting our values in support of ethical principles in areas of low value ostensibility and repeatability. For facts, the traditional justifications for privileging science are attenuated when ostensibility and repeatability are low. One response is a call for more specificity about the limits of scientific understanding, more engagement with those possessing traditional ecological knowledge, and strong links between scientific analysis and public deliberation. The goal is to enhance understanding of, and trust in, the science available, including its limits. Such processes also help in understanding how to apply general knowledge to the context about which decisions are to be made. In a sense, this is a case where we need a move away from viewing scientists as autonomous experts and toward a view of scientists as carriers of special knowledge that must be complemented with other forms of knowledge. It is a context in which respect for public understanding is enhanced.

Collins and Evans (Collins and Evans 2007) call for increased use of what they call "interactional expertise" in scientific controversies. In their conceptualization, interactional expertise is the province of those who know enough of a domain of science to carry on an informed conversation with experts but not enough to carry out research in that area, an ability they label "contributory expertise."[22] Putting aside the question of the distinction between these two types of expertise, I want to consider a key point that follows from their arguments: when societal decisions depend substantially on science and technology we might be well served by engaging multiple forms of expertise to help us all think through the implications of the science.[23] When we are dealing with ethical questions of limited ostensibility and repeatability, it can be hard for us to see the implications for our values of what might happen. We are subject to the pitfalls of fast cognition, heuristics and biases in risk perception, biased assimilation, and homophily in our affiliations and information seeking. We may start with an almost random value position, or one overly influenced by the efforts of the powerful to shape public views, and adhere to and strengthen that view over time.

This may be a problem where applied ethicists could help inform public debates, not so much by arguing for their favored position and against other stances as by pointing out clearly the multiple ways in which a set of decisions might affect things we value. Researchers have begun to examine a number of methods for structuring discussions so that people can explore what values come to bear in thinking about a decision (Arvai et al. 2001; Crocker et al. 2008) and more work is surely needed. When faced with assessing our values around an issue with low ostensibility and repeatability we need help. It may be that methods that help make us aware of a full range of ethical considerations and that encourage thoughtful reflection and respectful discussion might help avoid premature closure and polarization.

We should not be naïve about the ability of such processes to influence political discourse and decision making, especially at a national level. The debate on climate change, for example, is strongly shaped by those who have a material interest in the outcome of the debate and they have proven very effective at misrepresenting the science of climate change in order to achieve their policy objectives. Such forces always offer well-crafted arguments that consciously tie into the prior beliefs and the values of those new to an issue. As Cialdini noted, there are many who actively manipulate the cognitive short cuts on which we depend. Too often, these manipulations are to our detriment and their benefit (Cialdini 2007 [1984]).[24]

I would also suggest that in circumstances of low ostensibility and repeatability we need to redefine expertise in a different way than do Collins and Evans. They are concerned primarily with expertise about facts and thus about science as a source of accurate information about the state of the world. Certainly scientific expertise of this sort is critical for most important decisions. But even if we knew what would happen under different courses of action with certainty, that would not be sufficient to make an individual or collective decision. In most cases there is no solution that is optimal across all values that are brought to the decision. We have to make decisions in the face of multiple values, some of which will conflict with others. And in reality there will always be considerable uncertainty about how decisions might influence things we value.

Social scientific expertise can be useful in describing the value positions that exist around an issue and how prevalent they are. Social science can also provide insights into how processes that are intended to elicit value positions and integrate them into a decision actually work when put into practice. But scientific expertise does not have any special privilege in determining what values should be favored and what values should be harmed when a decision is made. We often confuse competencies, thinking scientific expertise is sufficient, not just necessary, for good decisions.

We have to supplement scientific expertise with at least two other forms of expertise (Dietz 1987; Dietz 2013; Dietz and Pfund 1988). One I have labeled community expertise but I am really referring simply to Dewey's interested or affected public. In cases of low ostensibility and repeatability, community experts may need help in thinking through the implications for their values. But ultimately, the interested and affected parties must speak to the values at stake in a decision; usually that input cannot be delegated to others.

In many cases it is essential to engage political expertise. Those who are actively engaged in policy systems will often have substantial knowledge of what is feasible to implement, how a decision will interact with existing policies, programs, and institutions, and what approaches have any hope of succeeding. In principle these are questions that might be answered via scientific inquiry. Certainly scientific study of policy systems is much needed as a part of structural human ecology. But just as the generalized knowledge of science must be supplemented with local understandings to "get the science right" in a particular context, so too must general understandings of policy and politics be supplemented with local knowledge to apply them to specific decisions.

Engagement with political expertise is a mixed blessing in decision making. Those engaged in the policy system can clarify many issues. They also may bring rather rigid value positions to the discussion. In many circumstances institutions can be designed to overcome the "tragedy of the commons" that can otherwise obtain from individual and organizational self-interest (Dietz et al. 2003; Ostrom et al. 2002). But we also know that policy systems can become highly polarized and antagonistic (Sabatier and Weible 2007; Weible and Sabatier 2007). This is one reason to identify political expertise as a separate domain from community expertise. Not all values from the public may receive reasonable representation in the policy system when it has become fragmented and polarized.

The logic of ostensibility and repeatability clarifies the difference between community and political expertise. A key job of a political expert is to examine carefully the implications of a decision for the interests she or he represents. That is, they must examine the implications of a potential decision for the values of their client. Often political experts can see the consequences of an action even when those consequences may not be very visible to others. They create value ostensibility. And since they work on such issues routinely, it is much more likely that they see and learn from parallel problems appearing repeatedly.[25] So they, unlike the general public/community experts, are working in a space where we may anticipate that value positions are well developed and less subject to quick heuristics. The problem is that they represent, because of personal passion or salary, specific subsets of the full range of values that may be affected by a decision. Thus we cannot expect them to be even-handed. So while they have a context that allows them to be reasonably sure of the value implications of a decision for what they and their clients care about, we must be cautious in using such positions to represent the larger community, where each individuals will bring multiple and even conflicting values to bear on every decision.

Conclusion

In Meta, Gene provided a wonderful synthesis that clarifies the ontology and epistemology of risk-related science. But he goes beyond that to map the terrain where "traditional" science can guide us, and a different terrain where we have to be especially attentive to the limits of traditional science. I have argued that his emphasis on ostensibility and repeatability lays a strong foundation for thinking about deliberative process and how they should be structured. Further, I have argued that this groundwork can support our thinking not only about science and facts but also about ethical discourses and values. Here the machinery by which we proceed is less well developed. Indeed, I have argued elsewhere that we often avoid discussion of value differences and value uncertainty in order to focus on differences in beliefs and uncertainty about facts (Dietz 2001; Dietz 2013).

The logic of Meta has opened up important debates in the risk literature about the role of science (Aven and Renn 2009; Aven and Renn 2010; Aven et al. 2011; Ravetz and Funtowicz 1998; Rosa 1998a; Rosa 2010). I suggest that it can also be a very useful, and very badly needed, stimulus to thinking about how we should analyze and conduct deliberations about values as well as about facts. This essay takes a few tentative steps on the path that Meta shows us.

Notes

1. By meta-theory I mean "grand theory" of general processes (Dietz and Burns 1992; McLaughlin 1998; McLaughlin and Dietz 2008), work delineating the relationship between positive and normative theory (Dietz 1994; Dietz and Stern 1998), work on ontology and epistemology (Rosa 1998b), and, especially for this essay, work that links these themes.

2. Gene wrote extensively on these issues, including in two major monographs (Jaeger et al. 2001; Rosa et al. 2013). But "Meta" is the core piece.

3. There are several exceptions to this general pattern, including *Understanding Risk,* a report from the U.S. National Academies (U.S. National Research Council 1996) that considered how deliberative processes help to "get the science right." Paul Stern (Stern 2005) has built on this and related work (Dietz and Stern 1998) to emphasize that deliberative processes build better understanding of the science especially when we are in Gene's area of low ostensibility and repeatability.

4. Of course, uncertainty is an intrinsic feature of the universe (or universes) in quantum theory, but in most other areas of science, phenomena are considered to be predictable in principle even if in practice the best theory will be stochastic (e.g. statistical mechanics).

5. In discussing science it has been common practice to draw the distinction between normative and positive analysis. But because the norms of scientific practice are discussed here, I will use the term ethical rather than normative to avoid confusion.

6. Galison (1997) invokes the idea of pidgin and Creole languages that evolve in order to allow shared ostensibility in high energy physics.

7. The ongoing saga of retractions of seemingly important research results is evidence that this process is at work in contemporary science.

8. While the focus of my discussion is on the environmental and social sciences, a lack of ostensibility and repeatability also characterizes much of evolutionary biology, astronomy, climatology, and other biological and physical science areas where

evidence usually comes from carefully assessing the implications for theory of observational rather than experimental data. (I thank Ortwin Renn for emphasizing this point.)

9. Iodine-131 is a radioactive isotope of iodine that is quite dangerous to humans and other animals and often generated in nuclear explosions and reactor accidents but is rather short lived. The half-life is critical in determining risk after events like Chernobyl or Fukushima.

10. Levins (1966; 1993); Orzack and Sober (1993) established the point the models can be realistic, precise, or general but that no model can optimize all three. Rosa et al. (2012) have applied this insight to risk comparisons.

11. Repeatability matters because each repetition is another test that pressures the scientific community to move toward the view that best matches reality. Ostensibility matters because when there can be debate about what is being observed, it is easier to cling to prior beliefs based on different interpretations of what different observers report.

12. My argument about the need for context specific understanding applies to situations where we have to understand the dynamics of complex systems and especially complex adaptive systems, such as coupled human and natural systems. There are certainly decision-making problems where conventional science can be readily adapted to the local context. Much of civil engineering is about just such applications. The difference revolves around whether or not there are substantial non-linearities and feedback loops that need to be considered in projecting what will happen. Hubris can occur when it is assumed that all systems behave in the relatively simple ways that some physical systems do.

13. This is hardly surprising given that Allan Mazur, a pioneer in the study of technological controversies (Mazur 1981; Mazur 2004), was Gene's dissertation advisor.

14. The approach has come to be called linked analysis and deliberation or analytic deliberation for short. The framework draws on Dewey (1888/1969; 1923) and Habermas (1970; 1991). There have been a number of arguments for deploying the theory around risk, environmental decision making, and sustainability (Dietz 1987; Renn et al. 1995). The U.S. National Academies have issued a number of reports reviewing the relevant literature and calling for the approach (U.S. National Research Council 1996; U.S. National Research Council 2008; U.S. National Research Council 2010).

15. Schnaiberg made the useful distinction between production sciences that facilitate growth and production on the one hand, and impact sciences that delineate the results of growth and production on the other (Schnaiberg 1980). He noted, as has Paul Ehrlich, that we systematically under-invest in the impact sciences. This is yet another way that power influences the content of science without distorting specific scientific results.

16. My informal impression is that the usual political tactic is rather crude. Rather than adding items to the research agenda and thus diluting efforts on any one topic, political interference usually takes the form of trying to block research. Thus gun advocates in the United States have included language in legislation to block federal research agencies from studying gun related violence (Kassirer 1995). Another tactic is harassment of scientists working on topics threatening to powerful interests, which

has been commonplace around climate change and gun control (Brown 2008; Shulman 2006).

17. Of course, in the sixteenth and seventeenth centuries, planetary astronomy did have strong implications for values and politics. To follow Gene's argument, as the evidence for a heliocentric solar systems became more ostensible and repeatable, other views became untenable and dropped from discourse. Some who take the Christian Bible as literally true question evolution and much of science that depends on "deep time" (Roos 2012) but few still question that the Earth revolves around the sun.

18. Paul Stern (personal communication) has also suggested, and I concur, that having multiple disciplines involved in the discussion can be helpful in uncovering unintentional influences of values on factual conclusions.

19. The relationship between the rational actor model and collective decision making is more complex that can be described here, involving consideration of Arrow's impossibility theorem on aggregating ordinal preferences (Arrow 1951) and the first fundamental theorem of welfare economics on efficient resource allocation in competitive markets as well as the huge literature that has expanded on these basic ideas. One particular vexing problem is how to handle risk, which quickly entrains the added problem of how to discount future events. There is considerable debate even among economists working in the utilitarian tradition on how to discount the future (Dasgupta 2008; Nordhaus 2012; Portney and Weyant 1999; Weitzman 2009). We know that members of the public also have sharply differing views about how best to handle uncertainty. For example, nearly all guidance on how to make personal investments includes an attempt to assess individual tolerance for risk because it varies so much from person to person. Research can help identify public views on these matters and can evaluate tools to help people think through their preferences about how to handle risk, but science cannot resolve how we *should* handle risk—that is an ethical issue. Renn, in his comprehensive volume *Risk Governance* (2008: 64-65, 146-147), suggests that there are three issues that must be addressed by deliberative processes: what facts matter, how risk should be handled, and how to value each possible outcome.

20. That is not to deny that interpersonal interactions are increasingly mediated by technology.

21. Of course there is substantial evidence that humans were a major cause of the extinction of Pleistocene megafauna. But those hunters were probably not aware that they were driving these species extinct, so the ethical considerations we face around mass extinctions today are novel.

22. Gene recommended this interesting book to me.

23. While *Rethinking Expertise* spawns many useful thoughts, I am not convinced that the distinction between contributory and interactional expertise is especially useful when we think about science applied to decision making. Thus I am not sure it is a useful guide to interactions between scientific communities and the public. First, many scientists partake of both forms of expertise—Gene's and my good friend Stephen Schneider was an exemplar of this. But not everyone has such abilities. Scientists who can make major contributions to science but not communicate effectively with the public don't have talent for or training in an area of expertise different from their core science—effective communication with audiences outside

their specialty. Of course there are many calls for scientists to do a better job. But these calls seldom acknowledge the time costs, and in contentious domains such as climate change, the costs in stress, of moving from the role of the scientist as researcher to the scientist as communicator. The problem may rest more in the fora where we ask for participation rather than with the scientists themselves. Scientists are asked to become skilled in communicating in venues that are poorly designed for the communication of science. Perhaps we should emphasize redesigning the venues. Second, the distinction between contributory and interactional makes much of "tacit" knowledge that goes with the former. But I wonder if such knowledge is tacit only because no one has taken the time to write the lab manual or produce the instructional video. The difference between those who contribute in major ways and those who don't is a mixture of luck (some Nobel laureates know they are pursuing major questions, some end up addressing major questions because they are very thoughtful about anomalous results) and insight about what questions to ask and how to ask them. This may be what is meant by "tacit knowledge" but it seems an odd definition. Two students could have identical training and know exactly the same techniques and have the same command of the literature but one asks deep questions that change the field and the other does routine work. To say one has tacit knowledge and the other does not seems stretching what the term might mean. My larger point is that what we need is not so much interactional expertise as Collins and Evans define it (or perhaps as I am misinterpreting what they mean) but rather expertise in how to structure interaction among the kinds of expertise needed for decisions.

24. Cialdini's concerns with this manipulation stand in sharp contrast to the tone found in the recent rediscovery of cognitive and social psychology by economics. There the idea of a "nudge" is usually raised with little concern about the power relations involved (Dietz 2011). Compare Cialdini's classic (Cialdini 2007 [1984]) with Thaler and Sunstein (Thaler and Sunstein 2009).

25. Of course, this may come at the cost of oversimplification and focusing on only one aspect of a problem or even stereotyping a policy proposal. Scientists think a great deal about the nuances of various climate mitigation policies. But those opposed to such policies often seem to focus on only one criterion—that mitigation imposes regulation and/or increased costs.

References

Arrow, Kenneth. 1951. *Social Choice and Individual Values*. New York: John Wiley and Sons.

Arvai, Joseph L., Robin Gregory, and Tim McDaniels. 2001. "Testing a Structured Decision Approach: Value-focused Thinking for Deliberative Risk Communication." *Risk Analysis* 21:1065-1076.

Aven, Terje, and Ortwin Renn. 2009. "On Risk Defined as an Event Where the Outcome is Uncertain." *Journal of Risk Research* 12:1-11.

———. 2010. "Response to Professor Eugene Rosa's Viewpoint to Our Paper." *Journal of Risk Research* 13:255-259.

Aven, Terje, Ortwin Renn, and Eugene A. Rosa. 2011. "On the Ontological Status of the Concept of Risk." *Safety Science* 49:1074-1079.

Bennett, Deborah J. 1998. *Randomness*. Cambridge, Massachusetts: Harvard University Press.

Brown, Michael. 2008. *Censoring Science*. New York: Dutton.

Campbell, Donald T. 1960. "Blind Variation and Selective Retention in Creative Thought as in Other Knowledge Processes." *Psychological Review* 67:380-400.

———. 1987. "Evolutionary Epistemology." Pp. 47-89 in *Evolutionary Epistemology, Rationality and the Sociology of Knowledge*, edited by G. Radnitzky and W. W. I. Bartley. La Salle, Illinois: Open Court.

Cialdini, Robert B. 2007 [1984]. *Influence: The Psychology of Persuasion*. New York: HarperCollins.

Clark, William C. and Nancy M. Dickson. 2003. "Sustainability Science: The Emerging Research Program." *Proceedings of the National Academy of Sciences, USA* 100:8059-8061.

Collins, H., and R. Evans. 2007. *Rethinking Expertise*. Chicago: University of Chicago Press.

Crocker, Jennifer, Yu Niiya, and Dominik Mischkowski. 2008. "Why Does Writing About Important Values Reduce Defensiveness? Self-Affirmation and the Role of Positive Other-Directed Feelings." *Psychological Science* 19:740-747.

Dasgupta, Partha. 2008. "Discounting Climate Change." *Journal of Risk and Uncertainty* 37:141-169.

Dewey, John. 1888/1969. "The Ethics of Democracy." Pp. 227-249 in *The Early Works of John Dewey, 1882-1898*, vol. 1, edited by J. A. Boydston. Carbondale, Illinois: Southern Illinois University Press.

———. 1923. *The Public and Its Problems*. New York: Henry Holt.

Dietz, Thomas. 1987. "Theory and Method in Social Impact Assessment." *Sociological Inquiry* 57:54-69.

———. 1988. "Social Impact Assessment as Applied Human Ecology: Integrating Theory and Method." Pp. 220-227 in *Human Ecology: Research and Applications*, edited by R. Borden, J. Jacobs, and G. R. Young. College Park, Maryland: Society for Human Ecology.

———. 1994. "'What Should We Do?' Human Ecology and Collective Decision Making." *Human Ecology Review* 1:301-309.

———. 2001. "Thinking about Environmental Conflict." Pp. 31-54 in *Celebrating Scholarship*, edited by L. Kadous. Fairfax, Virginia: George Mason University.

———. 2003. "What is a Good Decision? Criteria for Environmental Decision Making." *Human Ecology Review* 10:60-67.

———. 2011. "The Art of Influence." *Nature* 479:176.

———. 2013. "Bringing Values and Deliberation to Science Communication." *Proceedings of the National Academy of Sciences* 110:14081–14087.

Dietz, Thomas, and Tom R. Burns. 1992. "Human Agency and the Evolutionary Dynamics of Culture." *Acta Sociologica* 35:187-200.

Dietz, Thomas, Elinor Ostrom, and Paul C. Stern. 2003. "The Struggle to Govern the Commons." *Science* 301:1907-1912.

Dietz, Thomas, and Alicia Pfund. 1988. "An Impact Identification Method for Development Program Evaluation." *Policy Studies Review* 8:137-145.

Dietz, Thomas, and Paul C. Stern. 1998. "Science, Values and Biodiversity." *BioScience* 48:441-444.

Dietz, Thomas, and Paul C. Stern. 1995. "Toward a Theory of Choice: Socially Embedded Preference Construction." *Journal of Socio-Economics* 24:261-279.

Folke, Carl. 2006. "Resilience: The Emergence of a Perspective for Social–Ecological Systems Analyses." *Global Environmental Change* 16:235-267.

Freudenburg, William F. and Eugene A. Rosa. 1984. *Public Reactions to Nuclear Power: Are There Critical Masses?* Boulder, Colorado: Westview Press/American Association for the Advancement of Science.

Galison, Peter. 1997. *Image and Logic: A Material Culture of Physics.* Chicago, Illinois: University of Chicago Press.

Gould, Stephen Jay. 1965. *The Mismeasure of Man.* New York: W.W. Norton & Company.

Habermas, Jürgen. 1970. *Towards a Rational Society.* Boston: Beacon Press.

———. 1991. *Moral Consciousness and Communicative Action.* Boston: Beacon Press.

Jaeger, Carlo, Ortwin Renn, Eugene A. Rosa, and Thomas Webler. 2001. *Risk, Uncertainly and Rational Action.* London: Earthscan.

Kahneman, Daniel. 2011. *Thinking Fast and Slow.* New York: Farrar, Straus & Giroux.

Kassirer, Jerome P. 1995. "A Partisan Assault on Science: The Threat to the CDC." *The New England Journal of Medicine* 333:793-794.

Kates, Robert W., William C. Clark, Robert Corell, J. Michael Hall, Carlo Jaeger, Ian Lowe, James J. McCarthy, Hans-Joachim Schellnhuber, Bert Bolin, Nancy M. Dickson, Sylvie Faucheux, Gilberto C. Gallopin, Arnulf Grubler, Brian Huntley, Jill Jager, Narpat S. Jodha, Roger E. Kasperson, Akin Mabogunje, Pamela Matson, Harold Mooney, Berrien Moore III, Timothy O'Riordan, and Uno Svedin. 2001. "Sustainability Science." *Science* 292:641-642.

Knorr-Cetina, Karin D. 1981. *The Manufacture of Knowledge: An Essay on the Constructivist Contextual Nature of Science.* Oxford: Pergamon.

———. 2005. "The Fabrication of Facts." Pp. 175–198 in *Society and Knowledge*, edited by N. Stehr and V. Meja. New Brunswick, New Jersey: Transaction.

Kuhn, Thomas S. 1962. *The Structure of Scientific Revolutions.* Chicago, Illinois: University of Chicago Press.

Latour, Bruno, and Steven Woolgar. 1986. *Laboratory Life: The Construction of Scientific Facts.* Princeton University Press: Princeton, New Jersey.

Levins, Richard. 1966. "The Strategy of Model Building in Population Biology." *American Scientist* 54:421-431.

———. 1993. "A Response to Orzack and Sober: Formal Analysis and Fluidity of Science." *Quarterly Review of Biology* 68.

Liu, Jianguo, Thomas Dietz, Stephen R. Carpenter, Marina Alberti, Carl Folke, Emilio Moran, Alice N. Pell, Peter Deadman, Timothy Kratz, Jane Lubchencko, Elinor Ostrom, Zhiyun Ouyang, William Provencher, Charles L. Redman, Stephen H. Schneider, and William W. Taylor. 2007a. "Complexity of Coupled Human and Natural Systems." *Science* 317:1513-1516.

Liu, Jianguo, Thomas Dietz, Stephen R. Carpenter, Carl Folke, Marina Alberti, Charles L. Redman, Stephen H. Schneider, Elinor Ostrom, Alice N. Pell, Jane Lubchencko, William W. Taylor, Zhiyun Ouyang, Peter Deadman, Timothy Kratz, and William Provencher. 2007b. "Coupled Human and Natural Systems." *Ambio* 36:639-649.

Mazur, Allan. 1981. *The Dynamics of Technical Controversy*. Washington, DC: Communications Press.

———. 2004. *True Warnings and False Alarms: Evaluating Fears about the Health Risks of Technology, 1948-1971*. Washington, DC: Resources for the Future.

McCright, Aaron M. 2000. "Challenging Global Warming as a Social Problem: An Analysis of the Conservative Movement's Counter-Claims." *Social Problems* 47:499-522.

McCright, Aaron M., and Riley E. Dunlap. 2010. "Anti-Reflexivity: The American Conservative Movement's Success in Undermining Climate Science and Policy." *Theory, Culture, and Society* 27:100-133.

McLaughlin, Paul. 1998. "Rethinking the Agrarian Question: The Limits of Essentialism and the Promise of Evolutionism." *Human Ecology Review* 5:25-39.

———. 2012. "Climate Change, Adaptation, and Vulnerability: Reconceptualizing Societal–Environment Interaction Within a Socially Constructed Adaptive Landscape." *Organization & Environment* 24:269-291.

McLaughlin, Paul, and Thomas Dietz. 2008. "Structure, Agency and Environment: Toward an Integrated Perspective on Vulnerability." *Global Environmental Change* 18:99-111.

Michaels, David. 2006. "Manufactured Uncertainty: Protecting Public Health in the Age of Contested Science and Product Defense." *Annals of the New York Academy of Sciences* 1076:149-162.

———. 2008. *Doubt is Their Product: How Industry's Assault on Science Threatens Your Health*. New York: Oxford University Press.

Michaels, David, and Celeste Monforton. 2005. "Manufacturing Uncertainty: Contested Science and the Protection of the Public's Health and Environment." *American Journal of Public Health* 95:S39-S48.

Nordhaus, William. 2012. "Economic Policy in the Face of Severe Tail Events." *Journal of Public Economic Theory* 14:197-219.

Oreskes, Naomi, and Erik M. Conway. 2010. *Merchants of Doubt: How a Handful of Scientists Obscured the Truth on Issues from Tobacco Smoke to Global Warming*. New York: Bloomsbury.

Orzack, Steven Hecht, and Elliott Sober. 1993. "A Critical Assessment of Levins's *The Strategy of Model Building* (1966)." *Quarterly Review of Biology* 68.

Ostrom, Elinor, Thomas Dietz, Nives Dolsak, Paul C. Stern, Susan Stonich, and Elke Weber. 2002. *The Drama of the Commons*. Washington, DC: National Academy Press.

Portney, Paul, and John Weyant. 1999. *Discounting and Intergenerational Equity*. Washington, DC: Resources for the Future.

Radnitzky, Gerard, and W.W. Bartley III. 1987. *Evolutionary Epistemology, Rationality, and the Sociology of Knowledge*. La Salle, Illinois: Open Court.

Ravetz, Jerry, and Silvio Funtowicz. 1998. "Commentary." *Journal of Risk Research* 1:45-48.

Renn, Ortwin. 2008. *Risk Governance: Coping with Uncertainty in a Complex World*. London: Earthscan.

Renn, Ortwin, Thomas Webler, and Peter Wiedemann. 1995. *Fairness and Competence in Citizen Participation: Evaluating Models for Environmental Discourse*. Dordrecht: Kluwer Academic Publishers.

Roos, Micha. 2012. "Measuring Science or Religion? A Measurement Analysis of the NSF Sponsored Science Literacy Scale 2006-2010." *Public Understanding of Science.*

Rosa, Eugene A. 1988. ""NAMBY PAMBY and NIMBY PIMBY: Public Issues in the Siting of Hazardous Waste Facilities." *Forum for Applied Research and Public Policy* 3:114-123.

———. 1998a. "Comments on Commentary by Ravetz and Funtowicz: 'Old Fashioned Hypertext'." *Journal of Risk Research* 1:111-115.

———. 1998b. "Metatheoretical Foundations for Post-Normal Risk." *Journal of Risk Research* 1:15-44.

———. 2007. "Long-Term Stewardship and Risk Management: Analytic and Policy Challenges." Pp. 227-255 in *Long-Term Management of Contaminated Sites*, edited by T. Leschine. Amsterdam: Elsevier.

———. 2010. "The Logical Status of Risk – to Burnish or to Dull." *Journal of Risk Research* 13:239-253.

Rosa, Eugene A., Thomas Dietz, Richard H. Moss, Scott Atran, and Susanne Moser. 2012. "Risk and Sustainability: A Look at Two Global Threats." *Solutions* 3:59-65.

Rosa, Eugene A. and Riley E. Dunlap. 1994. "The Polls-Poll Trends: Nuclear Energy: Three Decades of Public Opinion." *Public Opinion Quarterly* 58:295-325.

Rosa, Eugene A., Aaron McCright, and Ortwin Renn. 2013. *The Risk Society Revisited: Social Theory and Governance.* Philadelphia: Temple University Press.

Rosa, Eugene A., Seth P. Tuler, Baruch Fischhoff, Thomas Webler, Sharon M. Friedman, Richard E. Sclove, Kristin Shrader-Frachette, Mary R. English, Roger E. Kasperson, Robert L. Goble, Thomas M. Leschine, William Freudenburg, Caron Chess, Charles Perrow, Kai Erikson, and James F. Short. 2010. "Nuclear Waste: Knowledge Waste?" *Science* 329:762-763.

Rosa, Eugene A., and Donald L. Clark Jr. 1999. "Historical Routes to Technological Gridlock: Nuclear Technology as Prototypical Vehicle." *Research in Social Problems and Public Policy* 7:21-57.

Sabatier, Paul A., and Christopher M. Weible. 2007. "The Advocacy Coalition Framework: Innovation and Clarification." Pp. 189-222 in *Theories of the Policy Process*, edited by P. A. Sabatier. Boulder, Colorado: Westview Press.

Salsburg, David. 2001. *The Lady Tasting Tea: How Statistics Revolutionized Science in the Twentieth Century.* New York: W.H. Freeman and Company.

Schnaiberg, Alan. 1980. *The Environment: From Surplus to Scarcity.* New York: Oxford University Press.

Shulman, Seth. 2006. *Undermining Science.* Berkeley: University of California Press.

Sterman, John D. 2008. "Risk Communication on Climate: Mental Models and Mass Balance." *Science* 322:532-533.

Sterman, John D., and Linda Booth Sweeney. 2007. "Understanding Public Complacency about Climate Change: Adults' Mental Models of Climate Change Violate Conservation of Matter." *Climatic Change* 80:1573-1480.

Stern, Paul C. 2005. "Deliberative Methods for Understanding Environmental Systems." *BioScience* 55:976-982.

Stigler, Stephen M. 1986. *The History of Statistics: The Measurement of Uncertainty Before 1900.* Cambridge, Massachusetts: Belknap.

Thaler, Richard H., and Cass R. Sunstein. 2009. *Nudge: Improving Decisions about Health, Wealth, and Happiness.*

Turner, B. L. II. 2010. "Vulnerability and Resilience: Coalescing or Paralleling Approaches for Sustainability Science?" *Global Environmental Change* 20:570-576.

Turner, B. L. II., Eric F. Lambin, and Annette Reenberg. 2007. "The Emergence of Land Change Science for Global Environmental Change and Sustainability." *Proceedings of the National Academy of Sciences, USA* 104:20666-20671.

U.S. National Research Council. 1996. *Understanding Risk: Informing Decisions in a Democratic Society*, edited by P. C. Stern and H. Fineberg. Washington, DC: National Academy Press.

———. 2008. *Public Participation in Environmental Assessment and Decision Making*, edited by T. Dietz and P. C. Stern. Washington, DC: National Academy Press.

———. 2010. *Advancing the Science of Climate Change.* Washington, DC: National Academies Press.

Vayda, Andrew P. 1988. "Actions and Consequences as Objects of Explanation in Human Ecology." Pp. 9-18 in *Human Ecology: Research and Applications*, edited by R. J. Borden, J. Jacobs, and G. L. Young. College Park, Maryland: Society for Human Ecology.

———. 2009. *Explaining Human Actions and Environmental Change.* Lanham, Maryland: Altamira Press.

Weible, Christopher M. and Paul A. Sabatier. 2007. "The Advocacy Coalition Framework: Innovations and Clarifications." In *Theories of the Policy Process*, edited by P. A. Sabatier. Boulder, Colorado: Westview Press.

Weitzman, M. L. 2009. "On Modeling and Interpreting the Economics of Catastrophic Climate Change." *The Review of Economics and Statistics* 91:1-19.

II. Risk

CHAPTER 4

Perspectives on Risks and Concerns with Respect to Climate Engineering

Ortwin Renn, Nadine Bratchatzek, Sylvia Hiller,
and Dirk Scheer, University of Stuttgart

Introduction

ENVIRONMENTAL SOCIAL SCIENCE RESEARCH has long investigated public perceptions and responses to technological risk (see review in York et al. 2010; Rosa and Freudenburg 2001; Rosa and Clark 1999). Eugene Rosa has been an early pioneer of theoretical as well as empirical work on public attitudes toward new technologies and political protest movements against unwanted technology or infrastructure, most prominently nuclear installations (Rosa et al. 2010; Whitfield et al. 2008; Rosa and Rice 2004). Some of his ideas are important for understanding new technological options on a grand scale, so-called *geoengineering* or *climate engineering measures* that are designed to offset the harmful consequences of anthropogenic climate change (Burns and Strauss 2013; The Royal Society 2009). Climate Engineering (CE) includes many options that can be summarized in two major categories: carbon dioxide removal (CDR) and solar radiation management (SRM). Carbon dioxide removal is linked to long-term sequestration of atmospheric carbon dioxide in forests, agricultural systems, or through direct air capture and geological storage (U.S. National Research Council 2011). SRM technologies promise to increase the reflectivity of the Earth's atmosphere or surface. Possibilities include whitening of roofs from private homes, inserting particles into the atmosphere, creating artificial clouds (cloud seeding), and others. CE is of special interest to social scientists from a theoretical as well as political angle: it involves both large-scale "high" technology and a combination of global planning and local siting (Short and Rosa 2004).

The prospect of using CE as a means for combatting climate change is of major concern to society. It has been fiercely advocated by scientific communities and policy circles and has been just as fiercely been rejected by other groups representing science, politics, and civil society (see overview in Burns 2012; Morgan 2012; Moreno-Cruz and Keith 2012; The Royal Society 2009; Badescu et al. 2006). Uncertainty about the potential side effects of CE is one of the most significant factors determining its acceptance by society (see the various aspects of uncertainty in Chapter 5 by Kasperson). Quantifying these risks is difficult, as CE involves major interactions between human interventions and natural phenomena. Gaps in our current state of knowledge make it difficult, if not impossible, to estimate the likelihood of individual CE technologies for causing particular effects, the intensity of those particular effects, and the severity of the damage should these effects occur. Furthermore, the characteristics of CE meet all the criteria for a complex and closely coupled system, which in the analysis of Charles Perrow is an invitation to "Normal Accidents" (Perrow 1984; review in Rosa 2005).

The possibility that application of CE technologies could cause severe damage on a global scale might be reason enough to avoid them, even if the probability of such a disaster occurring is estimated to be extremely low (Jackson and Salzman 2010). Analyses of the risks posed by CE have been founded on plausible (but still unverified) assumptions, with most analyses using Bayesian or portfolio approaches that combine random variation with expert knowledge for assessing risks (see chapters in Launder et al. 2010). The perception of these risks by the public and the media is, however, only partially influenced by scientific assessments (Renn 2008, 98ff.). It is also the product of personal opinion and general attitudes towards risk. Arguments based on ethical considerations or theories of justice must also be taken into account (von Schomberg 1995; Preston et al. 2012). They are quite likely to be combined with arguments about technical and scientific uncertainty, and in some cultures they may go hand in hand with a general distrust of technology or even of civilization in general.

This contribution concentrates on a comparative review of social responses to CE in several countries and illustrates some central insights from the current literature of the subject in the social sciences. It also includes a review of some empirical studies about public knowledge on the subject. Particular attention is given to the social conflict potential of CE research and the large-scale deployment of CE technologies in the eyes of the public. Based on this analysis, the paper also addresses the issue of risk communication and the design of future public debates on this topic, with a specific emphasis on the groundbreaking work that Eugene Rosa has brought to the field of risk governance and communication.

Understanding Risk Perception in the Context of CE

Public perceptions of risk are only marginally determined by the scientifically derived probability of particular outcomes (Rosa and Matsuda 2005; Boholm 1998; Stern in this volume). Psychological studies show that low-probability, high-consequence risks are often associated with the pattern of pending danger (Renn 2008, 112). Risk in this pattern is seen as a random threat that can trigger a disaster without prior notice and without sufficient time to cope with the hazard involved. This image is linked to artificial risk sources with large catastrophic potential. Risk sources in this category include major facilities like nuclear power plants, liquid natural gas (LNG) storage facilities, chemical production sites, and other human-made sources of potential danger, which could have catastrophic effects on humans and the environment in the event of a serious accident. The impact of this risk class on risk perception depends on three factors:
- the random nature of the event,
- the expected maximum (catastrophic) impact, and
- the time-span for risk control measures.

Studies on risk perception show that in these cases the numerical probability of these rare random events plays hardly any role for the perceived seriousness of the risk under review: it is the random nature of the event that poses the feeling of threat (Jaeger et al. 2001, 105; Rohrmann and Renn 2000; Renn 2004). Human beings are more comfortable with threats that they can foresee and plan for rather than threats that could materialize at any time regardless of how unlikely that might be.

The prospect of being exposed to such random effects makes many people feel threatened and powerless. The debates on CE research and possible deployment of corresponding technologies also provoke images of big power versus public interests and associations with equity violations (Leiserowitz 2010; Mercer et al. 2011). Conflicts over public goods such as the climate are particularly difficult to resolve, as individual stakeholders, including states, have virtually no incentive to provide the collectively desirable outcome on their own (Rosa and Dietz 2010; Rosa 2001). It is therefore necessary for all stakeholders to cooperate with one another (Ostrom 1990; 2010; Ostrom et al. 2002; and Renn 2011). Furthermore, conflicts over global public goods are characterized by very diverse interests on the part of the stakeholders involved and by cultural and political circumstances. For example, the conflict triggered by the search for a suitable location for CO_2 capture and storage (CCS) can be identified as a typical distribution conflict (Schulz et al. 2010). The public perceives that the distribution of costs and risks is unequal: the risk is borne by a few, while many others, or the community as a whole, reap the benefits (York and Rosa 2005; Rosa 1988).

CE technologies may involve insidious hazards. To cite one example, the use of sulfur to modify the stratosphere may involve globally distributed effects that include new ecological and health risks (Ricke et al. 2010). Experience with environmental contamination resulting from human activity (pesticide residues in drinking water, genetic engineering, etc.) reveals that risks of this kind are intuitively perceived to be particularly severe and are often feared more than comparable risks posed by everyday routines or natural sources (Sjöberg 2000; Stern in this volume). For example, the risk of contracting cancer as the result of being exposed to environmental pollution causes greater fear than as the result of smoking cigarettes (Renn 2004). This is because individuals rate risks imposed on them higher than risk that they take voluntarily (Slovic 1987). Accordingly, it is in line with human psychology for a person to fear the risks posed by genetically modified food and at the same time to indulge in risky behavior like speeding (Rohrmann and Renn 2000). In assessing risks that appear imposed on someone and not discernible via the senses, people depend on experts for information. When people do not trust the institutions whose job it is to provide the necessary information, conflicts will result (see Kasperson in this volume on trust). Most people demand a zero-risk approach if they do not trust those institutions. They are unwilling to make tradeoffs between benefits and risks (Jaeger et al. 2001, 251). Those who do not trust experts or policy makers on CE will reject any attempt to implement CE technologies, regardless of the actual level of risk involved. This risk-avoidance has been observed in many other similar contexts, such as the nuclear debate (Whitfield et al. 2009; Short and Rosa 2004).

Societal Risk Discourses and Risk Perception in the Social Sciences

Until now, only a handful of social science studies have been published focusing on risk perception and public responses to CE. Most of them focus on international relations, governance, ethics, and economic analysis (Burns et al. 2013; Davis 2012; Gardener 2011). The few existing social science studies on public responses to CE mainly consist of articles weighing the pros and cons on the basis of theoretical considerations or arguments derived from analogies with other sectors of technology (overview in Leiserowitz 2010; Spence et al. 2011; Mercer et al. 2011). They also examine the resonance of such arguments in the political sphere and among the wider public. Jackson and Salzman (2010) doubt whether the public will ever accept radiation management technologies such as reflectors in space and the spreading of nanoparticles in the stratosphere, or carbon dioxide removal technologies such as ocean fertilization. They recommend forest protection and reforestation and the use of bioenergy in combination with Carbon Capture and Storage as alternative options. But they also remark that actual cases in the Netherlands and Germany indicate that major public opposition to carbon storage facilities must be reckoned with (cf. Schulz et al. 2010). Their conclusion is that the debate on CE should focus on the technologies with the best chances of being accepted by the public (Jackson and Salzman 2010).

The assumption widely held in the current literature is that the factors most strongly supporting the protest against CE technologies are (1) concerns about the impossibility of assessing the risks involved; (2) the global scale of these risks (issues of irreversibility of changes); and (3) ethical, legal, governance-related, and geopolitical concerns (Burns et al. 2013). Related to the risks involved, a number of potential risk areas have been identified, ranging from the mere preparation of CE field experiments to the physical application of CE technologies, the impacts on political stability, the possible interruption of CE deployment, and the misuse of the these technologies for political power purposes (Grunwald 2010; Scheer and Renn 2010; Corner and Pidgeon 2010). In the context of the political implementation of CE technologies and its impacts on political stability, the unilateral deployment of these technologies is perceived as particularly critical and potentially disastrous in its consequences (Corner and Pidgeon 2010). It follows that the acceptance of these technologies by the public will depend not only on how risks are perceived, but also on how much trust in the regulatory institutions is involved, on how transparent CE activities appear, and how much confidence exists in the nature of the liability regimes (Jackson and Salzman 2010; Bracmort et al. 2010). This debate is also focused on equity concerns, in particular that regions that might benefit from CE are not those that are at risk from potential adverse effects such as shifts in precipitation (Gardiner 2011; Ricke et al. 2010). Again this concern resonates with similar concerns that were raised with nuclear waste management and other controversial siting issues in large-scale technologies (Short and Rosa 2004; Rosa 1988).

Furthermore, potential health issues and psychosomatic impacts complicate the acceptance of such technologies. The latter might materialize if radiation management deployment caused more vibrant sunsets or duller skies (Scheer and Renn 2010). This concern echoes the recent problems with siting wind generators in the United States or Europe (see Kasperson, Chapter 5). A more fundamental concern relates to the suspicion that the prospect of CE deployment might undermine sensitivity to the need for sustainable patterns of production and consumption. These concerns are not restricted to actual deployment; it has also been asserted that CE research itself might be enough to undermine other efforts undertaken to avoid or mitigate climate change (Corner and Pidgeon 2010). This state of affairs might also be exacerbated by lobby groups that have no interest in reducing emissions (Humphreys 2011). However, some studies suggest that the opposite might also be true. As CE measures demand so much resource capability and are associated with many unknown risks they could be a powerful reminder that avoidance and mitigation might be the more suitable and acceptable options. The fear that these technologies could actually be deployed might therefore serve as an incentive to reduce emissions. In this view, research on CE is highly welcomed to demonstrate the risks and side effects resulting in higher acceptance for mitigation (Corner and Pidgeon 2010).

Research of the Royal Society has yielded interesting results on the topic of social acceptance and public dialogue. Their 2009 report includes results of a preliminary study based on discussions between focus groups representing various interests and values among the UK public. The focus groups were stratified in terms of their commitment to environmental values and behavioral patterns. Each group discussed potential risks, benefits, and areas of uncertainty in relation to various CE technologies (The Royal Society 2009, 43). The study showed that the perceptions of CE among the focus groups were largely negative. In the light of these results, the Royal Society recommends that further and more thorough investigations of public attitudes, concerns, and mental images of uncertainty be conducted parallel to technological research and development work. They also advocated an intense public dialogue with citizens based on the model of the deliberative-analytical discourse (see Stern in this volume). Other studies produced similar recommendations. The American Meteorological Society, for example, has recommended that the scientific and technical exploration of the potential of CE technologies should be accompanied by broadly based studies of their social and ethical implications (AMS 2009).

The acceptance problems arising in connection with carbon capture and storage (CCS) demonstrate the necessity of involving stakeholders and affected citizens at an early stage (Schulz et al. 2010; Bracmort et al. 2010). Such involvement may not produce automatic acceptance, but it is a necessary condition for gaining the trust needed to at least consider the arguments of those in favor of such installations (U.S. National Research Council 2008). It would also help in assessing the degree of tolerance present and in pinpointing potential sources of controversy between those who bear more than their fair share of the risks and those who enjoy the benefits (Reynolds 2011; Schulz et al. 2010). This would call for a dialogue between scientists and academics, political decision-makers, and the general public (Bracmort et al. 2010). It seems prudent to initiate an international public dialogue in the form of an analytic-deliberative discourse before any serious attempt of implementation is conducted. Public scrutiny should play an active advisory role throughout the period during which scientific research and development is going on and, even more importantly, before any significant intervention will take place, in particular if it is driven by commercial interests. Deliberative workshops (similar to focus groups) and citizens' juries (similar to planning cells, with a panel of citizens selected on the basis of certain criteria to represent the spectrum of opinions and attitudes present in the population) have been recommended as formats facilitating such participation (Corner and Pidgeon 2010).

A dialogue of this kind must be informed by an awareness that risk cultures and worldviews vary. Attitudes towards the deployment of technologies such as CCS may differ from one country to the next (Scheer and Renn 2010; Rohrmann and Renn 2000). It is also important to evaluate the whole array of available technologies in order to determine the scale of the opportunities and risks they pose, the extent to which the public trusts the science and expertise involved, and the effects of the technologies on social justice, as these technologies are part of a broader strategy designed to mitigate anthropogenic climate change (Jackson and Salzman 2010).

Empirical Results on Individual Public Perception

Even though social science studies on RSM technologies are rare, there are a few investigations focusing on individual attitudes and concerns. Surveys in the United States have shown that 74 percent of those questioned have never heard of climate engineering and only 3 percent had a realistic idea of what it actually is (Leiserowitz 2010). The study also showed that only 3 percent of Americans were able to provide a correct definition and prescription of geoengineering. A UK survey showed that only 7 percent of the respondents reported they would know a fair amount or more about CE while 75 percent had never heard or knew almost nothing about it (Spence et al. 2010, 20). A cross-country survey covering the United Kingdom, the United States, and Canada, however, showed substantially higher awareness rates. The term geoengineering is known by 20 percent; the term climate engineering even tops this level with 24 percent (Mercer et al. 2011, 4). In a more refined survey design differentiating between geoengineering and climate engineering in an open-ended question, roughly 70 percent of the sample responded to this question (Mercer et al. 2011, 4). According to the authors, only 8 percent of the respondents had an approximately adequate understanding of geoengineering whereas a surprisingly high figure of 45 percent were able to provide a coherent and adequate explanation of climate engineering (Mercer et al. 2011, 4).

Concerning individual attitudes on CE, survey questions focus on the *level of agreement to use CE technologies* for combatting climate change. Almost half of all respondents in the United Kingdom (47 percent) tend to support geoengineering approaches to fight global warming while surprisingly only 4 percent were strictly opposed to this method. The majority (50 percent), however, was uncertain about their preferences and did not express a positive or negative opinion (Spence et al. 2010). Within the cross-country study carried out by Mercer et al. the majority of respondents held a moderately positive view on the issue of whether Solar Radiation Management (SRM) should be used as a solution to global warming. The mean value amounted to 2.35 on a four point scale from 1 (strongly disagree) to 4 (strongly agree). And 25 percent of respondents refused to use any response category on the four-point scale (Mercer et al. 2011, 4).

In contrast to the British study where whitening roofs was seen as most acceptable, most of those questioned in the U.S. surveys by Mercer et al. (2011) were in favor of reforestation and the production of bio-charcoal, as these tend to be seen as what are often called no-regret measures leading to other advantages in addition to climate protection (the option of coloring their roofs were not included in the U.S. list of options). Methods involving the ocean, such as iron fertilization, were seen as particularly risky with regard to their effects on ecosystems. Participants were in favor of combining various international attempts of CE with individual, national, and international efforts to control emissions. In general, adopting sustainable lifestyles was seen as the only possible long-term solution.

A cluster analysis conducted by Mercer et al. (2010, 5) revealed two emerging patterns among the respondents: the supporters and detractors. Within the whole sample they identified 29 percent supporters and 20 percent detractors. In other words, almost half the sample demonstrated a clear position in favor of or in opposition to SRM technologies. There were some country-specific differences. While supporters were evenly distributed between all three countries (33 percent USA, 32 percent UK, and 26 percent Canada), detractors were largest in the US (41 percent USA, 28 percent UK, 31 percent Canada).

Since the level of media coverage in Germany has been lower than the countries covered by Mercer et al., it can safely be assumed that knowledge and awareness of CE are even more limited there. Although comparative surveys do not yet exist, it is fair to assume that the majority of the German population currently either have no opinion on CE or view it with caution and skepticism. Further, it is likely that increasing media coverage, especially relating to the risks and the moral hazards implicit in these technologies, will lead to increased skepticism about and hostility toward climate engineering in general.

There has been a controversial discussion on the LOHAFEX project (a research project dealing with the potential of ocean fertilization) that resulted in a large volume of comments and critical remarks in the press and on the web (Ruhenstroh 2009). This outrage of protest provides further evidence for our claim that Germans will be specifically critical to CE, albeit on a small scale relating to experimental application of iron fertilization of oceans.

Empirical Results on Group and Institutional Perception

In contrast to some of the reported individual surveys, focus group research produced a much more negative image of public opinions and positions towards CE. In the UK, the focus groups of the Royal Society (2009) showed that attitudes to CE technologies are predominantly negative, although acceptance varied dramatically among the participants, who were selected for differences in their overall commitment to environmental causes. The stronger the commitment to environmental values, the stronger were the objections to CE. The reasons for concern were very diverse and partially dependent on the technology under review. The option of painting roofs and buildings with white color was seen as most acceptable (however, also as not highly realistic) while the option of ocean fertilization was seen as most problematic. Irrespective of the methods, many respondents raised fundamental ethical objections to all forms of CE, while others had none. In addition, a telephone survey involving 1,000 participants was conducted on behalf of the Royal Society. Responses to this survey were particularly negative whenever the interviewers touched on technologies for the modification of the stratosphere. 47 percent were opposed to the deployment of such technologies. Another 39 percent rejected ocean iron fertilization (The Royal Society 2009, 43).

CE technologies are often seen as a substitute for emission abatement, which reduces its acceptance. While economic analysis does show that such substitution is possible under certain circumstances (Morgan 2012; Klepper and Rickels 2011), management activities will need to be sustained and even expanded indefinitely if emissions are going to continue at present rate (The Royal Society 2009). Thus a crucial question arises—whether an engagement in CE acts as an incentive to reduce emissions or as a free pass for continuing emissions. The answer to this question determines to a large degree the severity and extent of the potential impacts.

This issue of how CE will affect actual emission rates was also reflected in the focus group discussion of the Royal Society as well as in the study of Corner and Pidgeon (2010). A number of participants in the Royal Society focus groups stated that planned investments in CE technologies and measures had motivated them to act in a more climate-friendly manner (reducing their own emissions, etc.) so as to avert the necessity for such global measures in the future. Corner and Pidgeon (2010, 31) also highlight the current uncertainty about whether and how strongly feedback from the deployment of CE technologies would affect future emission rates. They suggest that social scientists should do more research on the link between CE deployment and incentives for emission reduction and mitigation. While the moral hazard phenomenon has been statistically demonstrated in conjunction with other technical innovations, such as the introduction of seat belts in vehicles, no empirical evidence supporting the moral hazard argument has yet materialized in the CE debate.

Studies carried out by the International Risk Governance Council (IRGC 2006) and the U.K. Natural Environmental Research Council (2010) show that CE technologies engender more controversy among NGOs and other organized groups than carbon dioxide removal technologies because respondents felt that CE could produce irreversible global effects and that these technologies could not be deployed in a manner that would only affect specific regions. The fact that most CE technologies only tackle the symptoms and do not get to the root of the matter is also seen as a problem. In addition to their potential risks for the environment, social group concerns included: controllability, deployment reversibility, cost-effectiveness, timeliness (whether technologies can be brought on line in time), and fair regulation practices in a transboundary setting.

The results of the public dialogue initiated by the study of the U.K. Natural Environmental Research Council (2010) suggest that a majority of the population are not opposed to CE in principle, but are deeply concerned about the implications of deploying particular technologies. As could be expected, opinions on climate change turned out to be strongly influenced by the degree to which those questioned perceive climate change to be a serious problem and by how successful they judge emission control efforts to be.

Comparisons with Other Technology Discourses

In sum, the future of CE debate and the public response to its implications are uncertain. The empirical results about public perception and social acceptance are still ambiguous and there is little conclusive evidence about how the debate will evolve. Another source of insight into likely social reactions to CE is the comparison with similar technological debates, a topic that Eugene Rosa has extensively covered (Rosa and Matsuda 2005; Whitfield et al. 2009; Short and Rosa 2004). Conclusions derived from drawing parallels to other technologies might provide some indication of how the population might react to CE.

Our research team convened an expert workshop in 2010 to have experts in technology assessment and attitude studies discuss the lessons learned from similar debates for the future of CE, specifically within the German context (Renn et al. 2011, 43). The case studies that were used for the comparisons were genetic engineering, nuclear energy, nuclear waste disposal, waste incineration, and natural hazard management (Renn et al. 2011, 43). The results of this workshop can be summarized as follows:

- For the modification of the stratosphere, clear parallels with nuclear energy were drawn, principally because of the fact that the effects span generations.

- For ocean fertilization, parallels with debates over organic agriculture and genetic engineering were drawn, as effects could be expected on biodiversity and ecology.
- For reforestation, parallels were drawn with anti-flooding measures, the designation of flood overflow areas, and general conflicts over land use.

According to the group of experts, the cases of nuclear installations, genetic engineering, and nanotechnology would show the closest proximity to CE. All these technologies have in common that the opportunities were presented first, with a certain degree of euphoria, while the risks were either neglected or downplayed (see also Rosa and Freudenburg 2001; Rosa 2001). In particular, nanotechnology may prove an interesting analogy for understanding public reactions to the introduction of new technologies (Renn and Roco 2006). Deliberative workshops held in the UK and Portugal by the European project Deepening Ethical Engagement and Participation in Emerging Nanotechnologies (DEEPEN) have identified five key positions often associated with nanotechnology. These five concerns can also be associated with CE (Davies et al. 2009):

- "Be careful what you wish for": getting exactly what you want may not ultimately be the ideal outcome.
- "Opening Pandora's box": interventions in the complex Earth system may lead to disaster.
- "Messing with nature": redesigning nature so that it more closely suits with our needs occasions moral scruples about destroying the existing order of the natural world.
- "Kept in the dark": CE measures should be rejected until decision-makers stop leaving the public in the dark about important aspects of the technology and its side effects.
- "The rich get richer and the poor get poorer": CE might exacerbate existing inequalities and injustices.

Interestingly, participants in the project tended to reject a vision that technology will continue to advance and will inevitable bring progress to human society.

Recommendations for Information and Discourse Strategies

Consensus exists in the literature and among experts (Renn et al. 2011, 47) that even at this early stage in the development of CE, it is necessary to provide the public with sufficient opportunities to get all the information they need to form their own balanced judgment as well as to become involved in the debate. A comprehensive communication and dialogue program is needed that frames CE in the light of the wider debate on climate change, emission control, mitigation, and adaptation. Guided by the precautionary principle, a dialogue program should focus more on the potential opportunities and risks than on explaining technical details of how it works. Together with sufficient information on opportunities and risks, the level of uncertainty involved should also be highlighted as a central issue of communication. The Royal Society study (2009) highlights three particular conditions for such a wider public debate: (i) transparency about actions, motives, and aims, (ii) absence of commercial lobbies, and (iii) comprehensive coverage of all concerns that are in the public debate.

Dialogue with the public should keep pace with scientific research on the advantages and disadvantages of CE. This way, it would be possible to keep track of the current debate about the extent and probability of side effects in the light of the latest research. This would enable outside observers to evaluate CE technologies as one option among many other climate protection policies. The experts that our research team in Stuttgart had consulted during the workshop suggested a four-stage plan to be used for citizen participation in this process:

1. Provision of extensive information and communication via the Internet and through public institutions (from science, politics, and civil society) that are active in the wider context of the climate change debate.
2. Organization of round tables or forums with stakeholders to identify the interests and preferences of organized groups in matters relating to CE research and deployment.
3. Organization of (web-based) citizen forums or citizen conferences to assemble information on the preferences, concerns, and ideas of citizens who are not affiliated with specific organizations and to feed this information back into the policy formation process.
4. When and if concrete CE deployments are considered in the future, specific round tables or other formats should be used to convey informed preferences to decision-makers.

Knowledge, attitudes, and mobilization potential should be systematically recorded at regular intervals. The background conditions and the priorities set by actors must be understood better as they progress over time and in the complex, dynamic context of opinion-formation and mobilization mechanisms. For that reason, the interplay between the parameters of information reception, understanding of risk, and uncertainty should be investigated in order to gain a clear idea of (i) the degree to which consensus is possible, (ii) where the opportunities actually lie for participating in deliberative decision-making on this topic, and (iii) what restrictions exist on stakeholder and public involvement in this area.

Conclusions

Irrespective of whatever role individual CE technologies might play in climate protection in the future, it is obvious that the discussion about research into these tools and their implementation cannot be considered in a political and social vacuum. The policies that lie ahead of society need to find approval by stakeholders and the public at large. At this point, there is still very little social science research on the social implications of CE. Some scientific publications do draw attention to social aspects of climate change, and the importance of dialogue with the public is highly emphasized. Yet empirical studies about people's attitudes or social group positions are rare.

Based on the few existing studies one can conclude that the current level of knowledge in the population regarding climate engineering is low. A positive attitude toward CE among stakeholders and the public at large appears to be highly unlikely. Yet this may differ from country to country. The U.S. studies show surprisingly higher rates of opposition than the studies of the UK and the Netherlands. Studies on attitude formation show that many respondents are still undecided while the others fall into two distinct categories of supporters and distractors. There is a lot of potential for conflict and political mobilization.

The work of Eugene Rosa can serve as an important orientation for how the debate might evolve and what public authorities can do in order to find societal consensus and public approval. First, as Rosa has pointed out, do not expect conflicts to disappear when there is no burning bush; second, put all your effort into developing a legitimate and inclusive governance culture that includes full transparency, opportunity for public consultation, and stakeholder involvement as well as a system of checks and balances (Rosa et al. 2010; see also Kasperson as well as Stern in this volume); and thirdly, do not misjudge NIMBY phenomena as an indicator of public irrationality and egoism but as an expression of social concerns that remain unaddressed (Rosa and Rice 2004; Rosa 1988). Following this advice is not a guarantee that effective risk communication and participation will produce a societal agreement on the future of CE, but without these recommended measures a consensus is almost impossible to reach.

References

American Meteorological Society. 2009. *Policy Statement on Geoengineering the Climate System.* Boston: AMS.

Badescu, Viorel, Richard Brook Cathcart, and Roelof D. Schuiling (eds.). 2006. *Macro-Engineering: A Challenge for the Future.* Dordecht: Springer.

Bracmort, Kelsi, Richard K. Lattanzio, Emily C. Barbour. 2010. "Geoengineering: Governance and Technology Policy." In Congressional Research Service (ed.) *CRS Report for Congress.* Washington, DC: Library of Congress.

Burns, William C. G. 2012. "Geoengineering the Climate: An Overview of Solar Radiation Management Options." *Tulsa Law Review* 46: 283-304.

Burns, William C. G., and Andrew L. Strauss. 2013. *Climate Change Geoengineering: Philosophical Perspectives, Legal Issues, and Governance Frameworks.* Cambridge: Cambridge University Press.

Boholm, Asa. 1998. "Comparative Studies of Risk Perception: A Review of Twenty Years of Research." *Journal of Risk Research* 1(2): 135–163.

Corner, Adam, and Nick Pidgeon. 2010. "Geoengineering the Climate: The Social and Ethical Implications." *Environment* 52 (1): 24-37.

Davies, Sarah, Phil Macnaghten, and Matthew Kearnes. 2009. *Reconfiguring Responsibility: Deepening Debate on Nanotechnology. A Research Report from the DEEPEN Project.* European Commission, Brussels. Durham: Durham University.

Davies, Gareth T. 2012. "Framing the Social, Political, and Environmental Risks and Benefits of Geoengineering: Balancing the Hard-to-Imagine against the Hard-to-Measure." *Tulsa Law Review* 46: 261-282.

Gardiner, Stephen M. 2011. *A Perfect Moral Storm: The Ethical Tragedy of Climate Change.* New York: Oxford University Press.

Grunwald, Armin. 2010. "Der Einsatz steigt: globale Risiken." *Politische Ökologie* 120: 37-39.

Humphreys, David. 2011. "Smoke and Mirrors: Some Reflections on the Science and Politics of Geoengineering." *The Journal of Environment & Development* 20: 99-120.

International Risk Governance Council (IRGC). 2006. *White Paper on Risk Governance Towards an Integrative Approach.* Geneva: IRGC.

Jackson, Robert B., and James Salzman. 2010. "Pursuing Geoengineering for Atmospheric Restoration." *Issues in Science & Technology* 26(4): 67-76.

Jaeger, Carlo C., Ortwin Renn, Eugene A. Rosa, and Thomas Webler. 2001. *Risk, Uncertainty and Rational Action.* London: Earthscan.

Kasperson, Roger. Chapter 5, this volume.

Klepper, Gernot, and Wilfried Rickels. 2011. "Climate Engineering—Wirtschaftliche Aspekte. Report to the Federal Ministry of Education and Science." Kiel: Kiel Earth Institute.

Launder, Brian, and J. Michael T. Thompson. (eds.) 2010. *Geo-engineering Climate Change: Environmental Necessity or Pandora's Box?* Cambridge: Cambridge University Press.

Leiserowitz, Anthony A. 2010. "Geoengineering and Climate Change in the Public Mind." Presentation to the Asilomar International Conference on Climate Intervention Technologies: Minimizing the Potential Risk of Research to Counter-Balance Climate Change and its Impacts. Pacific Grove, California, 24 March 2010.

Mercer, Ashley, David Keith, and Jacqueline Sharp. 2011. "Public Understanding of Solar Radiation Management." *Environ. Res. Letters* 6, 044006; doi: 10.1088/1748-9326/6/4/044006.

Moreno-Cruz, Juan B., and David W. Keith. 2012. "Climate Policy under Uncertainty: A Case for Solar Geoengineering." *Climatic Change*, doi 10.1007/s10584-012-0487-4.

Morgan, M. Granger. 2012. "Effectiveness of Stratospheric Solar-Radiation Management as a Function of Climate Sensitivity." *Nature* 2: 92–96.

Morgan, M. Granger, and Katharine Ricke. 2010. *Cooling the Earth through Solar Radiation Management: The Need for Research and an Approach to its Governance.* IRGC Opinion Piece. Geneva: International Risk Governance Council.

Ostrom, Elinor. 1990. *Governing the Commons: The Evolution of Institutions for Collective Action.* Cambridge: Cambridge University Press.

Ostrom, Elinor, Thomas Dietz, Nives Dolsak, Paul C. Stern, Susan Stonich, and Elke U. Weber. 2002. *The Drama of the Commons.* Washington, DC: National Academy Press.

Ostrom, Elinor. 2010. "Polycentric Systems for Coping with Collective Action and Global Environmental Change." *Global Environmental Change* 20: 550–557.

Perrow, Charles. 1984. *Normal Accidents: Living with High Risk Technologies.* New York: Basic Books.

Preston, Christopher J., Albert Borgmann, and Holly Jean Buck. 2012. *Engineering the Climate: The Ethics of Solar Radiation Management.* Lanham: Lexington Books.

Renn, Ortwin. 2004. "Perception of Risks." *The Geneva Papers on Risk and Insurance* 29(1): 102–114.

Renn, Ortwin. 2008. *Risk Governance: Coping with Uncertainty in a Complex World.* London: Earthscan.

Renn, Ortwin. 2011. "The Social Amplification/Attenuation of Risk Framework: Application to Climate Change." *Wiley Interdisciplinary Reviews: Climate Change* 1(1) doi: 10.1002/wcc.99 (2011).

Renn, Ortwin, and Mike Roco. 2006. "Nanotechnology and the Need for Risk Governance." *Journal of Nanoparticle Research* 8 (2-3): 23-45.

Renn, Ortwin, Nadine Brachatzek, and Sylvia Hiller. 2011. "Risikowahrnehmung, gesellschaftliche Risikodiskurse und Optionen der Öffentlichkeitsbeteiligung." Report to the Federal Ministry of Education and Science. Dialogik, Stuttgart.

Reynolds, Jesse. 2011. The Regulation of Climate Engineering." *Law, Innovation and Technology* 3: 113-130.

Ricke, Katharine L., M. Granger Morgan, and Myles R. Allen. 2010. "Regional Climate Response to Solar-Radiation Management." *Nature Geoscience* 3: 537-541.

Rohrmann, Bernd, and Ortwin Renn. 2000. "Risk Perception Research - An Introduction." In *Cross-Cultural Risk Perception: A Survey of Empirical Studies*, edited by Ortwin Renn and Bernd Rohrmann, 11-54. Dordrecht: Kluwer Academic Publishers.

Rosa, Eugene A. 1988. "NAMBY PAMBY and NIMBY PIMBY: Public Issues in the Siting of Hazardous Waste Facilities." *Forum for Applied Research and Public Policy* 3: 114–123.

———. 2001. "Global Climate Change: Background and Sociological Contributions." *Society and Natural Resources* 14: 491-499.

———. 2005. "Celebrating a Citation Classic—and More: Symposium on Charles Perrow's Normal Accidents." *Organization and Environment* 18: 229-234.

Rosa, Eugene A., and Donald L. Clark. 1999. "Historical Roots to Technological Gridlock: Nuclear Technology as Prototypical Vehicle." *Research in Social Problems and Public Policy* 7: 21-57.

Rosa, Eugene A., and Thomas Dietz. 2010. "Human Dimensions of Coupled Human-Natural Systems: A Look Backward and Forward." In *Human Footprints on the Global Environments*, edited by Eugene A. Rosa, Andreas Diekmann, Thomas Dietz, and Carlo C. Jaeger, 295-314. Cambridge: MIT Press.

Rosa, Eugene A., and Nicholas Freudenburg. 2001. "The Sociology of Risk." In *International Encyclopedia of the Social and Behavioral Sciences*, edited by Neil J. Smelser and Paul B. Baltes, 13356-13360. New York: Pergamon.

Rosa, Eugene A., and Noriyuki Matsuda. 2005. "Risk Perceptions in the Risk Society: The Cognitive Architecture of Risk Between Americans and Japanese." In *Toward a Peaceable Future: Peace, Security and Kyosei from a Multicultural Perspective*, edited by Yoichiro Murakami, Noriko Kawamura, and Shin Chiba, 113-130. Pullman: Washington State University Press.

Rosa, Eugene A., and James Rice. 2004. "Public Reaction to Nuclear Power Siting and Disposal." In *International Encyclopedia of Energy*, Vol. 5, edited by Cutler J. Cleveland, 181-194. New York: Elsevier.

Rosa, Eugene A., Seth P. Tuler, Baruch Fischhoff, Thomas Webler, Sharon M. Friedman, Richard E. Sclove, Kristin Shrader-Frachette, Mary R. English, Roger E. Kasperson, Robert L. Goble, Thomas M. Leschine, William Freudenburg, Caron Chess, Charles Perrow, Kai Erikson, and James F. Short. 2010. "Nuclear Waste: Knowledge Waste?" *Science* 329: 762-763.

Ruhenstroth, Miriam. 2009. "Streit um LOHAFEX." Spektrum der Wissenschaft. 1 (18.1.2009).

Scheer, Dirk, and Ortwin Renn. 2010. "Klar ist nur die Unklarheit: die sozio-ökologischen Dimensionen des Geo-Engineering." *Politische Ökologie* 120. S. 27-29.

Schulz, Marlen, Dirk Scheer, and Sandra Wassermann. 2010. "Neue Technik, alte Pfade? Zur Akzeptanz der CO_2 Speicherung in Deutschland." *GAIA* 19 (4): 287-296.

Short, James F., and Eugene A. Rosa. 2004. "Some Principles for Siting Controversy Decisions: Lessons from the U.S. Experience with High Level Nuclear Waste." *Journal of Risk Research* 7: 115-135.

Sjöberg, Lennart. 2000. "Perceived Risk and Tampering with Nature." *Journal of Risk Research* 3: 353–367.

Slovic, Paul. 1987. "Perception of Risk." *Science* 236 (4799): 280–285.

Spence, Alexa, Dan Venables, Nick Pidgeon, Wouter Poortinga, and Christina Demski. 2010. *Public Perceptions of Climate Change and Energy Futures in Britain: Summary Findings of a Survey Conducted in January-March 2010*. Technical Report (Understanding Risk Working Paper 10-01). Cardiff: School of Psychology.

The Royal Society. 2009. *Geoengineering the Climate: Science, Governance and Uncertainty.* September 2009, RS Policy document 10/09. London.

U.K. Natural Environment Research Council. 2010. *Experiment Earth? Report on a Public Dialogue on Geoengineering.* Performed by IPSOS Mori. Swindon: NERC.

U.S. National Research Council of the National Academies. 2008. *Public Participation in Environmental Assessment and Decision Making.* Washington, DC: The National Academies Press.

————. 2011. *America's Climate Choices*. Committee on America's Climate Choices. Washington, DC: The National Academies Press.

Von Schomberg, René. 1995. "The Erosion of the Valuespheres: The Ways in Which Society Copes with Scientific, Moral and Ethical Uncertainty." In *Contested Technology: Ethics, Risk and Public Debate*, edited by René von Schomberg, 13-28. Tilburg: International Centre for Human and Public Affairs.

Whitfield, Stephen C., Eugene A. Rosa, Amy Dan, and Thomas Dietz.. 2008. "The Future of Nuclear Power: Value Orientations and Risk Perception." *Risk Analysis* 29: 425-437.

York, Richard, and Eugene A. Rosa. 2005. "Societal Processes and Carbon Dioxide (CO2) Emissions." *Social Forces*, online rejoinder (http://socialforces.unc.edu/).

York, Richard, Eugene A. Rosa, and Thomas Dietz. 2010. "Ecological Modernization Theory: Theoretical and Empirical Challenges." In *The International Handbook of Environmental Sociology*, edited by Michael Redcliff and Graham Woodgate, 77-90. Cheltenham: Edward Elgar.

CHAPTER 5

Opportunities and Dilemmas in Managing Risk and Uncertainty

Roger E. Kasperson, Clark University

U NCERTAINTY IS AN INESCAPABLE INGREDIENT of life. Even for familiar situations—such as crossing a street—some level of uncertainty inevitably exists. Past experience is relevant for decisions involving the future but contexts change and new elements affecting risk may unexpectedly appear. Usually, this residual uncertainty remains within reasonable bounds and humans make their way in an uncertain and changing world where existing knowledge and experience suffice as a guide to future expectations. But where highly complex systems with extensive connectivity and interaction exist, or where novel problems or technology limit experience as a resource, decisions often must be made under conditions of high uncertainty. Typically, those decisions cannot wait (see below). It is not surprising that in a world of complex systems involving rapid technological change, highly coupled human and natural systems, and a kaleidoscope of social, economic, and political institutions, high levels of uncertainty challenge existing assessment methods and familiar decision and management procedures.

Some examples of uncertainty problems may be instructive. If we take a familiar problem—such as the continuing toll of automobile accidents—the causality of collisions is generally well understood, even including how human behavior interacts with the physical system so that events (collisions) can be minimized through traffic regulations and highway and vehicle designs. Compare this with climate change, where an array of changes in temperature, precipitation, sea level rise, and severe storms may extensively alter the nature of ecosystems, disrupt coastal systems, and threaten human health. As yet, the timing and spatial distribution of such changes remain beyond our assessment capabilities. Wind energy has been mired in seemingly unending

73

debate over fish and wildlife threats even though land-based wind turbines appear to be a minor contributor to overall population and species risk compared to other stressors. Or take the case of radioactive waste disposal with first-of-a-kind facilities in different geologic settings for periods of time stretching to 100,000 years, when completely different human societies and technologies may exist.

These latter cases cannot be analyzed by conventional risk analysis methods, so alternative approaches to assessing and managing uncertainty must be found. Because of the "systems" properties of these issues, the well-honed strategy of "divide and conquer" of positivist science may need to give way to newer, more holistic and integrative assessment; and command-and-control management may need to give way to adaptive management and building resilience against the unexpected and unknown.

Three Types of Uncertainty

It is essential at the outset to clarify what is meant by *uncertainty* and how it enters into risk analysis and management. By *uncertainty* we mean that the direction of change is relatively well known but the probability of events and the magnitude of consequences, and perhaps even the receptors at risk, cannot be estimated with any precision. For this discussion, we identify three major sources of uncertainty: where insufficient data exist to estimate probabilities and magnitude; where insufficient models exist to characterize risk genesis and consequences; and where basic processes in physical and human phenomena are not understood, the direction and causes of change are not known to science, and thresholds and nonlinear relationships are present but not understood (Morgan and Henrion 1990). Also, Rosa (1998) examines the meta-theoretical basis of risk and uncertainty.

The first source of uncertainty—data inadequacies, which are sometimes referred to as *aleatory uncertainty,* is perhaps the most tractable. This is where the admonition to work harder, gather more data, and rely more on science and local knowledge may make most sense. But even here the scope of the data and the inherent random variation in the physical and human worlds may be problematic. Statistical techniques may be used which minimize, but do not eliminate, inevitable remaining uncertainty. Also, there are often confounding factors, such as those with population changes and other sources of low-level radiation or chemical exposures, that complicate and limit risk estimates.

A second source of uncertainty lies in the models that are used to project possible components of the risk process, such as releases, exposures, dose-response relations, and consequences. This is often referred to as *model-parameter uncertainty*. Models are only simplified representations of reality, it must be acknowledged. As such, subtle and contingent factors are often omitted. Such models typically simplify assumptions concerning data gaps and confounding factors.

Not surprisingly, the third, and undoubtedly the most difficult source of uncertainty, is what is termed *deep uncertainty*, or alternatively *ignorance* or *epistemic uncertainty*. These are uncertainty situations in which the phenomena posing potential threats to human societies are characterized by high levels of ignorance, are still only poorly understood scientifically, and modeling and subjective judgments must substitute extensively for estimates based upon experience with actual events and outcomes, or ethical rules must be formulated to substitute for risk-based judgments.

For those who must make decisions, deep uncertainty can be a major swamp—but, paradoxically, an opportunity as well. On the one hand, deep uncertainty is a field for creativity and experimentation. Well-established approaches may or may not be appropriate, and so arguments may well be made for initiatives that strike out in new directions. Timing is also uncertain, so one can wait for political "windows" of opportunity. Scenario analysis takes on added importance. On the other hand, escape from the imperative to come to decision is also abundantly there. In the political context, *delay* is a major resource and deep uncertainty provides wonderful cover. For those who seek to escape the exigencies of a decision where the outcome and political fallout remain highly uncertain, or to postpone to the next lucky incumbent, abundant rationale can be made to delay for further research and assessment with the admonition that "we will know better." It is important to note that whatever the political objective, delay itself further adds to uncertainty just as the science to narrow uncertainties proceeds. Exporting decisions to unknown future political environments inevitably adds new and often unforeseeable elements to the decision context.

Essential in all these uncertainties is clarifying which uncertainties are crucial to understanding risk issues and making decisions. The full list of uncertainties for any complex problem will be long, opaque, and often subtle. Accordingly, it is essential to relate uncertainties to risks that dominate the overall risk challenge. In short, not all uncertainties matter, or some uncertainties matter much more than others. The Clark University hazard chain model (Figure 1) shows that a myriad of uncertainties exist for any given risk.

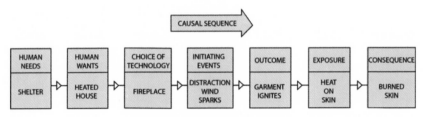

Figure 1. Hazard Chain Model
Source: C. Hohenemser, R. E. Kasperson, and R. W. Kates, 1985

In this model, uncertainties typically occur at each stage in the evolution of a hazard or risk. Some of these will be very large and important in the overall hazard; some will be related to very minor risks. Then distinctions are important not only in allocating risk assessment resources and effort but also in decision making under uncertainty. With uncertainties what really matters is choosing overall strategies, such as command-and-control or adaptive management strategies, and also choosing where to intervene in the hazard chain and which options may be most effective.

Funtowicz and Ravetz (2001) have provided an important perspective not only by distinguishing among types of uncertainty but by relating these types to decision-making stakes and considerations (Figure 2).

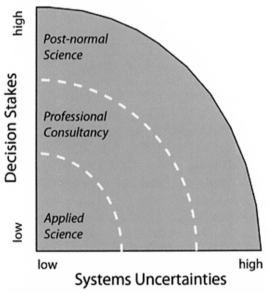

Figure 2. A Diagram of Problem-solving Strategies

They have persuasively pointed out that major management strategies have evolved geared to the interrelationships between types of uncertainty and the pattern of decision stakes. In short, risk problems where the uncertainties are high, the sources of uncertainty are complex, the decision stakes complex, and the problems urgent, are quite different than other kinds of risk decision problems. And, as they point out, the means of assessment and coping that have evolved are quite different. For example, when both uncertainties and decision stakes are low, standard routines and procedures are typically employed and usually suffice for acceptable decisions. On the other hand, when system uncertainties are poorly understood and decision stakes are high, what they term as "post-normal" science must be employed and decision-making is inevitably contentious. All this is instructive for uncertainty research and decision making under uncertainty. Depending on the type and source of uncertainty, new information and more data do not always reduce uncertainty. Much depends upon whether the uncertainty arises from gaps in data, insufficient models, or inadequate scientific understanding. It must be appreciated, as the 2005 National Resource Council (NRC) report on *Thinking Strategically* has nicely shown, that scientific progress may not only reduce certain uncertainties but also uncover new ones. Accordingly, the proper characterization of uncertainty is of great value, to scientists and decision makers alike, where new information and data are related to the type of uncertainty and risk at stake.

While there is little question that risk uncertainty is challenging for the scientific community, it is not an issue for the scientists alone. Uncertainty also has much to do with the differential pattern of vulnerability to nature and to human communities, and to the ambiguities surrounding optimal management approaches and interventions. To take a prominent example, risk assessment assumes that sufficient knowledge and quantification can be achieved so that command-and-control strategies and regulation can be employed. Much depends on how large the residual uncertainties are, whether they can be reduced significantly, and how they affect the acceptability of the risk. Where deep uncertainties exist, other management approaches may be called for, such as adaptive management. *Adaptive management* recognizes that large uncertainties may still exist and that knowledge is co-evolving with the risk, so an alternative management approach—going with the flow and making mid-course corrections—may be required. Much depends upon the risk, however, and the extent to which mid-course corrections can be made in technology, siting, and the project design. But the importance of collaboration is clear, as recognized in the 1996 model of risk analysis set forth by the NRC (Figure 3).

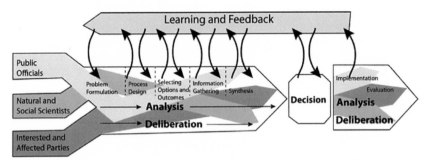

Figure 3. A Schematic Representation of the Risk Decision Process
Source: U.S. National Research Council 1996, 120

Social Trust and Uncertainty

The greater the uncertainty, the greater the need for social trust. This has been recognized since Luhmann (1989) clearly articulated this relationship. If it is clear that many unknowns permeate a particular environmental or risk problem, then confidence that the analyst and decision maker are deeply committed to protecting those at risk and care about their well-being is essential.

Gaining such trust does not come easily. Some societies (including the United States) have undergone a basic loss of trust in science and in major institutions (Kasperson, Golding, and Tuler 1992). Debates continue as to the degree to which lack of social trust is general and structural in nature (connected with social stratification and inequalities in wealth), the result of historical experiences (the civil rights movement and Vietnam in the United States), or the product of experience with decision makers in particular arenas. In any event, if conditions of low social trust prevail, they pose major challenges to decision making.

These are difficult enough if the problems are familiar and uncertainties are low. In situations of large (and especially deep) uncertainty, however, social trust becomes an essential resource. The combination of deep uncertainty and high social distrust is often a recipe for conflict and stalemate. As studies of facility siting across various countries (Shaw 1996; Lesbirel 1998; Lesbirel and Shaw 2005) and policies addressing nuclear power and managing nuclear waste have made clear, social distrust can be a fatal source of conflict and ultimately political stalemate (Whitfield et al. 2009). It is also known that despite well-intentioned efforts by planners and decision makers, social trust once lost is extremely difficult to recover and often cannot be gained within the time frames that decisions require (Slovic 1993).

What are the Decision Options?

What options are open to decision making when high uncertainty prevails? Several approaches exist, as shown in bullets following the box. In all cases, adhering to general principles is essential as the NRC (2009) has recently made clear (see Box 1):

Box 1. Recommended Principles for Uncertainty and Variability Analysis

Risk assessments should provide a quantitative, or at least qualitative, description of uncertainty and variability consistent with available data. The information required to conduct detailed uncertainty analyses may not be available in many situations.
1. In addition to characterizing the full population at risk, attention should be directed to vulnerable individuals and subpopulations that may be particularly susceptible or more highly exposed.
2. The depth, extent, and detail of the uncertainty and variability analyses should be commensurate with the importance and nature of the decision, and should be informed by the risk assessment and with what is valued in a decision. This may best be achieved by early engagement of assessors, managers, and stakeholders in the nature and objectives of the risk assessment and terms of reference (which must be clearly defined).
3. The risk assessment should compile or otherwise characterize the types, sources, extent, and magnitude of variability and substantial uncertainties associated with the assessment. To the extent feasible, there should be homologous treatment of uncertainties among the different components of a risk assessment and among different policy options being compared.
4. To maximize public understanding of and participation in risk-related decision-making, a risk assessment should explain the basis and results of the uncertainty analysis with sufficient clarity to be understood by the public and decision-makers. The uncertainty assessment should not be a significant source of delay in the release of an assessment.
5. Uncertainty and variability should be kept conceptually separate in the risk characterization.

Source: NRC 2009, 120

- *Delay to gather further information* and conduct more studies in the hope of reducing uncertainty across a spectrum of risk. For many problems, this is a sensible procedure. Value of information methods now seek to weigh the value of seeking more information and analysis against the costs of further delay. Not all decision elements are typically included in such assessment, but relevant analysis for many decisions to proceed or to delay further can be had. But for deep uncertainty problems, throwing science at problems and gathering more data and improving models may not contribute much to solving the risk problem.

- *Interrelate risk and uncertainty* to target critical uncertainties for priority further analysis and compare technology and development options to determine whether clearly referable options exist for proceeding. Uncertainties abound in most difficult decisions, but not all are of equal importance. Which uncertainties, it needs to be asked, are critical for decisions to be made and to what extent can risks be clarified or be reduced by further research and assessment? Without such a priority determination, uncertainty is a limitless track of unending work, as new uncertainties appear as old ones are put to bed.

- *Enlarge the knowledge base for decisions through greater lateral thinking and perspective.* Vertical thinking is customary in risk analysis—research for the source of the risk and means of risk mitigation thinking are important. Two types of lateral thinking are possible. The first involves placing a particular problem or risk into a broader category of similar problems to assess where complementarities exist and relevant risk experience can be tapped. Many people have noted that the thousands of chemicals facing potential regulation cannot be managed by one-by-one procedures. The need clearly exists to define "like" clusters of problems or hazards to determine whether they can be managed as a group and where hazards or problems rank within the group and thus indicate priority. This broadening also needs to examine the embedding of problems within other policy domains—such as industrial sectors as the structure of agriculture, energy, or transportation. Another example is facility siting which has emerged as a common problem in many societies. Whether one is looking at nuclear plants, wind energy farms, or hazardous waste sites, common problems in assessment and engaging the public exist across facilities. Rosa et al. (2012) have nicely explored this issue for climate change and terrorism. So learning from other relevant societal experience is essential.

The second type of lateral thinking involves the need for explicit risk/benefit comparisons among the options available to the decision maker. If some options are decisively better than others, considering the range of risk that may exist (even when large uncertainties are taken into account), then delay is not a sensible option. This is not to suggest that efforts to understand and reduce (where possible) existing uncertainties should not continue. Of course, they should. But if the development is deemed essential to decision goals, if benefits clearly are judged to exceed costs, and if a concert of political support exists or can be built, then development can proceed while effort to build the knowledge base continue.

• *Invoke the precautionary principle.* The precautionary principle emerged from the Rio Declaration on Environment and Development of 1992, holding that "where there are threats of serious or irreversible damage, the lack of full scientific understanding shall not be used as a reason for postponing cost-effective measures to prevent environmental deterioration" (Whiteside 2006, viii). The principle leaves much to determine in its application, as European experience has shown, but clearly it is germane to many situations of high uncertainty where serious or irreversible risks are involved. What is "serious" or "irreversible" must be determined, of course, but a decision in favor of precaution can escape the burden of endless studies aimed at assessing whether risk is involved and whether it is sufficient to justify societal intervention. So a decision choice in favor of precaution may be made on ethical grounds, while scientific work continues to reduce or clarify the nature of uncertainties and risks.

Two Major Opportunities: Adaptive Management and Resilience Building

Most environmental protection efforts have traditionally proceeded in "command and control" fashion, drawing upon military models of how decision objectives may be accomplished. In such an approach (Figure 4) it is assumed that risks and uncertainties can be defined with sufficient accuracy and the future can be anticipated sufficiently well that sound decision-making can move forth, usually to achieve quantitative standards. Detailed guidelines and procedures typically are an intrinsic part of this approach. So in emergency response regulations, for example, detailed guidance is provided aimed at an "engineered" societal response—when warning of an event should occur, the form it should take, when evacuation should occur, routes to be taken, etc.

Adaptive management proceeds in a fundamentally different way. The assumption is that uncertainties cannot all be reduced and that the future to a significant degree is unknowable or only partly knowable. Surprises must be expected. And so learning through experience and from evolving

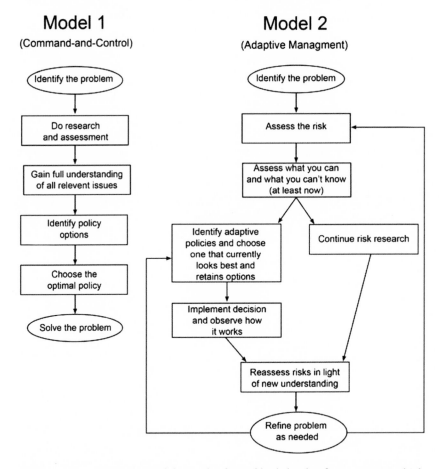

Figure 4. Two Decision Models. In the face of high levels of uncertainty, which may not be readily resolved through research, decision makers may avoid a linear decision stategy in which nothing is done until research resolves all key uncertainties (Model 1), but rather adopt an iterative and adaptive management strategy (Model 2) that can continually respond to new information while experience and knowledge evolve. (after Granger Morgan)

knowledge is essential, as Henry (2009) has shown. Societal efforts to control hazards are seen as essentially experiments through which learning may occur. When uncertainties abound, there is little reason to believe that we will get things right on first try. And so the approach is to proceed with humility. Given that the needed knowledge base is evolutionary and will grow over time, adaptive management proceeds in a manner to maximize effective use of increasing knowledge and learning from the application of intervention systems. Figure 4 contrasts the basic structure of command-and-control and adaptive management approach.

Adaptive management is, like sustainability, becoming a favorite slogan and enjoying broad popularity. It is not suitable, however, for all risk and uncertainty issues. While elements of nuclear accidents, for example, have a strong record of monitoring experience and learning from mishaps and accident precursors, this does not mean that we should be prepared to undergo catastrophic accidents from nuclear plants while we put in place an evolutionary regulatory system. By contrast, climate change is a challenge in which basic societal and economic institutions are deeply involved, potential impacts are as yet highly uncertain in spatial and temporal distribution, optimal mixes of mitigation and adaptation systems are unclear, and value issues are profound and highly contentious. Adaptive management is clearly more suitable for the latter than the former. It is a clear call where "one size does not fit all."

Resilience Building. Fundamental and longer term systems-approach is possible. This approach would begin the longer-term effort to reconstruct society to build the institutions, structure of economy, and social capital needed for a society focused on an effective coupling of society and technology with nature. Thomas Friedman (2007), viewing America's plight in 2007, called for a transformation to a new "green geopolitics":

> "[This transformation] is about creating a new cornucopia of abundance for the next generation by inventing a whole new industry. It's about getting our best brains out of hedge funds and into innovations that will not only give us the clean-power industrial assets to preserve our American dream but also give us the technologies that billions of others need to realize their own dreams without destroying the planet. It's about making America safer by breaking our addiction to a fuel that is powering regimes deeply hostile to our values. And finally it's about making America the global environmental leader, instead of a laggard." (Friedman 2007, 72).

A resilient society, as Walker and Salt (2006) have argued, is one predicated on the understanding that it is constantly in the midst of dynamic changes. This continuing process of change challenges institutions and policy makers to construct a course for society in which the society, economy, and ecosystems constantly work for policies that create adaptive functional systems that provide people with valued goods and services across scales and over time. It is a course that seeks to keep options open continuously, creating new options as old ones close (Walker and Salt 2006, 140). It is a new basic paradigm for guiding society and the economy, and their relationship with nature, to goals of sustainability and resilience and away from preoccupation with short-term profits and gains. Sustainability efforts in Europe are beginning initial steps for this new paradigm but as yet this vision remains on the horizon for old advanced industrial societies (such as the United States).

What Do Opportunities Require From Institutions?

Adaptive management and resilience-building require institutions that function very differently than those in the well-honed and familiar "command-and-control" world of environmental protection that has emerged over decades in the twentieth century (Rosa et al., 2012). These institutional prerequisites include such far-reaching properties as:

- highly flexible management structures, capable of recreating themselves in short time frames;
- horizontal interaction as well as vertical authority, information flow, and reporting;
- high permeability of institutional boundaries to external environments, stakeholders, and clients;
- candid and open acknowledgement of uncertainties, gaps in knowledge, and errors in past decisions;
- multiple centers of learning within the institutions;
- effective monitoring systems to test projections and estimates against actual experience;
- capabilities that embrace the concept of socio-technical and socio-ecological systems and the broad capabilities they require for assessment and decision making;
- ongoing active involvement of major stakeholders at all levels of the institution and all phases of the decision process.

These institutional properties are consistent with the call for an "integrative and implementable science" (Bammer and Smithson 2008). Existing management institutions, whether in the public or private sector, typically do not score well on these attributes and accordingly have major constraints on their abilities to learn. But enhanced institutional assets for learning and adaptive capacity come with other problems. For example, open acknowledgement of high uncertainty or past errors can well erode public confidence and credibility. Mid-course corrections in management strategy can raise questions as to whether managers really understand the issues and whether they may have been incompetent in the past. Openness to stakeholders may erode the role of high-quality internal expertise. The problems abound and the existing knowledge of how to address these issues is weak. The various options for coping with large uncertainties are not mutually exclusive, of course. Even the use of standard risk assessment and command-and-control regulation typically employ some element of precaution and adaptation to evolving knowledge or new experiences. On the other hand, there are important choices among the archetypes of these different approaches. Heavy reliance on the precautionary principle, as Whiteside (2006) points out, moves significantly away from an approach of risk balancing with benefits, in which the burden of proof is strongly on the advocates of precaution. In cases of deep uncertainty, all approaches can benefit from more integrative systems thinking, involving greater use of lateral (comparative) thinking and analogue cases.

But There Are Vexing Dilemmas

Although opportunities abound, there are also perplexing dilemmas, as follows:

Dilemma 1: Openness vs. institutional coherence.

> The call for greater openness in the assessment process and in institutional functioning is everywhere. Initial results often are accompanied by large uncertainties. Should decision makers and scientists quickly convey initial results, even if they are highly tentative? If the results prove to be mistaken, responsible institutions will pay some price in social trust, confidence, and even internal conflict. Yet withholding even preliminary results also carries some burden in public trust.

Dilemma 2: Framing the risk problem.

> It is not unusual for long-standing risk problems to have conventional and widely accepted framing. New problems, and especially surprises, often raise major contentions about the nature of the problem. This is an issue, for example, that has beset the nuclear industry where conflict rages over the risks of meltdown, potential links to nuclear weapons, and threats to civil liberties.

Dilemma 3: Learning and adaptation.

Experience is a valuable asset in risk assessment and management. Moving adaptation from simply rebound to an equilibrium, however, fails to recognize the dynamic nature of human-environment systems, where constant change is the rule. Learning from events and experience is not something that happens automatically. The right lessons are not always defined and the right lessons are not always learned. Even if important learning occurs, the wrong adaptations may be chosen. Dealing with uncertainty carries its risks, and so while constant adjustment is needed, mistakes must also be anticipated.

Dilemma 4: Risk du jour and integrated assessment.

Experience can be a drawback as well as a plus. The last event is inevitably the first in memory. But most risk problems are highly site-specific—what happens at Place A may have very little relevance for Place B. Also, what happens in the past needs to be assessed but may have limited relevance for what happens in the future. But it is not uncommon that the risk of the day ("risk du jour") or the risk of yesterday often shapes the assessment of what the risk problem is. This is the case with wind energy. Early experience with siting wind turbines focused on impacts upon raptors in California and bird fatalities at other sites (Ram 2011). Despite the fact that the largest proposed offshore wind energy site in the United States has focused on visibility issues, or that the more extensive European experiences have focused on sea mammals and other issues, the United States risk assessment program has appropriated heavy resources to the last "du jour" risk problem. This is not unusual. On the one hand, risk experience is important and needs to be considered; on the other, an integrated knowledge base is essential in variable site risks and policy decisions. So all the day-to-day forces push to risk-du-jour management and all the past systematic assessment pushes to a partial (unintegrated) knowledge base. How does the ordinary decision maker cope?

Dilemma 5: Vigilance and skepticism.

It is important to be confident and build upon what is known. On the other hand, uncertainties always exist and will continue, and so decisions must be made under uncertainty. Knowledge covers multiple domains of science and experience while human systems are highly variable and often chaotic. Accordingly, skepticism should always prevail. There are always important things to be learned, even when existing knowledge is impressive and robust. As a result, *vigilance* is an important dimension of risk assessment and learning. Long-held assumptions may exist for good reason but can also be traps for comprehensive assessment. Accordingly, a skeptical view of knowledge must be maintained. This can happen in several ways. One is maintaining a high diversity of expertise in the institution. Another is maintaining dialogue with critics rather than debunking them. A plural process to assessment and decision making is a valuable asset in the decision process and should be actively encouraged.

Dilemma 6: Trust and credibility.

As noted above, dealing with uncertainty is far more difficult when levels of social trust and credibility are in short supply. Making assessments and communicating information and analyses are difficult when the communicator is not respected and trusted. As research by Slovic (1993) has made clear, it is much harder to build trust than to lose it. Since trust is also embedded in large structures of society, here the loss of trust among institutions is instructive—even actions designed to build trust are often not successful. Accordingly, dealing with uncertainty may have to proceed in the face of declining trust levels. There is, of course, no simple remedy for this problem, but it is clear that collaborative efforts may minimize the trust burden on managers while placing greater authority and power on those at risk. Accordingly, the process used for addressing uncertainty may move outside the scientific assessment process to enhancing the trust in how assessments and decisions are made.

Moving Ahead

With the increasing complexity of the interaction among society, economy, technology, and nature, uncertainty problems are likely to be a major part of the political landscape. They will almost certainly continue among the more difficult policy decisions that societies face, particularly if global environmental change and sustainability issues continue to move to a more prominent place on national and international agendas, and in public values. But, as this paper argues, we are not without strategies and tools for moving forward. Recognition is needed that progress is a question of long-term transformations and the urgency to begin these changes and paradigm shifts is growing rapidly. Rosa's work on structural human ecology provides an important pathway for progress.

References

Bammer, Gabriele, and Michael Smithson, eds. 2008. *Uncertainty: Multi-disciplinary Perspectives on Risk.* London: Earthscan.

Blue Ribbon Commission on America's Nuclear Future. 2012. *Report to the Secretary of Energy.* Washington: Department of Energy.

Friedman, Thomas L. 2007. "The Power of Green." *The New York Times Magazine* (April 15): 40-51, 67, and 71.

Funtowicz, Silvio O., and Jerome R. Ravetz. 2001. "Global Risk, Uncertainty, and Ignorance." In *Global Environmental Risk*, edited by Jeanne X. Kasperson and Roger E. Kasperson, 173-194. London: UNU and Earthscan Press.

Henry, Adam D., and Thomas Dietz. 2011. "Information, Networks, and the Complexity of Trust in Commons Governance." *International Journal of the Commons* 5:188-212.

Henry, Adam Douglas. 2009. "The Challenge of Learning for Sustainability: A Prolegomenon to Theory." *Human Ecology Review* 16: 131-140.

Jaeger, Carlo C., Ortwin Renn, Eugene A. Rosa, and Thomas Webler. 2001. *Risk, Uncertainty, and Rational Action.* London: Earthscan.

Kasperson, Roger E., and Mimi Berberian, eds. 2011. Integrating Science and Policy: Vulnerability and Resilience in Global Environmental Change. London: Earthscan.

Kasperson, Roger E., Dominic Golding, and Seth Tuler. 1992. "Social Distrust as a Factor in Siting Hazardous Facilities and Communicating Risks." *Journal of Social Issues* 48: 161-187.

Kinzig, Ann, David Starett, et al. 2003. "Coping With Uncertainty: A Call for a New Science-Policy Forum." *Ambio* 32(5): 330-335.

Lesbirel, S. Hayden, and Daigee Shaw, eds. 2005. *Managing Conflict in Facility Siting: An International Comparison.* Cheltenham: Edward Elgar.

Lesbirel, S. Hayden. 1998. *Nimby Politics in Japan.* Ithaca: Cornell University Press.

Luhmann, Niklas. 1989. *Ecological Communication.* Translated by J. Berdnarz. Chicago: University of Chicago Press.

Morgan, M. Granger, and Max Henrion. 1990. *Uncertainty: A Guide Toward Dealing with Uncertainties in Quantitative Risk and Policy Analysis.* Cambridge: Cambridge University Press.

National Research Council (NRC). 1996. *Understanding Risk.* Washington, DC: National Academies Press.

National Research Council (NRC). 2005. *Thinking Strategically.* Washington, DC: National Academies Press.

National Research Council (NRC). 2009. *Science and Decisions: Advancing Risk Assessment.* Washington, DC: National Academies Press.

Ram, Bonnie. 2011. "Assessing Integrated Risks of Offshore Wind Projects: Moving Towards Gigawatt-scale Deployments." *Wind Engineering* 35(2): 247-265.

Rosa, Eugene. 1998. "Metatheoretical Foundations for Post-Normal Risk." *Journal of Risk Research* 1:15-44.

Rosa, Eugene A., Thomas Dietz, Richard H. Moss, Scott Atran, and Susanne Moser. 2012. "Managing the Risks of Climate Change and Terrorism." *Solutions* 3: 59-65.

Rosa, Eugene A., Aaron McCright, and Ortwin Renn. In press. *The Risk Society: Social Theory and Governance.* Philadelphia: Temple University Press.

Shaw, Daigee, ed. 1996. *Managing Conflict in Facility Siting: An International Comparison.* Cheltenam: Edward Elger.

Slovic, Paul. 1993. "Perceived Risk, Trust, and Democracy." *Risk Analysis* 13: 675-682.

U.S. Climate Change Science Program. 2003. *Strategic Plan for the U.S. Climate Change Science Program.* Washington: The Program.

———. 2007. *Best Practice Approaches for Characterizing, Communicating, and Incorporating Scientific Uncertainty in Climate Decision Making.* SA Product 5.2. Washington: The Program.

Walker, Brian, and David Salt. 2006. *Resilience Thinking: Sustaining Ecosystems and People in a Changing World.* Washington, DC: Island Press.

Whiteside, Kerry H. 2006. *Precautionary Politics: Principle and Practice in Confronting Environmental Risk.* Cambridge: MIT Press.

Whitfield, Stephen, Eugene A. Rosa, Thomas Dietz, and Amy Dan. 2009. "The Future of Nuclear Power: Value Orientations and Risk Perceptions." *Risk Analysis* 29: 425-437.

CHAPTER 6

Design Principles for Governing Risks from Emerging Technologies

Paul C. Stern, National Research Council

TECHNOLOGICAL INNOVATIONS ARE DEVELOPED and promoted for the benefits they are expected to bring to the innovators, the adopters, and sometimes also to the broader society. The benefits tend to be readily apparent, with data that are ostensible and repeatable in the sense defined by Rosa (1998; see also Dietz, Chapter 3); the costs, particularly those that are delayed or borne by non-adopters, are usually less so, at least at first. Consequently, initial judgments about the relative benefits and costs of innovations must often be revised in light of experience. This process is often contentious, especially when some people or groups perceive that they are paying the costs without getting the benefits. Sometimes, as in the case of the management of high-level radioactive waste and genetically modified foods, new technologies that most experts believe can be managed adequately have been prevented from development by the actions of groups that have political legitimacy and some of the evidence on their side. It is plausible that when decisions are made entirely by private actors, a technology may be developed in ways that yield greater societal risks and fewer societal benefits than under a regime in which public interests have some of the decision authority.

This logic underlies the argument that rules or regulations sometimes need to be imposed on markets to internalize the negative externalities of emerging technologies. The potential for some such technologies to result in avoidable harms and social conflict is sufficiently large that it makes sense to seek lessons from past experience and apply them to the governance of emerging technologies so as to better anticipate and reduce risks and to lower the social costs of technologies and of conflict over them.

I report here on a project that began in the National Research Council's Committee on the Human Dimensions of Global Change (now the Board on Environmental Change and Society) when I was staff director and Gene Rosa was a member of the committee. The project initially sought to distill general lessons on the governance of emerging technologies from two sources. We sought insight inductively from experience with emerging technologies, drawing mainly on analyses of experience with technologies that are now in place (nuclear power, radioactive waste management, and DNA manipulation), but looking also at some technologies that were emerging at the time the project began in 2008 (nanotechnology, biotechnology, and information science and technology). We also sought insight deductively from social scientific research on potentially relevant social processes, such as perception, assessment, and management of societal risks; management of common-pool resources; the workings of international institutions and networks; and science communication and utilization. The first phase of this project, which developed an initial assessment of lessons from these sources of insight, was summarized in a 2009 technical report that has not previously been published in a readily accessible place (Stern, Wilbanks, Cozzens, and Rosa 2009). After reporting on that work, I propose a set of design principles for the governance of emerging technological risks, and then briefly discuss how those principles might be applied to consider the risks associated with the extraction of natural gas and oil from shale formations by horizontal drilling and hydraulic fracturing.

Insights Induced from Experience with Technological Risks

Insights from the development of nuclear energy. Although public attitudes toward "the peaceful atom" were quite positive for the early decades after World War II, by the 1970s, opposition to the construction of new nuclear power plants began to emerge and grow, to the point that not a single reactor built in the United States was ordered for almost forty years beginning in 1973. A considerable body of research (e.g., Freudenburg and Rosa 1984; Rosa and Dunlap 1994; Rosa 2001) suggests at least two possible explanations for the growing public concern: an association of nuclear technology with an imagery of some dread (Weart 1982; Rosa and Clark 1999; Rosa 2001), and a growing recognition of risks associated with nuclear power plant operation and the nuclear fuel cycle, leading to a rational response to perceived risks, which was to slow down development until concerns about risks could be addressed. Evidence tends to be more supportive of the latter explanation (Mitchell 1984). Some writers have drawn the following generic lessons from this experience:

- "Emerging technologies that are perceived as risking large-scale catastrophe tend to be treated differently from emerging technologies whose impacts are less visible or appear to be less profound.
- "While scientists tend to focus on distinguishing between substantial vs. very small risks, the public tends to focus on zero risks vs. non-zero risks.
- "While scientists tend to focus on the probability a risk will be realized, the public tends to focus on the consequences.
- "Large-scale technology applications are more likely to cause public concern than small-scale applications (Wilbanks 1984).
- "An important aspect of risk estimation is 'human factors,' for example, in the operation of technology, not just technology characteristics and performance in the abstract.
- "Public concerns are related to the extent to which a possible consequence of technological development and use is unknown vs. consequences based on evidence-based knowledge.
- "Where technologies involving advanced science are developed in ways that present obstacles to public participation, relatively-uninformed public attitudes are more likely to impede than promote progress.
- "Public concerns are conditioned by institutional factors, particularly public confidence and trust in institutions responsible for risk management" (Stern et al. 2009, 6-7).

Insights from radioactive waste management. Geological disposal of radioactive waste from nuclear power production has long been recommended as the best way to control the risks. However, absent a social consensus on how to handle such wastes over the long term (e.g., Duncan 2003; Greenberg et al. 2007a and b), the United States continues to maintain the wastes in temporary storage. Experts increasingly conclude that the biggest challenges to waste disposition are societal (e.g., Slovic et al. 1979; Dunlap, Kraft, and Rosa 1993; Rosa and Freudenburg 1993; NRC 2001; Rosa et al. 2010). According to the National Research Council (NRC) Board on Radioactive Waste Management (2001, 30), "Most countries have made major changes in their approach to waste disposition to address the recognized societal challenges. Such changes include initiating decision processes that maintain choice and that are open, transparent, and collaborative with independent scientists, critics, and the public." Research on strategies for managing radioactive wastes has led writers to draw generic lessons such as:

- "Judgments about hazards often differ between the public and the technical community, and regardless of whose judgments are better, public perceptions matter in technology acceptance.
- "Public judgments of the seriousness of hazards are related to the extent to which a possible consequence is dreaded, especially if the consequence is potentially unbounded in its effects.
- "The same risks are considered to be more serious by some population segments than others; e.g., in general, white, male, affluent, and/or highly-educated people see radioactive waste as less risky than other people do.
- "Public participation is often an effective way to promote public confidence in both institutions and technologies" (Stern et al. 2009, 8).

Insights from DNA manipulation. When the first reports of gene splicing technology appeared, concerns quickly arose from within the scientific community that the technology might deliberately or inadvertently be used to create organisms with increased virulence or other novel characteristics. One result was that early on, in 1976, the National Institutes of Health issued guidelines governing the conduct of recombinant DNA research, including the review of proposed experiments. More recently, serious concern has arisen about the possibility that DNA or related new technologies could be deliberately misused for terrorism or to create new types of biological weapons (NRC 2004a, 2004b, 2006b; WHO 2005; OECD 2004). Some lessons drawn from this experience include (Barinaga 2000; Singer 2001):

- "Risk assessment is not a scientific issue alone; it is also a social issue.
- "Risks should be analyzed and assessed not only as scientists view them but also as society is likely to view them.
- "It is easier to discuss risk issues before they become chronic and positions become hardened.
- "In many cases, risk assessment needs to be case-specific, not generic, because possible consequences may depend on relatively subtle differences in substance composition and/or use" (Stern et al. 2009, 9).

Other lessons from experience with risk assessment and management. A large body of primarily inductive work, often described under the rubric of "risk assessment and risk management" has looked for lessons across a range of technologies management issues. Much of this has been reviewed in reports from the National Research Council (NRC). Several of these (e.g., NRC 1983, 1989, 1994b, 1996, 2008a) track a major development in this field—the increasing recognition that scientific analysis of risks needs to be supplemented with methods for integrating input from "interested and affected parties" (NRC 1996, 3), not only for managing the risks, but even for understanding them. These and other NRC reports (e.g., NRC 1994c, 1995, 1997a, 1997b, 2006d, 2006e) provide valuable sources of insight into what must be done to guide an emerging technology to successful implementation and how to design management systems to perform those functions. Among the insights that have been developed from this line of research and analysis are:

- "There are multiple metrics of risk, not only probability and magnitude.
- "Qualitative aspects of hazards are important (e.g., dread, controllability; e.g., Slovic 1987; Gould et al. 1988).
- "Different parties to societal decisions about risks have different value priorities and even different understandings of a risk situation.
- "Analytic-deliberative processes that include the "spectrum of interested and affected parties" (NRC 1996) are highly useful in risk assessment and management, particularly for directing analysis toward questions that are important to decision participants.
- "Such processes are often advisable because of several characteristics of decisions about emerging technologies: complexity of choices, multidimensionality of risk, scientific uncertainty, value conflict and uncertainty, long time horizons, difficulty of excluding actors from taking action, high stakes, potential for mistrust, and time pressure (Dietz and Stern 1998).
- "It can be helpful to structure decisions in ways that make value differences and tradeoffs explicit" (e.g., Slovic and Gregory 1999; Gregory and McDaniels 2005).

Insights from experience with public participation in environmental decision making. Hundreds of case examples of efforts to engage the interested and affected parties in environmental decision making have been examined in order to derive lessons for best practice (e.g., Beierle and Cayford 2002; NRC 2008a). A review by the NRC (2008a) concluded that different decision situations posed different challenges for organizing public participation and that participatory processes should be designed based on a diagnosis of the situation. The review recommended (NRC 2008a, 3) that "[p]rocess design should be guided by four principles: inclusiveness of participation, collaborative problem formulation and process design, transparency of the process, and good-faith communication." When decisions have substantial scientific content, the study recommended that they be supported with analytic-deliberative processes that ensure transparency of information and analysis, that pay explicit attention to both facts and values, that are explicit about assumptions and uncertainties, that involve independent review of analyses or collaborative analysis, and that allow for iteration to reconsider conclusions based on new information. Techniques and processes for analysis and for considering information should, the study recommended, be chosen collaboratively with the opportunity for change as needed to overcome difficulties.

Insights Derived Deductively from Social Science Research

Insights from research on science communication and utilization. A significant body of social science research has indicated that decision-relevant scientific information is not necessarily used by those who can benefit from it, even when, as with public officials, it is their responsibility to make decisions on the basis of the best available information (e.g., Sabatier 1978; Weiss and Bucuvalas 1980; Freudenburg 1989; Landry et al. 2003; Romsdahl 2005). Other research indicates that individual citizens do not make optimal use of information available for their environmental choices. This conclusion is reported in research on environmental communication (e.g., McKenzie-Mohr and Smith 1999; Schultz 2002), disaster communication (e.g., Mileti 1999; NRC 2006a), public health communication (e.g., Valente and Schuster 2002), and information from climate forecasts (e.g., NRC 1999, 2008b). This literature provides support for several explanations of the non-use of information, including cognitive limitations of the potential users, the extra effort needed to use new information, inadequate communication between information producers and users, and scientific research agendas that are shaped more by the scientists' intellectual curiosity than by users' information needs (e.g., Clark and Majone 1985; NRC 1984b, 1989, 1999, 2002d; Cash et al. 2003; McNie 2007).

Effective use of information has often been found to depend on the efforts of intermediaries or "boundary organizations" (Cash et al. 2003; Miles et al. 2006; van Kerkhoff and Lebel 2006), which can help scientists understand which information would be most useful to decision makers, help make decision-relevant information accessible to users, and provide a credible source of information for them. Whether decision makers seek and use scientific information appears to depend on "the existence of good communication links between information providers and users, the degree to which information is easily incorporated into users' decision routines, the credibility of the information providers from the users' perspective, the strength of communication networks among the information users, and the potential for decisions to be challenged" (Stern et al. 2009, 26). It is plausible that new technologies could be an exception to some of these generalizations. Potential users of a new technology may be motivated to seek out information, particularly about its potential benefits, while ignoring information about potential risks. Thus, a major governance problem may be inadequate early attention to information about the risks.

This family of research activities points to the following lessons:

- "Information about benefits is often developed more aggressively than information about risks, leading to governance challenges later.
- "Boundary organizations can be important in closing the gap between the producers and consumers of risk-related information.
- "Social impediments are more likely to arise in risk management processes if risk communication comes late (e.g., NRC 1989).
- "Building trust through public participation can increase the likelihood of acceptance of a technology, though doing this well is often challenging" (e.g., NRC 2008a).

Insights from research on international networks. Research on international networks considers ways in which multiple institutions—governments, corporations, "civil society" organizations, and a range of other "stakeholders"—engage together in decision making. This research draws heavily on cases in international finance and environmental protection. Some of this work emphasizes the roles of "epistemic communities" (e.g., Haas 1989, 1992a, 1992b; Haas et al. 1993), often prominently including scientists, which are linked by common understandings and which, through those understandings, have sometimes been instrumental in achieving international agreements on risk governance; for example, in the case of the Montreal Protocol on substances that harm the atmosphere's ozone layer (e.g., Haas 1992a). What have been called global public policy networks (Reinicke and Deng 2000) have also helped in risk governance by "putting issues on the policy agenda, negotiating and setting global standards, gathering and disseminating knowledge, creating and improving markets, helping to implement international agreements, and improving participation of those needed to fulfill" other functions (Stern et al. 2009, 23). Research on global policy networks identifies principles for creating and nurturing networks that might be useful for emerging technologies: getting the right people on board, creating a shared vision, emphasizing the need for collective thinking, setting achievable milestones, maintaining some structure while avoiding bureaucratization, and including both local and global actors and the developed and developing worlds. The research also suggests ways to implement these principles.

Insights from research on governing common-pool resources. Research on common-pool resource (CPR) management (e.g., Hardin 1968; McCay and Acheson 1987; Ostrom 1990; Baland and Platteau 1996; NRC 2002a) has focused mainly on institutions for managing private use of resources that are depletable by extraction, such as forests (Gibson et al. 2000), fisheries (e.g., Acheson 1981; Berkes et al. 2001), and irrigation water supplies (e.g., Wade 1988; Bardhan and Dayton-Johnson 2002). This focus may appear to be an opposite to risk management, in the sense that environmental risks typically involve private actions that add undesirable things to a publicly shared environment. In both cases, however, the problem is to govern the negative shared consequences of private actions.

Research in the CPR tradition pays special attention to non-governmental institutions organized by those whose private actions cause negative shared consequences in order to create and enforce management rules. This extensive body of research has led to the identification of several generic governance challenges and "design principles" for preventing private destruction of public goods (Ostrom 1990; Stern et al. 2002a, 2002b; NRC 2002a; Dietz et al. 2003). In the first phase of our investigation into the governance of emerging risks, we found this line of research particularly intriguing and instructive, as it suggested the idea that there might be generic design principles for systems of risk governance and, moreover, it proposed a set of such principles that might be applied or adapted.

The following governance requirements from those identified in the literature on traditional resource commons (Stern et al. 2002a, 2002b; Dietz et al. 2003) seemed relevant to emerging technologies:

- "Provide timely, understandable information about the technology and human interactions with it, matched to the scale of decision making and with accountability for the information providers.
- "Deal with conflicts about the development and use of the technology.
- "Induce compliance with rules at low cost.
- "Provide needed infrastructure, particularly institutional infrastructure;
- "Encourage adaptation and change" (Stern et al. 2009, 21).

Three governance principles have been identified as especially relevant for global-scale problems (Dietz et al. 2003): (1) Employ *analytic-deliberative processes* to structure dialogue among scientists, technology developers, and interested publics; consider key information about the technology and its use and effects; and repeat the dialogue over time, for example, at different phases of research, development, demonstration, and application, and when important new information appears about the technology's uses and potential consequences (NRC 1996; Dietz and Stern 1998; Mitchell et al. 2006). (2) Organize *nested governance,* at levels from local to global, to coordinate technology developers who usually have the best knowledge of local developments with the technology and may have some informal influence over each other, and governmental authorities at various levels. (3) Establish *institutional variety* involving mixtures of institutional types (e.g., hierarchies, markets, and community self-governance) with a variety of decision rules to foil rule evaders (Gardner and Stern 1996; NRC 2002a).

Identifying Design Principles for Governing the Risks of Emerging Technologies

Governance of emerging technologies has several things in common with governance of common-pool resources, but is also different in fundamental ways. The main similarities are that both have two key aspects of commons: a divergence of interests between individuals and larger collectivities, commonly known as a public goods or collective action problem (Olson 1965) and a divergence between short-term and long-term interests, in which seeking short-term benefits leads to longer-term costs (Stern 1976). There are important differences, too, which pose challenges for any effort to extend past work on design principles in the tradition of research on common-pool resource management from local natural resources to emerging technological risks. One set of differences results from the fact that unlike the commonly-studied common pool resources, which are localized geographically, emerging technological risks are normally global because technologies can be implemented anywhere in the world and because the knowledge to develop them is global. Another set of differences results from the differences between adding risks to an environment and extracting depletable resources. I explored these differences and their implications in a recent paper (Stern 2011), which built on the seminal work of Ostrom (1990) and on related efforts undertaken at the NRC or inspired by those efforts (Dietz et al. 2003; NRC 1996, 2002a, 2008a; Stern et al. 2002b).

Local versus Global Commons

The global commons that are most like the commons studied in the Ostrom tradition are degradable natural resources that can be adequately understood only at a global scale. The atmosphere and the global ocean are the paradigmatic examples and the problem of climate change, with its effects on both atmosphere and ocean, is the paradigmatic problem requiring governance. The concept of global commons may also be applicable to degradable anthropogenic resources, such as the Internet, global markets for goods and services, international treaties, and the global networks that provide news and economic, social, and environmental information. Such possibilities are beyond the scope of this paper. The concept of global commons may also be applicable to emerging technologies, as already noted.

Insights drawn from research on local resource commons might not generalize to global commons for several reasons: (1) the geographic extent of the activities that must be controlled is usually tens to thousands of square kilometers for local natural resources, but it is global for technologies; (2) the number of people involved is tens to thousands for local resources, but potentially billions for technological risks; (3) degradation of global resources is usually much less salient to those involved than is the case with local resources, so those responsible may not be aware that a degradation process is ongoing; (4) both the benefits and costs of local natural resource use are shared by the users, but the users of a global resource may not be the same as the main bearers of the risks; (5) the users of a local natural resource usually share common institutions and culture, but with global commons, those who get most of the benefits and those who bear most of the costs may be in different countries or even different continents; and (6) most local natural resources regenerate on a human time scale, which allows learning from experience, whereas this is often not the case with many global commons. Table 1 summarizes these differences between local resources and global commons, several of which might be important for risk governance. Those of Ostrom's design principles that are strongly place-based seem particularly difficult to extend. For instance, it does not seem possible to *define boundaries for the appropriators and the resource* with global phenomena, and *defining rules congruent with ecological conditions* does not have a clear meaning because of the difficulties of identifying the conditions and enforcing global rules.

Others of Ostrom's design principles seem applicable if interpreted appropriately, although their implementation on a global scale presents challenges.

Table 1. Some differences between local natural resources and global commons that may be important for governance.

	Local natural resources	Global commons
1. Geographic scale	Local	Global
2. Number of resource users	Tens to thousands	Millions to billions
3. Salience: actors' awareness of degradation	Resource use is conscious purpose, resource provides major portion of livelihood, users monitor the resource	Resource degradation is unintended byproduct of intentional acts; actions causing degradation are of low importance for most users
4. Distribution of interests and power	Benefits and costs mainly internal to group of appropriators	Significant externalities between appropriators and others across places and generations; differences of interest and power among classes of appropriators
5. Cultural and institutional homogeneity	Homogeneous	Heterogeneous
6. Feasibility of learning:	Good	Limited
6a) Regeneration of degraded resource	Renewable over less than a human generation	Regeneration over more than a human generation
6b) Ease of understanding resource dynamics	Feasible without extensive scientific training	Scientifically complex with limited predictive ability
6c) Stability of resource dynamics	Stable, though variable	Dynamic systems with changing rules
6d) Ability to learn across places	Possible	Difficult

Source: Adapted from Stern (2011)

- *Allow most users to participate:* This principle could be applied to global commons if the "users" are redefined as the interested and affected parties and not only those who directly use the technology. It is often difficult, however, to allow most of them to participate meaningfully because there are so many and because participants need to understand the technology and the relevant science for participation to be meaningful. However, good guidance is available on how to organize effective public participation in environmental decisions (NRC 2008a, and see below).

- *Hold monitors accountable:* This important principle is challenging to implement because the monitoring may need to be global to cover all the places where a technology is used and where its effects may be felt. The monitoring tasks need to be coordinated among authorities in different jurisdictions that normally use different rules of accountability. In addition, there is often considerable uncertainty about what to monitor when the risks are not yet understood. New organizations or institutions may be needed to agree on what to monitor and on monitoring protocols, to coordinate monitoring efforts, and to agree on when and how to change monitoring protocols when new experience or information seems to call for change.

- *Apply graduated sanctions:* This is a good principle to try to apply, but challenging because sanctioning authority is usually divided among many entities, and enforcement is especially difficult if the technology users and those who bear the risks are not in personal contact and are in different jurisdictions. New institutions or organizations may be required to which the parties delegate sanctioning authority or that coordinate sanctioning efforts for consistency across jurisdictions.

- *Low-cost conflict resolution:* This is also a worthy principle, but it can be hard to implement because the parties are disconnected socially, spatially, organizationally, and in some cases, also temporally.

- *External authorities permit local control:* This principle may be applicable for some local enterprises that use a technology, but in many other cases, meaningful local control does not seem feasible. Consider a major industrial facility such as a nuclear power plant. The closer a governing unit gets in geographical scale to the location of the facility, the less likely it may be to have the funds and expertise needed for effective governance.

- *Nested layers of organization:* This principle may apply to monitoring and sanctioning, but major negotiation will typically be required for coordination to be achieved.

Resource Extraction versus Technological Risk

Insights from the analysis of local resource commons may not generalize to the governance of emerging technologies for several reasons in addition to those identified in the previous section. First, emerging technologies are global in ways that most classical commons are not. Some of them, such as technologies that operate over the Internet or that are integrated in global markets, are parts of linked global systems. Other emerging technologies, such as new biotechnologies, are global in that the knowledge needed to implement them is globally distributed. Their effects may also be felt in integrated global systems, for example, if they change the ecology of pathogens. The global nature of most emerging technologies makes local control and the design principles that rely on it very challenging to implement.

Second, unlike the classical commons, which involve resources that regenerate themselves under most conditions, irreversibility is the normal condition with the effects of new technologies. Innovation itself is an irreversible process. This difference means that effective governance of emerging technologies will depend more on anticipation of risks and less on reactions to experience than is the case with the classical common-pool resources.

Third, the uncertainty tied to the implications of emerging technologies is of a different character from that facing the users of a forest or fishery. With the classical commons, appropriators may not need to understand the resource and its dynamics in a scientific way because they can learn enough about the dynamics from long experience to manage the commons successfully. With new technologies, that option may not be available. There may be the possibility of catastrophic consequences. This makes scientific uncertainty a more serious issue for governing new technologies, especially those that may be used to intervene in complex, imperfectly understood systems such as global ecosystems or the climate system (see Renn et al., this volume, for a discussion of the case of climate "geoengineering"). It means that scientific analysis will typically be a key element in governance.

Fourth, emerging technologies often elicit strong conflicts of interests and/or of values between different collections of people: those who develop and expect to benefit from them, and those who do not and may expect to bear the risks. This has been the case with nuclear energy, genetically modified crops, and many other emerging technologies. Technology proponents often dismiss such concerns as NIMBY (not in my backyard) complaints (Rosa 1988). Because the groups whose interests conflict are not as likely to be in communication as they are in classical commons situations, governance of emerging technologies will typically require the creation of forums, venues, new lines of communication, or institutions for them to consider and address conflicts.

Proposed Design Principles

These sets of differences between the governance challenges of emerging technologies and those of traditional local resource commons suggest a list of design principles for governance of emerging technologies that is somewhat different from what has been developed for resource commons. (A complementary set of design principles for risk governance institutions can be found in Kasperson's contribution to this volume, along with a list of key dilemmas facing the governance of risks under uncertainty. Comparing these independently derived ideas is a task for future work.)

1. Invest in science to understand the technology, its interactions with its users, and the ways in which its use can pose risks to things people value. Scientific analysis needs to be explicitly incorporated in addressing the risks of emerging technologies. The need is evident from the history of nuclear power, agricultural chemicals, pharmaceuticals, and many other technologies. When concerns are raised about the risks of technologies, scientific analysis is needed to evaluate the concerns and to find ways to reduce unacceptable risks. In the literature on environmental regulation, these scientific activities are discussed in terms of risk assessment and risk management (NRC 1983), and the need for scientific analysis is unquestioned.

Although it is normal to engage science in the development of new technologies and often also in estimating their benefits, it is critical for governance that scientific analysis also be used to anticipate possible hazards. As already noted, the governance strategy of learning from experience and adapting to changes in the system as they appear, which often works well with classical commons, is perilous for managing emerging technologies because of irreversibility. The example of the creation of a new species by genetic manipulation is sufficient to make this point. Many other emerging technologies, including nuclear power, new drugs, and the Internet have also had major "unanticipated" consequences. In some of these cases, though, someone did anticipate the consequences but the warnings were ignored. Although anticipating risks may be difficult, serious efforts are worthwhile if it seems that *post hoc* coping with adverse events might prove too costly. Scientists who understand the technology well are often in the best position to anticipate the hazards. It is important to note, however, that they may lack expertise in sciences that focus on important potential consequences, such as ecology, epidemiology, and the social and behavioral sciences. In addition, for a variety of organizational, cultural, and psychological reasons, these scientists are sometimes blind to risks they might otherwise notice.

What is often missing and much needed are governance institutions that ensure that scientifically based risk anticipation is taken seriously, is conducted through a process that allows a full range of parties to influence the analytic agenda, and begins before the technology is widely implemented. Such governance institutions were created early in the history of recombinant DNA technology, with the establishment of the Recombinant DNA Advisory Committee (RAC) at the National Institutes of Health in 1974. The RAC is a federal advisory committee that functions as a venue for deliberating about management of this technology and that makes recommendations to the federal government for its governance. The original idea behind the United States Congressional Office of Technology Assessment was to undertake this kind of early assessment function (Kunkle 1995), and particularly to do so with independence from the federal executive branch. The Human Genome Project has devoted 3–5 percent of its budget to "studying the ethical, legal, and social issues surrounding availability of genetic information," according to the project's information site (http://www.ornl.gov/sci/techresources/Human_Genome/elsi/elsi.shtml, accessed January 9, 2013).

Approaches involving broad foresight are far from universal, however. For example, in the well-established practice of approval of new drugs in the United States, the main role of scientific analysis is much narrower: to determine whether a drug is "safe and effective," with safety normally defined only in terms of short-term effects on the individuals receiving the drug. Moreover, much of the drug research that goes into these determinations is carried out by the pharmaceutical developers, so that its independence is open to question. It is a common occurrence that the scientists who understand an emerging technology best are in the employ of the technology's developers, whose incentives lead them to support research on the technology's benefits more than its risks. This typical situation presents a significant governance challenge for organizing science to anticipate risks.

2. Ensure meaningful participation of the interested and affected parties in both scientific and governance matters. These matters include identifying risk concerns, framing questions for scientific analysis, interpreting science, and developing rules for technological development and implementation and for their oversight. As already noted, the potentially affected parties typically do not all have sufficient resources, particularly including scientific and technological knowledge, to engage in debates about risks and benefits on an equal footing. It is often necessary, and sometimes difficult, to level the playing field. Affected parties that lack technical knowledge need to be confident that their interests and values are adequately represented in technical discussions they may not fully understand. Government agencies with oversight responsibility are typically called upon to represent the interests of "the public," but some of the affected parties may not trust these agencies or their experts, and in fact, the agencies may not understand the risk concerns of greatest importance to all the various parties. If technically unsophisticated parties cannot employ their own technical experts and must rely on experts who are provided to them, long-term interaction may be required between these parties and their assigned specialists before the experts gain adequate understanding of their clients' concerns and the clients gain confidence in the experts. Another challenge of engaging the affected parties is that they may not know they will be affected until after the decisions that affect them have been made (see Dietz, Chapter 3). Useful guidance for designing participatory processes can be found in National Research Council (2008a).

3. Integrate scientific analysis and broadly based deliberation. Meaningful participation means not only that the various parties have sufficient technical competency to engage seriously and effectively in analysis of risks and benefits, but also that the processes for conducting and interpreting analysis are informed by deliberation among individuals expressing the concerns and perspectives of the range of parties. Such deliberation is important in deciding, for example, which parameters of a technology's implementation and effects are most important to monitor. Technical experts approaching the science from different parties' perspectives are likely to have different predilections about what is important to monitor, and an exchange of ideas is likely to lead to a monitoring regime with broader legitimacy than one designed by a narrower group of experts. Broadly based deliberation is similarly needed in interpreting information from science and from monitoring efforts. Under uncertainty or when information is incomplete in important respects, parties with different interests and values typically offer competing interpretations of available knowledge. Deliberation is also needed in considering governance rules: which norms of technology implementation to establish and emphasize, which violations deserve the most serious sanctioning, and so forth.

Well-designed analytic-deliberative processes can integrate cutting-edge science into governance regimes in ways that make the scientists, as well as the appropriators and monitors, accountable to the wider set of parties (see NRC 1996, 2008a, 2009; Dietz and Stern 1998). These processes involve well-structured dialogue among scientists, resource users, and interested publics to provide credible information, build trust in it, consider its import for resource management, and provide a basis for adaptation and change.

4. Higher-level actors should facilitate participation by lower-level actors. This principle is important because technological innovation is inherently global and raises issues that do not arise with local commons. The principle of nested layers of governance from the commons literature may be difficult to apply, however, because it is often the case that there is no overarching authority that has the power to regulate or set rules for the users of technology at lower levels of governance because technology development and its impacts occur in different countries. But even when higher-level actors lack regulatory power, they can coordinate and harmonize rules developed at lower levels, as they can with local resource commons. They may also be uniquely suited for enabling meaningful participation in lower-level governance by providing scientific expertise, information, or resources to develop information that is needed for such governance. Information about the workings of a new technology may be beyond the capacity of local actors to gather or understand without help. Higher-level institutions can also gather information about the risk governance experiences of multiple local-level institutions, which would be prohibitive for each local institution to get on its own, and make the collected experience accessible for decision makers in other places.

Such nested governance systems may be organized within national governmental structures; by private-sector organizations; by nonprofit, non-governmental organizations; or by combinations of these. Industry organizations, for example, have sometimes been created to set product standards or best-practice standards (see, e.g., Prakash and Potoski 2006; Busch 2011). Their motivations for doing this may not all be public spirited: standards may, for example, be developed to undercut demand for the products of competitors who do not adhere to them. Whatever the complex of motives, a far-sighted industry group can sometimes create institutions that reduce technological risks.

5. Engage and connect a variety of institutional forms, global to local, in making rules, monitoring, and sanctioning. Institutional variety is a fundamental principle of polyarchy as described by Ostrom (2010), although it was not highlighted in her earlier work on local resource commons. It deserves explicit attention as a governance principle for global resources and emerging technologies (Sovacool 2011). There are useful roles in governance for command-and-control, market-based, and informal forms of influence. The challenge is to find combinations of institutional forms that can effectively implement the other design principles.

6. Establish independent monitoring, accountable to the interested and affected parties. Scientific analysis requires credible data. Experience shows that in disputes over the development of new technologies, the initially available data related to benefits and risks, which are typically produced by technology promoters, are a common source of controversy. It is often the case that parties engage in disputes about technical issues of data quality or adequacy when an underlying issue is that little effort has been made to collect relevant data about some outcomes of great concern to some of the parties. Opening the processes of monitoring and data collection may not resolve conflicts of interests or values, but open monitoring is likely to focus attention more closely on fundamental matters of conflict rather than on technical issues. Monitoring protocols should be subject to change by mutual agreement.

7. Plan for institutional adaptation and change (iterative risk management). Given the inherent uncertainties in estimates of the risks and benefits of emerging technologies, changes in the state of scientific knowledge, and the possibility of surprise emerging as the technology is monitored in use, it is critical that governance regimes be organized to be adaptive to changing information, including scientific information. Adaptiveness in governance systems, sometimes called iterative risk management (NRC 2011), is therefore an important design principle. The key challenges of iterative risk management include designing institutions to learn rather than to simply follow standard operating procedures, possibly by making reconsideration into a routine, and incorporating science into organizational learning processes.

A Case Example: Risks in Development of Natural Gas in Shale Deposits

To illustrate the design principles, I turn to the example of a currently emerging set of unconventional technologies—horizontal drilling and hydraulic fracturing ("fracking" for short) for extracting natural gas and oil from shale deposits. Although the technologies are not new, their use has been rapidly expanding in the United States and elsewhere in recent years, and a great variety of new risk concerns has been raised about the technologies themselves, the ways they are implemented and regulated, and their effects on a variety of physical, biological, social, and economic conditions.

Development of these technologies to date has been following a familiar path in which information about risks and benefits is provided initially by developers and proponents of the technology, with the concerns of other interested and affected parties emerging later, in opposition to proponents' claims. This process seems inconsistent with the design principles proposed above. A useful thought experiment would be to imagine what a governance regime for unconventional shale gas and oil development might look like if it were designed according to the above principles.

Knowledge is insufficient to define a best governance regime in advance, but it seems evident that any future governance regime would have to evolve from current governance arrangements and would likely include a mix of existing governance institutions (e.g., laws and regulatory authorities at various governmental levels, insurance industry practices, oil and gas industry standards of practice, and the tort system); evolved versions of these institutions; and new institutions and organizations developed to perform functions for which existing entities are seen as insufficiently well suited. In short, a governance regime that effectively implements all the design principles would have to be developed over time and to involve multiple institutions performing in concert. Existing knowledge suggests that the best process for evolving such a regime would be broadly participatory, consultative, and deliberative, as suggested by design principle #7: plan for institutional adaptation and change.

As a stimulus to further discussion, I propose here an institutional form that could help to implement several of the design principles: investing in science, ensuring meaningful participation by the interested and affected parties in scientific matters, integrating scientific analysis and broadly based deliberation, facilitating broad participation by providing better information even for poorly resourced parties, and planning for its own institutional change. The proposal is for an independent Commission on the Development of U.S. Shale Gas and Oil Resources, created with support and funding from federal and state governments and from the industry, with the primary purpose of informing decisions about shale gas and oil development by examining the benefits, costs, and risks of various kinds of operations and practices as well as tradeoffs among them.

The commission would serve as a venue for deliberating about needs for scientific analysis and monitoring and about the import of the resulting information, and it would make decision-relevant information available to parties at various levels of social organization. It might also support and conduct some of the needed scientific analysis and monitoring. The commission would have the following functions:

- To identify potential benefits, costs, and risks of shale gas and oil development through the entire product life cycle and the lifetime of extraction and decommissioning of wells and associated infrastructure;
- To evaluate evidence on these potential benefits, costs, and risks at geographic scales from local to global (e.g., effects of global shale gas and oil development on global climate) and at various time scales;
- To establish protocols for monitoring the operation of the industry and the associated benefits, costs, and risks;
- To periodically review the evidence on all of the above on the basis of new data, experience, scientific analysis, and emerging concerns;
- To identify best practices in shale gas and oil exploration, extraction, transportation, waste management, occupational and public health and safety protection, industry self-regulation, governmental taxation and regulation, and the design of legal frameworks;
- To recommend changes in the practices of actors in the public and private sectors based on analyses of best practice and observed deviations between best and actual practice;
- To make data, analyses of evidence, and recommendations widely available to decision participants at all organizational levels in the public and private sectors; and
- To investigate claims of significant damage from the operations of the industry in order to improve understanding of benefits, costs, risks, and the nature of best practices for key private and public sector actors.

To perform these functions in ways consistent with the design principles, the commission membership would need to be diverse in terms of expertise and perspectives. It would need to include expertise across the relevant range of fields of knowledge, such as shale geology, hydrology, gas and oil production engineering, transportation, occupational and public health and safety, economics, community processes, regulatory analysis, industry self-governance, legal analysis, risk analysis, and insurance, among others. For additional expertise, the commission would need to be empowered to call on experts in relevant fields to inform its work as needed. In addition, members should be selected to ensure that the commission includes the perspectives and concerns of profit-making entities in the gas and oil industry and other industries potentially affected positively or negatively by shale development, workers in these industries, citizens in potentially affected communities, governments at all levels, and people concerned about the quality of the non-human environment.

The process for selection of commission members would likely prove critical to its credibility and to the extent of influence it will have. The selection process must credibly arrive at a balanced membership that is open to a wide range of types of evidence and that subjects all claims to critical analysis. The National Academy of Sciences/National Research Council (NAS/NRC) has developed a method of selecting boards and committees to address complex and controversial policy issues that has a good track record in terms of credibility, balance, and evidence-based analysis. Such a method would be appropriate for selecting commission members, and it is conceivable that the tasks of selecting members and ensuring balance in the membership could be delegated to the NAS/NRC. However its members are selected, it is critical that the membership selection process and the operation of the commission be independent of the organizations that supply its funding.

The commission would need to be endowed with sufficient resources to undertake, commission, or supervise some necessary scientific analysis and monitoring activities, particularly when other credible sources of such information are not available. It would also need resources to establish and manage processes that provide meaningful opportunities for input from the range of interested and affected parties, beyond the commission's members, regarding needs for and interpretation of scientific analyses and monitoring. Developing such processes may be challenging. Established procedures for public input into risk governance, such as notice-and-comment rulemaking and processes routinized under the Federal Advisory Committee Act, are typically less participatory than the design principles require, have mixed records for effectiveness and efficiency, and may not be good models. Guidance for the design of participatory processes for environmental assessment and decision making can be found in National Research Council (2008a). However, any process the commission develops for eliciting broadly based input should be treated as experimental and should be monitored and periodically reconsidered. Resources should be provided for this purpose.

The commission as envisioned here would have only analytic and advisory functions. It would not have power to legislate, regulate, establish monetary damages, enforce rules, or engage in other activities normally reserved for governmental entities. However, if its work is strong and credible, it could gain significant indirect influence over governmental and industry actors through its recommendations.

An independent commission of this type would be only one element of a governance regime. The regime's overall effectiveness would depend on not only on how well the commission performs its functions but also on the other preexisting governance institutions and on public reaction to the commission's work. All these parts of the governance system can be expected to evolve along with the commission. The fact that the commission would lack any legal authority would reduce its formal power, but has the practical advantage of making it implementable without changes in laws and regulations. For it to acquire influence, it will be important for the commission to take on a few initial activities that would demonstrate its independence and the quality and usefulness of its work. Thus, a short menu of possible initial tasks should be part of the initial mission statement for the commission.

For the governance regime as a whole to embody all the above design principles, the overall system would have to evolve to perform the functions the commission could not, such as ensuring meaningful participation in formal decision making by the interested and affected parties, coordinating nested levels of governance, and providing effective connections among institutions. A commission could help establish monitoring protocols, but it could not make monitoring accountable to the interested and affected parties unless it actually conducted or supervised the monitoring. Thus, even a well-functioning commission on this model would solve only some of the problems of designing a governance system according to the above principles.

In conclusion, it is important to reiterate that the above is only one suggestion for improving governance of the emerging technologies being used in shale gas and oil development. A more careful study of this idea and other possible institutional innovations and of past experience with similar institutional innovations (e.g., the Presidential Commission for the Study of Bioethical Issues, http://www.bioethics.gov/) might be a good first step toward developing a governance regime appropriate to this emerging set of technologies. In considering the institutional design issues, it may be worth following a major effort now being organized at the National Academy of Sciences that, according to the academy's press release of November 15, 2012, "will fund and carry out studies, projects, and activities over a 30-year period...to advance scientific and technical understanding to enhance the protection of human health and environmental resources in the Gulf Coast region including issues concerning the safety of offshore oil drilling and hydrocarbon production and transportation in the Gulf of Mexico and on the United States' outer continental shelf [and]…to contribute to the development of advanced environmental monitoring systems." This effort may perform some of the analytical and advisory functions proposed above for the shale gas commission with respect to a different set of oil and gas production technologies. Its experience may be instructive in thinking about how to organize these functions to inform decisions about development of oil and gas resources in shale deposits.

References

Acheson, James M. 1981. "The Lobster Fiefs: Economic and Ecological Effects of Territoriality in the Maine Lobster Industry." *Human Ecology* 3(3):183-207.

Baland, Jean-Marie, and Jean-Philippe Platteau. 1996. *Halting Degradation of Natural Resources: Is There a Role for Rural Communities?* Oxford: Clarendon Press.

Bardhan, Pranab, and Jeff Dayton-Johnson. 2002. "Unequal Irrigators: Heterogeneity and Commons Management in Large-scale Multivariate Research." In *The Drama of the Commons. Committee on the Human Dimensions of Global Change*, edited by Elinor Ostrom, Thomas Dietz, Nives Dolssak, Paul Stern, Susan Stonich, and Elke U. Weber, 87-112. Washington, DC: National Academy Press.

Barinaga, Marcia. 2000. "Asilomar Revisited: Lessons for Today?" *Science* 287:1584-1585.

Beierle, Thomas C., and Jerry Cayford. 2002. *Democracy as Practice: Public Participation in Environmental Decisions*. Washington, DC: Resources for the Future.

Berkes, Fikret, Robin Mahon, Patrick McConney, Richard C. Pollnac, and Robert S. Pomeroy. 2001. *Managing Small-Scale Fisheries: Alternative Directions and Methods*. Ottawa: International Development Research Centre.

Cash, David W., William C. Clark, Frank Alcock, Nancy M. Dickson, Noelle Eckley, David H. Guston, Jill Jäger, and Ronald B. Mitchell. 2003. "Knowledge Systems for Sustainable Development." *Proceedings of the National Academy of Sciences* 100(14): 8086-8091.

Clark, William C., and Giandomenico Majone. 1985. "The Critical Appraisal of Scientific Inquiries with Policy Implications." *Science, Technology, and Human Values* 10(3): 6-19.

Dietz, Thomas, Elinor Ostrom, and Paul C. Stern. 2003. "The Struggle to Govern the Commons." *Science* 302: 1907-1912.

Dietz, Thomas, and Paul C. Stern. 1998. "Science, Values, and Biodiversity." *Bioscience* 48: 441-444.

Duncan, Ian J. 2003. "What to Do with Nuclear Waste." *Nuclear Energy—Journal of the British Nuclear Energy Society* 42(3): 145-148.

Dunlap, Riley E., Michael E. Kraft, and Eugene A. Rosa. 1993. *Public Reactions to Nuclear Waste: Citizens' Views of Repository Siting*. Durham: Duke University.

Freudenburg, William R. 1989. "Social Scientists' Contributions to Environmental Management." *Journal of Social Issues* 45(1): 133-152.

Freudenburg, William R., and Eugene A. Rosa, eds. 1984. *Public Reactions to Nuclear Power: Are There Critical Masses?* Boulder: Westview.

Gardner, Gerald T., and Paul C. Stern. 1996. *Environmental Problems and Human Behavior.* Boston: Allyn and Bacon.

Gibson, Clark C., Margaret A. McKean, and Elinor Ostrom, eds. 2000. *People and Forests: Communities, Institutions, and Governance.* Cambridge: MIT Press

Gould, Leroy C., Gerald T. Gardner, Donald R. DeLuca, Adrian R. Tiemann, Leonard W. Doob, and Jan A.J. Stolwijk. 1988. *Perceptions of Technological Risks and Benefits.* New York: Russell Sage Foundation.

Greenberg, Michael, Karen Lowrie, Joanna Burger, Charles Powers, Michael Gochfeld, and Henry Mayer. 2007a. "Nuclear Waste and Public Worries: Public Perceptions of the United States' Major Nuclear Weapons Legacy Sites." *Human Ecology Review* 14 (1): 1-12.

———. 2007b. "The Ultimate LULU? Public Reaction to New Nuclear Activities at Major Weapons Sites." *Journal of the American Planning Association* 73(3): 346-351.

Gregory, Robin, and Timothy McDaniels. 2005. "Improving Environmental Decision Processes." In National Research Council, *Decision Making for the Environment: Social and Behavioral Science Research Priorities,* edited by Garry D. Brewer and Paul C. Stern, 175-199. Washington, DC: National Academies Press.

Haas, Peter M. 1989. "Do Regimes Matter? Epistemic Communities and Mediterranean Pollution Control." *International Organization* 43(4): 377-403.

———. 1992a. "Banning Chlorofluorocarbons: Epistemic Community Efforts to Protect Stratospheric Ozone." *International Organization* 46(1): 87-224.

———. 1992b. "Introduction: Epistemic Communities and International Policy Co-ordination." International Organization 46(1): 1-35.

Haas, Peter M., Robert O. Keohane, and Marc A. Levy. 1993. *Institutions for the Earth: Sources of Effective International Environmental Protection.* Cambridge: MIT Press.

Hardin, Garrett. 1968. "The Tragedy of the Commons." *Science* 162: 1243-1248.

Kasperson, Roger E. 2013. "An Integrative Framework for Risk Assessment, Vulnerability Analysis, and Resilience Building." Chapter 5, this volume.

Kunkle, Gregory C. 1995. "New Challenge or the Past Revisited? The Office of Technology Assessment in Historical Context." *Technology in Society* 17: 175-196.

Landry, Réjean, Moktar Lamari, and Nabil Amara. 2003. "The Extent and Determinants of Utilization of University Research in Government Agencies." *Public Administration Review* 63(2): 192-205.

McCay, Bonnie J., and James M. Acheson. 1987. *The Question of the Commons: The Culture and Ecology of Communal Resources.* Tucson: University of Arizona Press.

McKenzie-Mohr, Doug, and William Smith. 1999. *Fostering Sustainable Behavior: An Introduction to Community-Based Social Marketing* (2nd ed.). Gabriola Island, BC: New Society.

McNie, Elizabeth C. 2007. "Reconciling the Supply of Scientific Information with User Demands: An Analysis of the Problem and Review of the Literature." *Environmental Science and Policy* 10: 17-38.

Miles, Edward L., Amy K. Snover, Lara C. Whitely Binder, Ed S. Sarachik, Philip W. Mote, and Nathan Mantua. 2006. "An Approach to Designing a National Climate Service." *Proceedings of the National Academy of Sciences* 103: 19616-19623.

Mileti, Dennis S., 1999. *Disasters by Design: A Reassessment of Natural Hazards in the United States.* Washington, DC: Joseph Henry Press.

Mitchell, Robert. 1984. "Rationality and Irrationality in the Public's Perception of Nuclear Power." In *Public Reactions to Nuclear Power: Are There Critical Masses?*, edited by William R. Freudenberg and Eugene Rosa, 137-182. Boulder: Westview.

Mitchell, Ronald B., William C. Clark, David W. Cash, and Nancy M. Dickson, eds. 2006. *Global Environmental Assessments: Information and Influence.* Cambridge: MIT Press.

National Research Council (NRC). 1983. *Risk Assessment in the Federal Government: Managing the Process.* Washington, DC: National Academy Press.

———. 1984. *Energy Use: The Human Dimensions.* Paul C. Stern and Elliot Aronson, eds. New York: W.H. Freeman.

———. 1989. *Improving Risk Communication.* Washington, DC: National Academy Press.

———. 1994a. *Science and Judgment in Risk Assessment.* Washington, DC: National Academy Press.

———. 1994b. *Management and Disposition of Excess Weapons Plutonium.* Washington, DC: National Academy Press.

———. 1995. *Management and Disposition of Excess Weapons Plutonium–Reactor-Related Options.* Washington, DC: National Academy Press.

———. 1996. *Understanding Risk: Informing Decisions in a Democratic Society.* Committee on Risk. Paul C. Stern and Harvey V. Fineberg, eds. Washington, DC: National Academy Press.

———. 1997a. *Controlling Dangerous Pathogens: A Blueprint for U.S.-Russian Cooperation, A Report to the Cooperative Threat Reduction Program of the U.S. Department of Defense.* Washington, DC: National Academy Press.

———. 1997b. *Proliferation Concern: Assessing U.S. Efforts to Help Contain Nuclear and Other Dangerous Materials in the Former Soviet Union.* Washington, DC: National Academy Press.

———. 1999. *Making Climate Forecasts Matter.* Washington, DC: National Academy Press.

———. 2001. *Disposition of High-Level Waste and Spent Nuclear Fuel: The Continuing Societal and Technical Challenges.* Washington, DC: National Academy Press.

———. 2002a. *The Drama of the Commons.* Committee on the Human Dimensions of Global Change. Elinor Ostrom, Thomas Dietz, Nives Dolsak, Paul Stern, Susan Stonich, and Elke Weber, eds. Washington, DC: National Academy Press.

———. 2002b. *New Tools for Environmental Protection: Education, Information, and Voluntary Measures.* Thomas Dietz and Paul C. Stern, eds. Washington, DC: National Academy Press.

———. 2004a. *Seeking Security: Pathogens, Open Access, and Genome Databases.* Washington, DC: National Academies Press.

———. 2004b. *Biotechnology Research in an Age of Terrorism.* Washington, DC: National Academy Press.

———. 2006a. *Facing Hazards and Disasters: Understanding Human Dimensions. Committee on Disaster Research in the Social Sciences: Future Challenges and Opportunities.* Washington, DC: National Academy Press.

———. 2006b. *Globalization, Biosecurity, and the Future of the Life Sciences.* Washington, DC: National Academy Press.

————. 2006c *Biological Science and Biotechnology in Russia: Controlling Diseases and Enhancing Security.* Washington, DC: National Academy Press.

————. 2006d *U.S.-Russian Collaboration in Combating Radiological Terrorism.* Washington, DC: National Academy Press.

————. 2008a. *Public Participation in Environmental Assessment and Decision Making.* Thomas Dietz and Paul C. Stern, eds. Washington, DC: National Academy Press.

————. 2008b. *Research and Networks for Decision Support in the NOAA Sectoral Applications Research Program.* Helen M. Ingram and Paul C. Stern, eds. Washington, DC: National Academy Press.

————. 2011. *America's Climate Choices.* Committee on America's Climate Choices. Washington, DC: National Academies Press.

Olson, Mancur. 1965. *The Logic of Collective Action: Public Goods and the Theory of Groups.* Cambridge: Harvard University Press.

Organisation for Economic Co-operation and Development. 2004. "Promoting Responsible Stewardship in the Biosciences: Avoiding Potential Abuse of Research and Resources." Summary of Frascati, Italy, Meeting. Available: http://www.oecd.org/dataoecd/30/56/33855561.pdf.

Ostrom, Elinor. 1990. *Governing the Commons: The Evolution of Institutions for Collective Action.* New York: Cambridge University Press.

————. 2010. "Polycentric Systems for Coping with Collective Action and Global Environmental Change." *Global Environmental Change* 20: 550–557.

Prakash, Aseem, and Matthew Potoski. 2006. *The Voluntary Environmentalists: Green Clubs, ISO 14001, and Voluntary Environmental Regulations.* New York: Cambridge University Press.

Reinicke, Wolfgang H., and Francis Deng. 2000. *Critical Choices: The United Nations, Networks, and the Future of Global Governance.* Ottawa, Canada: International Development Research Centre.

Renn, Ortwin, Nadine Bratchazek, Sylvia Hiller, Dirk Scheer. 2013. "Perspectives on Risks and Concerns with Respect to Climate Engineering." Chapter 4, this volume.

Romsdahl, Rebecca J. 2005. "When Do Environmental Decision Makers Use Social Science?" In National Research Council, *Decision Making for the Environment: Social and Behavioral Science Research Priorities*, 139-174. Washington, DC: National Academy Press.

Rosa, Eugene A. 1988. "NAMBY PAMBY and NIMBY PIMBY: Public Issues in the Siting of Hazardous Waste Facilities." *Forum for Applied Research and Public Policy* 3:114-123.

————. 2001. "Public Acceptance of Nuclear Power: Déjà Vu All over Again?" Forum on Physics and Society, American Physical Society 30(2).

Rosa, Eugene A., and Donald L. Clark. 1999. "Historical Routes to Technological Gridlock: Nuclear Technology as Prototypical Vehicle." *Research in Social Problems and Public Policy* 7: 21-57.

Rosa, Eugene A., and Riley E. Dunlap. 1994. "Nuclear Power: Three Decades of Public Opinion," *Public Opinion Quarterly* 58: 295-325.

Rosa, Eugene A., and William R. Freudenburg. 1993. "The Historical Development of Public Reactions to Nuclear Power: Implications for Nuclear Waste Policy." In *Public*

Reactions to Nuclear Power: Citizens' Views of Repository Siting, edited by Riley E. Dunlap, Michael E. Kraft, and Eugene A. Rosa, 32-63. Durham: Duke University Press.

Rosa, Eugene A., Seth P. Tuler, Baruch Fischhoff, Thomas Webler, Sharon M. Friedman, Richard E. Sclove, Kristin Shrader-Frechette, Mary R. English, Roger E. Kasperson, Robert L. Goble, Thomas M. Leschine, William Freudenburg, Caron Chess, Charles Perrow, Kai Erikson, and James F. Short. "Nuclear Waste: Knowledge Waste?" *Science* 329: 762-763.

Sabatier, Paul. 1978. "The Acquisition and Utilization of Technical Information by Administrative Agencies." *Administrative Science Quarterly* 23: 396-417.

Schultz, P. Wesley. 2002. "Knowledge, Information, and Household Recycling: Examining the Knowledge-deficit Model of Behavior Change." In National Research Council, *New Tools for Environmental Protection: Education, Information, and Voluntary Measures*, edited by Thomas Dietz and Paul C. Stern, 67-82. Washington, DC: National Academy Press.

Singer, Maxine. 2001. "Commentary: What Did the Asilomar Exercise Accomplish, What Did it Leave Undone?" *Perspectives in Biology and Medicine* 44: 186-191.

Slovic, Paul. 1987. "Perception of Risk." *Science* 236: 280-285.

Slovic, Paul, and Robin Gregory. 1999. "Risk Analysis, Decision Analysis and the Social Context for Risk Decision Making." In *Decision Science and Technology: Reflections on the Contributions of Ward Edwards*, edited by James Shanteau, Barbara A. Mellers, and David A. Shum, 353-365. Boston: Kluwer Academic.

Slovic, Paul, Sarah Lichtenstein, and Baruch Fischhoff. 1979. "Images of Disaster: Perception and Acceptance of Risks from Nuclear Power." In *Energy Risk Management*, edited by Gordon Goodman and William Rowe, 223-245. London: Academic Press.

Sovacool, Benjamin K. 2011. "An International Comparison of Four Polycentric Approaches to Climate and Energy Governance." *Energy Policy* 30: 3832–3844.

Stern, Paul C. 1976. "Effect of Incentives and Education on Resource Conservation Decisions in a Simulated Commons Dilemma." *Journal of Personality and Social Psychology* 34: 12851292.

———. 2011. "Design Principles for Global Commons: Natural Resources and Emerging Technologies." *International Journal of the Commons* 5: 213-232.

Stern, Paul C., Thomas Dietz, Nives Dolsak, Elinor Ostrom, and Susan Stonich. 2002a. "Knowledge and Questions after 15 Years of Research." In National Research Council, *The Drama of the Commons*. Committee on the Human Dimensions of Global Change, Elinor Ostrom, Thomas Dietz, Nives Dolsak, Paul C. Stern, Susan Stonich, and Elke U. Weber, 445-489. Washington, DC: National Academy Press.

Stern, Paul C., Thomas Dietz, and Elinor Ostrom. 2002b. "Research On the Commons." *Environmental Practice* 4: 61-64.

Stern, Paul C., Thomas J. Wilbanks, Susan Cozzens, and Eugene Rosa. 2009. "Generic Lessons Learned about Societal Responses to Emerging Technologies Perceived as Involving Risks." Oak Ridge: Oak Ridge National Laboratory (ORNL/TM-2009/114).

van Kerkhoff, Lorrae, and Louis Lebel. 2006. "Linking Knowledge and Action for Sustainable Development." *Annual Review of Environment and Resources* 31: 445-477.

Wade, Robert. 1988. "The Management of Irrigation Systems: How to Evoke Trust and Avoid Prisoner's Dilemma." *World Development* 16: 489-500.

Weart, Spencer. 1982. "Nuclear Fear: A Preliminary History." *Working Papers in Science and Technology* 1(1): 61-88.

Weiss, Carol H., and Michael J. Bucuvalas. 1980. *Social Science Research and Decision Making*. New York: Columbia University Press.

Wilbanks, Thomas J. 1984. "Scale and the Acceptability of Nuclear Energy." In *Nuclear Power: Assessing and Managing Hazardous Technology*, edited by Martin J. Pasqueletti and K. David Pijawka, 9-50. Boulder: Westview.

World Health Organization. 2005. "Life Science Research: Opportunities and Risks for Public Health, Mapping the Issues." (WHO/CDS/CSR/LYO/2005.20). Available: http://www.who.int/csr/resources/publications/deliberate/WHO_CDS_CSR_LYO2005_20/en/index.html.

III. Structural Human Ecology of Nations

CHAPTER 7

Energy and Electricity in Industrial Nations

Allan Mazur

G ENE ROSA, TOM DIETZ, AND RICHARD YORK, with their students and colleagues, have developed such a forceful body of work on societal development that my goal in this chapter is simply to report recent work of my own as supplementary to theirs. I address two topics: (1) the importance of energy and electricity consumption for improving quality of life, and (2) the importance of population growth in raising a nation's energy and electricity consumption.

Energy Consumption and Quality of Life

The energy crisis of the 1970s—marked by the Yom Kippur War (1973) and ensuing OPEC oil embargo, and the Iranian revolution (1979)— alerted Americans that supplies of energy were not inevitably reliable and inexpensive. It was known empirically that nations with the highest energy consumption per capita had the highest gross domestic product per capita, and it was generally assumed that the former drove the latter. The implication was that choking off a nation's energy supply would inevitably cause deterioration in lifestyle.

Gene Rosa was at that time a graduate student at Syracuse University, and together we reexamined this view with a cross-sectional analysis of the world's nations. The study had two innovations. First, we used several indicators of quality of life in addition to GDP per capita; many of these were also correlated with energy consumption per capita. Second, we looked separately at the developed nations, and here our results suggested that once a nation reaches the high level of energy consumption typical of an industrial country, further increases in energy consumption yielded little gain in quality of life.

121

The implication was that highly energy-consuming nations were wasteful and probably could conserve without detriment to lifestyle (Mazur and Rosa 1974). But this conclusion was hardly ironclad and virtually ignored.

Three decades later, with considerably improved national time-series data, I revisited this issue with a longitudinal study, comparing changes in energy and electricity consumption per capita (from 1960 to 2005) to changes in diverse indicators of quality of life (Mazur 2011).

Methods

Most of my analysis is based on 21 industrialized countries, following the United Nations in counting the developed nations as Japan in Asia, Canada and the United States in North America, Australia and New Zealand in Oceania, and Europe, excluding Eastern Europe. I limited analysis to nations larger than two million in population because small countries add little to the overall picture.

Energy statistics by nation and year from 1980 are available from the U.S. Energy Information Agency (EIA 2008). Most indicators of quality of life are reported in the World Bank's World Development Index Online (2009). Suicides per capita are in the United Nations Demographic Yearbook (1985, 2006). I took a subjective measure of well-being from the World Values Survey (Inglehart et al. 2008). Until the unification of Germany in 1990, data for East and West Germany are combined. See Mazur (2011) for methodological details.

There is no completely satisfactory way to measure the well-being of a nation's people. In 1990 the United Nations adopted the Human Development Index (HDI), combining three indicators: life expectancy, adult literacy rate (and school enrollment), and GDP per capita. The HDI has the advantage of a simple summary variable, but since its components are not commensurable, they are necessarily combined in an arbitrary way.

Following earlier multiple-indicator studies and constrained by the availability of comparative data, I selected 13 variables that measure diverse aspects of well-being and are related to per capita consumption of energy and electricity among the world's nations. These are life expectancy and (somewhat redundantly) infant mortality rate; physicians and hospital beds per capita; rate of enrollment in college (tertiary education); internet users per capita; fixed and mobile phone subscribers per capita; percent of households with television; passenger cars per capita; GDP per capita (based on purchasing power parity, in constant international dollars), male suicides per capita, divorce rate, and percentage of population satisfied with their lives.

Each indicator is assailable as a normative measure of well-being. High GDP per capita or number of cars (or other consumer goods) per capita is especially subject to the criticism of wastefulness. Longer life expectancy has diminishing returns when accompanied by loss of vigor, disability, and depression, requiring social services for elderly citizens who are no longer productive and who no longer enjoy their lives. Divorce, usually considered the failure of a marriage, may be regarded as freedom to end an unhappy relationship. Low suicide rate might reflect the forbiddance of suffering people at the end of life to induce their own "death with dignity." Even decreasing infant mortality, to which hardly anyone would object, raises population size and hence environmental load. There is also the matter of how equitably benefits are distributed through a society, which is not captured by these variables. With such qualifications, it is still true that in the industrial democracies, the focus of this inquiry, there is general agreement that people are better off when each indicator moves one way rather than the other. When the same finding reliably occurs across a broad range of indicators, then misgivings one might have for any particular indicator become less weighty.

To date, the hypothesis that increased energy (or electricity) consumption produces improved quality of life has been tested only with cross-sectional data. Knowing changes in 11 of the indicators of quality of life, from approximately 1980 (1990 for internet usage) to 2006, allows the first test with longitudinal data.

Looking at all the world's nations, distributions of variables are often highly skewed with extreme outliers. Limiting the analysis to industrial democracies eliminates most outliers and skew. Therefore, correlations are calculated on untransformed data. (Correlations after log transformations are essentially unchanged.)

The propriety of using significance tests is dubious since the 21 nations do not comprise a random sample; also sample sizes vary depending on the indicator. Nonetheless, significance levels are often requested so I report them with the caveat that p values serve more as benchmarks than as true probabilities.

Results

Energy use is strongly correlated with diverse indicators of quality of life among the world's nations. Figure 1 is an illustration showing life expectancy in 2006 as a function of per capita energy consumption (triangles) for 135 countries with populations over two million. Nearly all nations using above

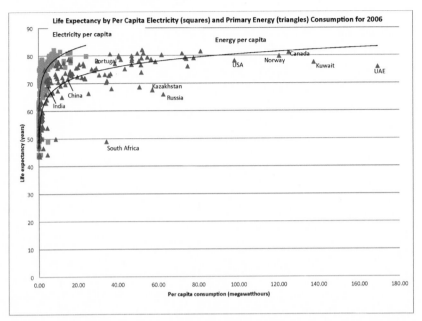

Figure 1. Life Expectancy by Per Capita Electricity and Primary Energy Consumption for 2006.

40 megawatt-hours of energy per person have life expectancies near 80 years, and consumption twice as high produces no increase in longevity. The scattergram is fit with a logarithmic curve, showing the leveling of longevity at higher levels of consumption. The left portion of the figure shows life expectancy as a function of per capita electricity consumption, again producing a logarithmic relationship. Nations using more than five megawatt-hours of electricity per capita have life expectancies around 80 years; there is no further improvement with up to three times more electrical usage.

Restricting ourselves to the industrial nations, correlations between energy or electrical consumption (per capita) and all life quality indicators are shown in Table 1. GDP per capita and rate of internet usage both increase with energy and electricity per capita. Percent enrolled in college and satisfied with life increase only with electricity consumption. Most correlations in Table 1 are small and insignificant. Some moderate correlations go the "wrong" way: high energy or electrical consumption per capita is associated with fewer physicians per capita, fewer telephones per capita, and higher divorce rate.

Table 1. Industrialized nations, 2006: Pearson correlations between energy or electricity consumption (per capita) and 13 indicators of quality of life.

Indicator	Consumption of primary energy per capita	Consumption of electricity per capita
Life expectancy	.00	.14
Infant mortality	-.30	.00
Physicians per capita	-.48	-.33
Hospital beds per capita	-.14	-.14
Male suicide rate	.17	.17
Divorce rate	.47	.31
Percent in college	.28	**.37**
Pct. households with TV	.10	.00
Phones per capita	-.52	-.33
Passenger cars per capita	.14	.00
Internet users per capita	**.60**	**.59**
GDP per capita	**.59**	**.62**
Percent satisfied with life	.33	**.55**

Bold indicates significant improvement with higher consumption ($p < .05$, one tail).

Cross-sectional data permit only a very weak test of the hypothesis that higher energy consumption causes improved well-being. It is preferable to compare change in energy consumption over time with corresponding changes in the quality of life. There are numerous determinants of energy/electricity consumption from nation to nation, and year to year, including relative cost of energy, patterns of imports and exports, and changing structure of an economy, but overall, if increasing consumption of per capita energy/electricity causes improvement in well-being, this ought to emerge as a signal over a period as long as a quarter century. Again using life expectancy as an example, Figure 2 represents each of the 21 developed nations with an arrow running from 1980 to 2006. Each arrow begins at that nation's coordinates of the graph for energy consumption (per capita) and life expectancy in 1980. The arrow ends at the coordinates for 2006.

All arrows point upward, showing that life expectancy improved considerably everywhere from 1980 to 2006; it is not a "saturated" indicator. Changes in per capita energy consumption were highly variable, with five nations slightly decreasing their per capita usage, another remaining nearly

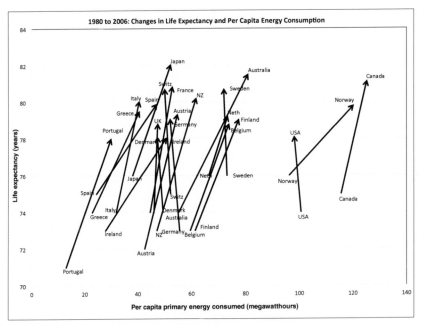

Figure 2. Changes in life expectancy by changes in per capita energy consumption for 21 industrial nations, 1980-2006.

the same, and the rest increasing. Overall, life expectancy rose irrespective of whether nations increased or decreased energy consumption per capita. Whatever caused this enhanced longevity, it was not in general an increase in the combustion of fuel.

Figure 3 is a similar display except now showing change in per capita electricity consumption from 1980 to 2006. It is noteworthy that electricity consumption per capita rose in every nation, even those that reduced their per capita energy usage. All arrows in Figure 3 point to the upper right, the result of across-the-board increases in both electricity consumption and longevity. However, increase in one variable is not proportional to increase in the other (r = .0), discrediting the hypothesis that the increased electrification contributed directly to increased longevity.

Table 2 shows correlations between changes in each indicator and changes in (per capita) energy and electricity consumption, over this quarter century. Nearly all correlations are small and insignificant. One exception is a sizable positive relationship between growth in energy consumption and increase in households having television. The cross-sectional links to energy or electricity

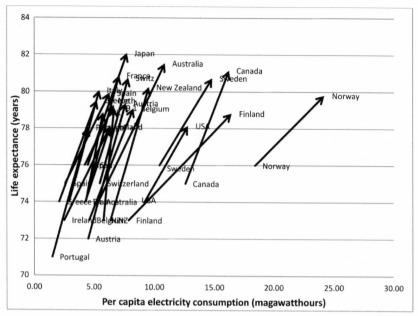

Figure 3. Changes in life expectancy by changes in electricity consumption (per capita) in 21 industrial nations, 1980-2006.

consumption in Table 1 (for internet use, GDP per capita, college enrollment, and satisfaction with life) are not sustained with longitudinal data.

Conclusion

Serious analysts agree that increased energy and electricity consumption is essential for improving the well-being of people in less developed nations. China and India, because of their population sizes and rapid growth, are the most salient examples of agrarian nations rapidly increasing their use of fuels and hydroelectricity to spur their economies, create jobs, and improve the material lives of their populations.

On a per capita basis, the wealthy industrial nations still consume far more energy and electricity than virtually any nonindustrial society. A minority of industrial nations, including the United States, has slightly reduced per capita energy consumption since the 1970s. But even among these nations, per capita electricity consumption continually increases, as does total energy consumption.

Prior analyses based on cross-sectional data have for years hinted that these rich nations may have reached a plateau upon which further increases

Table 2. Industrialized nations, 2006 (n = 13-21): Pearson correlations
between change in energy or electricity consumption (per capita)
and changes in 11 indicators of quality of life.

Change in	Change in consumption of primary energy per capita	Change in consumption of electricity per capita
Life expectancy	.27	.00
Infant mortality	-.24	.22
Physicians per capita	.20	-.10
Hospital beds per capita	.08	-.53
Divorce rate	.32	.00
Percent households with TV	**.53**	-.10
Phones per capita	.00	-.33
Passenger cars per capita	.37	-.06
Internet users per capita	-.32	.10
GDP per capita	.28	.32
Percent satisfied with life	.00	.20

Bold indicates significant improvement with higher consumption (p ≤ .05, one tail).

in energy and electricity consumption produce little if any benefits for quality of life. The present analysis, the first based on longitudinal data, fortifies that supposition. Among industrial nations, increases in per capita energy and electricity consumption over the quarter century between 1980 and 2006 were not accompanied by corresponding improvements in indicators of quality of life. The once common claim that energy and electricity consumption improves per capita GDP, which recent analysts have severely qualified, receives no support from this cross-national comparison of trends.

Why, in rich nations, does increasing energy/electricity consumption fail to cause commensurate improvements in quality of life? Some aspects of well-being may have improved so much during the past century that there is little room for further gain. With most houses having a television, this indicator is nearly saturated. Infant mortality rate cannot go much lower than its present average of four deaths per thousand births across the industrial nations. But life expectancy increased several years between 1980 and 2006, suggesting that it may continue to improve. Most of the indicators of well-being used here have no obvious near-term limits, and still they are not related to increased energy or electricity consumption.

Affluent societies consume energy in extravagant and inefficient ways. Of course, there will be specific new uses of energy that have undeniable value for some users. But often the perceived utility of an innovation is an illusion of consumer culture. This is especially true for further increases in electrification, one reason that electricity consumption increases faster than nonelectric consumption.

This analysis takes no account of differences among industrialized nations such as climate and geography that may affect the utility obtained from a unit of energy consumed. The Mediterranean climate requires less heating than northern Europe or most of North America, but Smil (2009) claims that controlling on climate explains little difference in overall energy consumption across Europe. The United States, Japan, urban Australia, and New Zealand are in temperate zones and on average (recognizing local variation) do not require inordinate heating or cooling. Other possibly relevant factors include a nation's endowment with energy sources and historical pattern of energy use. Each nation is treated here without regard to its internal energy flows or its interdependence with other nations, for example, the intimate interconnection between the United States and Canada of both fuel exports and electrical grids.

Perhaps the most sociologically potent theoretical explanation of continually increasing energy use came from historian Thomas Hughes (1983) in his study of early electrification in the United States, Britain, and Germany. In each nation, the people and institutions involved with electricity, whatever its industrial and institutional form, consistently pursued growth, comprising a kind of social "momentum" arising from the involvement of people whose professional skills are committed to the system. Corporations, government agencies, professional associations, and universities that profited from electrification, or were otherwise invested in it, provided—and still provide—the momentum. From this perspective, growing consumption is caused less by the pull of consumers than the push of institutions and industries that produce the fuels and electricity, or sell the products that use them.

In Industrial Nations, is Population Growth an Important Driver of Energy or Electricity Use?

Looking across the world's nations, the principle determinants of energy consumption are population size and affluence (York, Rosa, and Dietz 2003; Rosa et al. 2009). In the imagery of *New York Times* columnist Thomas Friedman, the world's resource problem is not due simply to too many people, but to too many people living a high-consumption "American" lifestyle (2008). The relative importance of these drivers has been a perennial point of contention, with neo-Malthusians giving most weight to population growth while others like Friedman emphasize our culture's extravagant use of energy.

Reviewing the past three decades of theoretical argument for and against population as the central driver of anthropocentric environmental change (of which fuels consumption is a major component), Dietz, Rosa, and York (2010) note the lingering impasse. To a considerable extent the opposing positions are at cross purposes. The role of affluence, so central in explaining consumption differences between developed and less developed nations, is far less important when inquiry is limited to industrial nations that are all affluent. Also, population growth is relatively low in the developed nations. Thus, the importance of any single driver depends on whether we consider the world overall, or only the richest nations. Even within the industrialized world, the situation of one country may differ importantly from that of another.

Affluence includes both the "pull" of consumer demand and the persistent "push" of fuel providers and electrical utility companies to increase the supply and consumption of energy, thereby increasing their profits. These are not the only factors besides population that affects energy and electricity use. Other drivers are the efficiency of a nation's energy technology; mix of fuels; mix of manufacturing, service, and transportation activities; climate and geography; environmental regulation of energy production; degree of electrification; availability of indigenous fuels; import and export of fuels and electricity; and consumption of energy by the nation's energy- and electricity-producing industries themselves.

In the second half of the twentieth century, was rising use of energy and electricity in industrial nations due more to population growth—the emphasis of the neo-Malthusians—or to other these causes?

Methods

I continue with the same set of 21 industrial nations but then focus on the United States. Energy and other national data used here are from "Energy Balances of OECD Countries" (2009), which provides the longest time series (since 1960) of energy trends that is reasonably comparable across nations. A nation's *total primary energy supply* (TPES) comprises all energy sources input to the society including fossil fuels, nuclear power, hydroelectricity, and other renewables. *Electricity consumption* refers to the amount of electricity distributed from domestic power plants to end users + imports of electricity – exports – distribution losses.

The total energy consumed by a nation in a year (E) equals the product of per capita energy consumption (e) and total population (P). If e and P are independent of one another, then differentiating this identity produces dE = e dP + P de. The term e dP is the portion of change in energy consumption that is due to changing population. Thus, the change in total energy consumption is decomposed into a population component (e dP) and a nonpopulation component (P de).

This partition is logically derived from a mathematical identity and does not necessarily have substantive meaning. Some increases in energy consumption are clearly the result of growing population, including construction of new housing subdivisions or apartment blocks, greater number of cars on the road and gallons of gasoline purchased, addition of new shopping malls, and increase in energy-consuming jobs. On the other hand, there is no clear rationale for distributing the enormous electricity consumption of a large aluminum smelter across the entire population when most people have no direct connection to it. For the partition to be meaningful, we must assume that each nation at a given time has a particular culture (or norm) of energy use, and that the modal person added to that nation will more or less use its per capita energy consumption (e). This is implicit in Thomas Friedman's complaint that too many people live an "American" lifestyle. I proceed on this assumption, recognizing that it will be justified or not depending on its utility and the evaluation of other researchers.

All terms in the equation are estimated from historical statistics. The differential equation is treated as a difference equation with the year as a time unit. International Energy Agency (IEA) data include each nation's yearly population, energy consumption, and electricity consumption. From these, year-to-year changes in the components of the equation are calculated arithmetically (Mazur 1994).

Results

The industrial nations vary considerably in per capita TPES and electricity. The highest users are in North America and Scandinavia, the lowest are near the Mediterranean. All industrial nations are high consumers by Third World standards. Per capita, even Portugal uses twice the energy and electricity of China, and seven to ten times as much as India.

Figure 4 compares increases in population, in TPES per capita and in electricity consumption per capita, from 1960 to 2008. Mean increases were 142% for population, 320% for TPES per capita, and 677% for electricity consumption per capita. With only three exceptions (United States, Australia, United Kingdom), per capita energy consumption increased more than population, especially in the Mediterranean region. Electricity consumption grew faster than TPES in all nations except Norway, and again the increases were greatest in southern Europe.

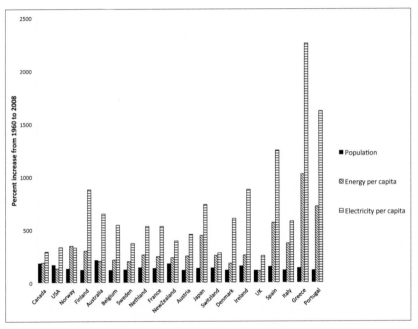

Figure 4. Increases in population, primary energy per capita, and electricity consumption per capita, 1960-2008

Population and nonpopulation components were calculated for each year's change in TPES. Components were normalized by dividing them by TPES that year, thus eliminating their connection to the nation's quantity of energy used. (i.e., for each year, the normalized population component = e $dP/TPES$; the normalized nonpopulation component = P $de/TPES$.) These components for the United States are plotted by year in Figure 5, which in broad view is similar to component plots for the other nations (not shown).

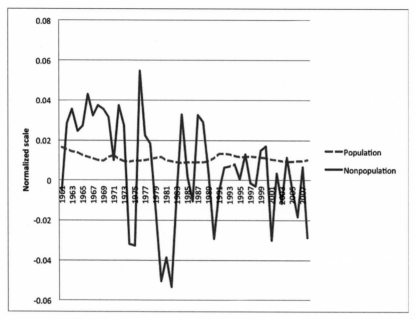

Figure 5. USA: Population and nonpopulation components of yearly change in TPES

The population component graph is smooth and nearly level, reflecting the fairly continuous year-by-year increase in U.S. population. In contrast, the graph of the nonpopulation component is erratic with the absolute magnitude of yearly fluctuations averaging twice the size of fluctuations due to population. Thus, population was less important than nonpopulation factors in driving TPES upward in most years; however, there were important changes by decade. During the 1960s, in the United States and elsewhere, nonpopulation factors produced yearly increases in energy consumption.

In recent years, nonpopulation causes are nearly as likely to diminish TPES as to increase it. The population component, though typically smaller than the nonpopulation component, invariably moves energy consumption upward. Perhaps population growth, integrated over many years, dominates nonpopulation factors—an example of "slow and steady wins the race." To evaluate this possibility, yearly changes in TPES (normalized) due to each component (population and nonpopulation) were summed over the years since 1960 (with 1960 set as a zero point). These cumulative changes for the United States are shown in Figure 6. Because population growth is fairly constant, its cumulative contribution moves smoothly upward.

Nonpopulation factors in the United States have a more interesting history, which is seen very clearly in Figure 6. Energy consumption (net of population) rose rapidly during the 1960s and early 1970s until interrupted by the OPEC oil embargo of 1973. After resuming its upward trend by the mid-1970s, there was a far greater downturn after the Iranian revolution of 1979. This initiated a period of modest growth (net of population) until the end of the century. Since 2000, while energy consumption due to population continues to rise, growth from nonpopulation factors actually declined. That is, apart from population growth, the United States has finally begun to reduce its energy consumption.

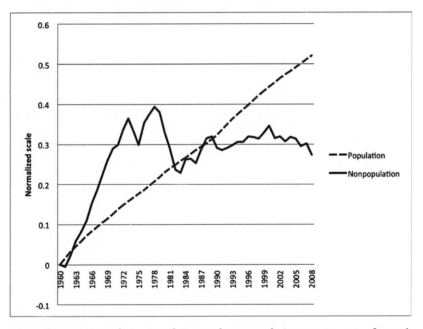

Figure 6. USA: Cumulative population and nonpopulation components of growth in TPES

Similar plots for the other major industrial nations are shown with commentary in Mazur (2012). Briefly, in Canada and Britain, unlike the United States, nonpopulation factors dominated population contributions to TPES until the last few years. In Australia, where the rate of population increase is most rapid, population is equally as important as nonpopulation factors in driving TPES upward. The European nations (France, Spain, Italy) and

Japan show similar pictures, with nonpopulation factors far more important than population as a driver.

Growth in electricity consumption was decomposed into population and nonpopulation components by the same method. Figure 7 shows cumulative increases since 1960 due to both components in the United States. Since the "energy crisis" of the 1970s, the nonpopulation component of U.S. electricity growth has leveled off. Pictures for other nations (not shown) are similar. In each country, nonpopulation factors greatly dominated population in spurring growth. This is a reflection of electricity growing far faster than population (and TPES) in all industrial nations.

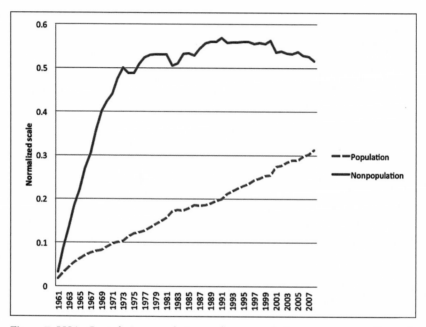

Figure 7. USA: Cumulative population and nonpopulation components of growth in electricity consumption

Conclusion

Did population growth or other causes most contribute to the rising use of energy and electricity in the industrial nations since 1960? The answer depends on the nation and how one interprets the question. Yearly fluctuations in TPES due to population growth averaged only one-sixth to one-half the magnitude of fluctuations due to nonpopulation factors. Thus, for a typical year in most nations, the population component was relatively small. However, in the 1970s and afterward, the yearly change in TPES due to nonpopulation factors was often negative, while the yearly change due to population growth, though smaller, was invariably positive. Therefore the cumulative effect of population growth from 1960 to 2008 eventually equaled or, in the United States, exceeded the cumulative effect of nonpopulation factors as was also true in Canada, the United Kingdom, and Australia, but not in France, Spain, Italy, or Japan. To some extent, this split is explained by relatively high population growth in Australia, Canada, and the United States (but not the United Kingdom), and relatively low population growth in Japan, France, and Italy (but not Spain).

The situation of electricity is different. Here we can say without qualification that population growth was a minor driver of the rapid increase in electrification of all industrial nations, especially in the years prior to the "energy crisis" of the 1970s. On average, from 1960 to 2008, per capita consumption of electricity increased twice as fast as per capita TPES and nearly five times as fast as population, though rapid escalation has abated since the price rises of the 1970s.

It may seem puzzling that U.S. population increase was an important driver of total primary energy consumption since 1960, but that population had only a modest effect on the growth of electricity consumption since 1960. This ostensible conundrum is explained by the year-to-year variation in TPES (net of population), sometimes rising, sometimes falling due to nonpopulation factors like oil prices. As a result, America's per capita consumption of TPES was lower in 2008 than in 1975. A continually larger share of America's yearly TPES was being used to generate electricity. It is plausible that the United States will soon devote most of its primary energy sources to the production of electricity, especially if there is a large move to electric cars.

A quick glance at Figure 6 might convey the impression that the United States was especially frugal with energy after 1975. This is correct in relative terms, but one must remember that American frugality began from an extraordinarily high base level of wastefulness, so it was relatively easy to eliminate the worst overuse by requiring, for example, higher miles-per-gallon automobile fleets. Most of the improvement was in the U.S. industrial sector, partly due to a changing mix of goods produced, possibly also because energy-intensive industrial activities were moved to the Third World, and likely because inefficient pre-World War II industrial plants, which remained undamaged by the war and functional into the 1970s, could be closed down without serious economic loss.

New electricity-dependent technologies are an obvious reason for some of the growth in the nonpopulation component of electrification, but at the same time, other newly introduced technologies including compact-fluorescent light bulbs and kitchen appliances are more electricity efficient. Some of the increase in electricity consumption is obviously gratuitous and wasteful, like needlessly extreme air conditioning or urban lighting to the extent that now it is often called "light pollution."

Discussion

The wholly technological and financial view of energy that prevails in the energy industries can be elucidated by contributions from the social sciences. There never was a "sociology of energy," but arguably there should be. One may say of social research in this field, as not in all other endeavors by social scientists, that the past decades have indeed improved our understanding of how things work in modern society.

References

Dietz, Thomas, and Eugene A. Rosa. 1997. "Effects of Population and Affluence on CO_2 Emissions." *Proceedings of the National Academy of Sciences* 94: 175-179.

Dietz, Thomas, Eugene A. Rosa and Richard York. 2009. "Environmentally Efficient Well-Being: Rethinking Sustainability as the Relationship between Human Well-being and Environmental Impacts." *Human Ecology Review* 16: 114-123.

————. 2010. "Human Driving Forces of Global Change: Examining Current Theories." In *Threats to Sustainability: Understanding Human Footprints on the Global Environment*, edited by Eugene A. Rosa, Andreas Diekmann, Thomas Dietz, and Carlo C. Jaeger, 83-132. Cambridge: MIT Press.

Friedman, Thomas. 2008. *Hot, Flat, and Crowded*. New York: Farrar, Straus and Giroux.

IEA. 2009. "Energy Balances of OECD Countries, 2009 Edition." Paris: OEDC/IEA.

Licklider, Roy. 1988. "The Power of Oil: The Arab Oil Weapon and the Netherlands, the United Kingdom, Canada, Japan, and the United States." *International Studies Quarterly* 32: 205-226.

Lightfoot, H. Douglas. 2006. "Understand the Three Different Scales for Measuring Primary Energy and Avoid Errors." *Energy* 32: 1478-1483.

Logan, John, and Harvey Molotch. 1987. *Urban Fortunes: The Political Economy of Place*. Berkeley: University of California Press.

Mazur, Alan. 1994. "How Does Population Growth Contribute to Rising Energy Consumption in America?" *Population and Environment* 15: 371-378.

————. 2011. "Does Increasing Energy or Electricity Consumption Improve Quality of Life in Industrial Nations?" *Energy Policy* 39: 2568-2572.

————. 2012. "Was Rising Energy and Electricity Usage in Industrial Nations (since 1960) Due More to Population Growth or to Other Causes?" *Human Ecology Review* 19: 50-57.

Mazur, Alan, and Eugene A. Rosa. 1974. "Energy and Life-style." *Science* 186 (14 November): 607-610.

Rosa, Eugene A., Andreas Diekmann, Thomas Dietz, and Carlo Jaeger. 2009. *Human Footprints on the Global Environment*. Cambridge: MIT Press.

Rosa, Eugene, Kenneth M. Keating, and Clifford L. Staples. 1980. "Energy, Economic Growth and Quality of Life: A Cross-National Trend Analysis." *Applied Systems and Cybernetics*, edited by George E. Lasker, 258-264. New York: Pergamon.

Rosa, Eugene, Gary E. Machlis, and Kenneth M. Keating. 1988. "Energy and Society." *Annual Review of Sociology* 14: 149-172.

Smil, Vaclav. 2009. "U.S. Energy Policy: The Need for Radical Departures." *Issues in Science and Technology* 25(4): 47-50.

Yergin, Daniel. 2011. *The Quest*. New York: Penguin Press.

York, Richard, Eugene Rosa, and Thomas Dietz. 2003. "Footprints on the Earth: the Environmental Consequences of Modernity." *American Sociological Review* 68: 279-300.

CHAPTER 8

Population, Affluence, and Greenhouse Gas Emissions: The Continuing Significance of Structural Human Ecology and the Utility of STIRPAT

Andrew K. Jorgenson, University of Utah

Introduction

THE HUMAN DIMENSIONS OF GLOBAL (and regional) environmental change are among the most pressing issues facing humanity and the natural world. In order for human civilization to effectively reduce its environmental impacts, rigorous empirical examinations are needed to identify the primary drivers of environmental and ecological degradation. Such rigorous, comparative work can inform mitigation polices and sustainable development strategies and assist in accurately informing global civil society of the burdens we place on nature and the likely inability of the latter to continue to sustain human social organization under current and projected economic and demographic conditions. Of particular importance are the human drivers of greenhouse gas emissions, given the scientific consensus regarding the role carbon dioxide and other greenhouse gases emitted into the atmosphere play in causing climate change and the observed patterns of global warming (e.g., IPCC 2007a, 2007b; U.S. National Research Council 2010).

Structural human ecology (SHE) and the related "STIRPAT" approach (i.e. Stochastic Impacts by Regression on Population, Affluence, and Technology) are analytical and methodological tools that allow researchers to tackle these critical issues concerning balanced and rigorous assessments of the human drivers of environmental change. Given their utility and flexible applicability, they have become central in multidisciplinary endeavors in recent decades. The purpose of this paper is to offer readers a modest overview of structural human ecology and STIRPAT, with attention paid to their origins as well as foundational and benchmark studies that engage the broader SHE framework while employing the STIRPAT approach to study human / environment relationships, primarily the effects of population and affluence on the environment in macro-level contexts. Particular attention is paid to empirical work on the human drivers of greenhouse gas emissions and the important contributions of the founders of STIRPAT, most notably Eugene Rosa, Thomas Dietz, and the later contributions of Richard York and others. In addition to summarizing the origins of SHE and STIRPAT as well as recent studies of greenhouse gas emissions, I report the results of new longitudinal STIRPAT analyses in the SHE tradition that take a closer look at regional and temporal variations in the effects of population size and affluence (i.e. levels of economic development) on the total levels of carbon emissions of nations. The results offer new insights into the nuances of these relationships, while further illustrating the continuing and perhaps increasing significance of both structural human ecology and STIRPAT.

Structural Human Ecology and STIRPAT

Structural human ecology (SHE) is a well-established perspective that truly blurs the boundaries between social and environmental sciences, with a keen focus on fundamental relationships between humans and nature. SHE emphasizes that human and environment relationships are characteristic of the human ecosystem, mainly consisting of four interacting components: population, social organization, environment, and technology. The systemic interrelationships between these four components are also commonly referred to as the P-O-E-T model, where each of them simultaneously affects and is affected by the others (e.g., Duncan 1964; Dietz and Rosa 1994; Rosa, York, and Dietz 2004). Broadly speaking, SHE is focused on the human drivers (in structural and demographic contexts) of environmental change or environmental impacts, and published research in the tradition tends to focus on such relationships at macro-levels of scale (see Rosa and Dietz 2012). However, I suggest the perspective can indeed be applied to such relationships at multiple and nested levels. The latter has been less common, primarily due to data and methodological limitations, but recent advances in measurement and modeling techniques provide fruitful avenues for future multi-scale SHE research that effectively combines social and ecological data.

SHE focuses on the many characteristics of population size, organization, and structure and how they drive environmental change (e.g., York, Rosa, and Dietz 2003a, 2003b, 2003c). The perspective also emphasizes the importance of considering ecological, biophysical, and climatologically-oriented factors that shape society / nature relationships, but this is far too often overlooked as a contribution of the perspective, a point I return to below. Others have correctly pointed out that SHE can be considered an aggravated version of coupled human and natural systems work (e.g., Knight 2009; Liu et al. 2007). Further, in the field of environmental sociology, scholars have successfully integrated SHE with other perspectives, most notably those of international political economy, in research on the human dimensions of global environmental change (e.g., Clark, Jorgenson, and Auerbach 2012; Jorgenson and Clark 2011; Shandra et al. 2004; see also Chapter 7 by Allan Mazur). Others have recently incorporated structural human ecology principles into sophistical multilevel analyses of individual-level attitudes about the environment (see Chapter 9 by Sandy Marquart-Pyatt).

While SHE is a broad theoretical perspective, STIRPAT, initially advanced by Dietz and Rosa (e.g. 1994), is a coordinated program of empirical research that attempts to evaluate the validity of SHE. In the words of those who have developed the program, "The goal of STIRPAT is to provide an analytic strategy for testing Structural Human Ecology Theory (SHE)" (http://stirpat.msu.edu/). STIRPAT, which stands for Stochastic Impacts by Regression on Population, Affluence, and Technology, is a reformulation of the IPAT equation. IPAT is a mathematical identity that has a long history of being employed as an accounting equation, and is appealing given its parsimonious specification of driving forces of environmental change and its grounding in ecological principles (for a thorough IPAT bibliography, see http://stirpat.msu.edu/IPATBib.htm). Further, the specification of the simple model indicates that the driving forces do not influence environmental impacts independently, since changes in one factor are multiplied by the other factors (York, Rosa, and Dietz 2003c).

While IPAT is helpful for conceptual framings, it is not suited for hypothesis testing since by design it assumes the effects of each driver (population, affluence, technology) to be proportional. Unlike IPAT, STIRPAT is not an accounting equation. It is a stochastic model appropriate for hypothesis testing. The baseline STIRPAT equation is as follows, where T (technology) represents everything that is not population and affluence (not represented in the equation), where *a* is the intercept, *b* and *c* are estimated coefficients, and e is the error term:

$$log\ Impact = a + b(log\ Population) + c(log\ Affluence) + e$$

Given that the variables are in logarithmic form, STIRPAT is by design an elasticity model. The coefficients of an elasticity model are relatively easy to interpret. Specifically, the coefficient for each continuous independent variable in such a model is the estimated percentage change in the dependent variable associated with a one percent increase in the independent variable, controlling for all other factors in the model. More broadly, the STIRPAT equation allows for the testing of theoretically-derived hypotheses from the SHE tradition as well as those derived from other perspectives since the model allows for the inclusion of factors and explanatory variables besides population and affluence, and within the model one can also decompose population, affluence, and technology. Besides allowing for the testing of hypotheses derived from perspectives other than SHE, the ability to include additional factors allows for more rigorous assessments of the environmental impacts of population and affluence, and much work has taken advantage of this opportunity, with results consistently suggesting that both are indeed key drivers of human-caused environmental degradation and pollution. As important, STIRPAT is well equipped to inform policy since it is designed to identify key drivers of environmental change and their relative effects, allowing for mitigation policies to more effectively target primary anthropogenic drivers. The approach can also be used for projection and forecasting models of future environmental impacts, as highlighted by recent published work (e.g., Dietz, Rosa, and York 2007; York 2006).

An ongoing challenge for STIRPAT researchers as well as for scholars in other areas is the difficulty in adequately operationalizing technology as a quantitative measurement suitable for comparative research. For example, one could argue that carbon emissions per unit of GDP could serve as a relatively valid indicator of technology, but employing such a measure in a study of total carbon emissions that also includes GDP per capita and population size as key explanatory variables could lead to serious if not fatal methodological and substantive problems. The ability to measure technology effectively and appropriately will likely continue to pose challenges, but this limitation does not take away from the utility of the STIRPAT approach in general and the overall validity of the work on population and affluence as key drivers in particular. In the next section I summarize foundational and benchmark studies that employ STIRPAT to evaluate the arguments of SHE concerning the environmental impacts of affluence and population.

STIRPAT Research on the Environmental Impacts of Population and Affluence

A large body of empirical work has emerged in a relatively short period of time that employs the STIRPAT formulation to assess the human drivers of global and regional environmental change, oftentimes focusing on the impacts of population size and other demographic characteristics and affluence, usually in the form of level of economic development (i.e., GDP per capita). The founding STIRPAT research team, consisting of Eugene Rosa, Thomas Dietz, and later joined by Richard York and others (e.g., Kyle Knight), provides a relatively complete online bibliography of published work employing the formulation (see http://stirpat.msu.edu/STIRPATBib.htm). In the following paragraphs I highlight what I consider to be some of the more notable published studies that make important contributions to the area.

Initially, research in this tradition was cross-sectional, mainly due to data availability, but these early studies were foundational in establishing the STIRPAT approach in empirical social and environmental sciences. As important, early cross-sectional studies were published in a diverse range of journals, including *Human Ecology Review* (Dietz and Rosa 1994), *Proceedings of the National Academy of Sciences* (Dietz and Rosa 1997), *International Sociology* (Rosa and Dietz 1998), *American Sociological Review* (York, Rosa, and Dietz 2003a), *Ambio* (Rosa, York, and Dietz 2004), *Journal of Industrial Ecology* (York, Rosa, and Dietz 2004), and *Frontiers of Human Ecology* (Dietz, Rosa, and York 2007). These earlier cross-sectional studies consistently showed that population and affluence are key drivers of environmental change (see also Burns, Davis, and Kick 1997 for an earlier cross-sectional study of greenhouse gas emissions that highlights the relevance of affluence and population as well as broader world-systemic factors). Another significant contribution of this earlier body of work (e.g., York et al. 2003a) was to empirically demonstrate the importance in treating ecological conditions themselves as independent variables, which has become relatively more common in recent studies of society/nature relationships (e.g., Jorgenson and Clark 2011; McKinney, Fulkerson, and Kick 2009). Unfortunately, the practice of treating environmental and ecological conditions as explanatory variables still faces resistance by many "mainstream" sociologists and other social scientists who continue to worry about being labeled as "environmentally deterministic" or abandoning what they consider classical sociological principles (Dunlap and Catton 1979).

Largely due to increasing data availability and software applications providing more powerful statistical techniques, much research in the STIRPAT tradition in recent years is longitudinal, consisting of repeated observations on relatively large number of cases, mainly countries (e.g. Clark, Jorgenson, and Auerbach 2012; Shi 2003, York 2006, 2007; York and Rosa 2012), but also smaller units of analysis, such as U.S. states (Clement and Schultz 2012). Longitudinal analysis, also commonly referred to as panel analysis, allows researchers to rigorously assess causal relationships as well as their temporal dynamics while more effectively controlling for omitted variable bias through the use of case-specific and time-specific fixed effects, specialized techniques that I discuss in greater detail in a later section of this paper.

Panel studies, like the prior cross-sectional analyses, consistently suggest that affluence and population are primary drivers of environmental change, and such studies have quickly become central in scholarship on the human drivers of greenhouse gas emissions (for a more extensive review of the published research, see Rosa and Dietz 2012). Further, recent research has employed interactions between time and explanatory variables to assess if the effects of the latter change through time. For example, consistent with the STIRPAT tradition, my colleague and I investigated the temporal stability of the effect of population size on national-level carbon emissions and found that for close to the past fifty years the effect of population is large in magnitude and stable in value through time, and this holds for samples restricted to only developed countries and only developing countries (Jorgenson and Clark 2010). In particular, the estimated elasticity coefficient for population size remained a value of 1.57 for the 1960 to 2005 period for a sample of developed countries, and also remained a value of 1.76 for a sample of less-developed countries during the same period.

In another recent cross-national study, we (i.e., Jorgenson and Clark 2012) engage STIRPAT as well as other established social science traditions to assess the temporal dynamics of the relationship between carbon emissions and levels of economic development (see also Jorgenson and Birkholz 2010 for a panel study of national-level anthropogenic methane emissions that investigates the temporal dynamics of the effects of population and affluence). Of particular relevance for structural human ecology and the STIRPAT approach, in models of total carbon emissions we found that for developed countries, the estimated coefficient for GDP per capita decreased by less than 5 percent in value from 1960 to 2005 (e.g., elasticity coefficient of .986 in 1960, decreasing to a value of .942 in 2005), while the estimated effect of GDP per capita for a sample of less-developed countries remained the same in value across the same 45-year period (elasticity coefficient of 1.003 in 1960 through 2005).

Thus, in the context of total anthropogenic carbon emissions, these recent panel studies indicate that both population and affluence have relatively large and temporally stable estimated effects for samples restricted to only developed countries and only less-developed countries, which highlights the continuing significance of population and affluence in particular, and STIR-PAT and SHE in general (see also Rosa et al. 2010). However, it is possible that the environmental impacts of population and affluence might differ for other types of national samples, such as samples for nations in particular macro-regions, and the temporal stability of the relationships between the environment and both of these drivers might also vary within or between macro-regions. The preliminary analyses reported in the following section are a modest attempt to answer such nuanced questions.

New Analyses of the Effects of Population and Affluence on Carbon Emissions

In this section of the paper I report the results of a longitudinal cross-national analysis for the 1960 to 2005 period that assesses the macro-regional differences in the estimated effects of population and affluence on total anthropogenic carbon dioxide emissions. I also assess the extent to which the estimated effects of population and affluence on emissions change through time for samples of nations unique to each macro-region. This new series of analyses build on my prior work with Brett Clark and others (e.g., Jorgenson and Clark 2010, 2012; Jorgenson, Clark, and Giedraitis 2012), where we instead focused on samples designated by relative levels of economic development (i.e., sample of developed countries and sample of less-developed countries) or focused solely on the transition economies of Central and Eastern Europe but for a much shorter and relatively recent period of time. In the current analyses I estimate elasticity models where all continuous predictors and the outcome are in logarithmic form, consistent with the approach advanced by the STIRPAT community in particular and the structural human ecology orientation in general. Prior to providing and discussing the findings, I briefly describe the samples of nations, the employed model estimation techniques, and the variables included in the estimated models.

I analyze a balanced dataset that consists of 10 observations per country at five-year increments from 1960 to 2005. With an overall number of 850 observations, the dataset consists of 85 countries. I include all nations with populations of at least one million for the entire period of investigation where data are available for all outcomes and predictors at each of the ten time points. Data availability at the time of this study precludes me from including time points before 1960 or after 2005. The countries included in the study are organized in four macro-regional categories, including (1) Africa, (2) Asia, (3) Latin America, and (4) Europe, North America, and Oceania combined. The countries, organized by macro-region location, are listed in Table 1. One weakness of the overall sample is that transition economy nations in Central and Eastern Europe are almost entirely excluded since data are not available for them for the entire period of study. Elsewhere I've conducted similar analyses on only those nations for the early 1990s to 2010 period (Jorgenson 2011; Jorgenson, Clark, and Giedraitis 2012).

For the STIRPAT panel analyses I use a time-series cross-sectional Prais-Winsten (PW) regression model with panel-corrected standard errors (PCSE), allowing for disturbances that are heteroskedastic and contemporaneously correlated across panels. I employ PCSE because the feasible generalized least-squares estimator that is often used to analyze panel data produces standard errors that can lead to extreme overconfidence with panel datasets that do not have many more time periods than panels. I correct for AR(1) disturbances (i.e., first-order autocorrelation) within panels, and since I have no theoretical basis for assuming the process is panel specific, I treat the AR(1) process as common to all panels. I control for unit-specific disturbances and include a linear control for time. For the linear time control (i.e., "year"), the values range from 1 for 1960 to 10 for 2005. The general panel model is as follows:

$$y_{it} = Bx_{it} + u_i + w_t + e_{it}$$

Subscript i represents each unit of analysis (i.e., country), subscript t represents the time period, and y_{it} is the dependent variable for each country at each time period. Bx_{it} represents the vector of coefficients for predictor variables that vary over time, u_i is the unit-specific (i.e., country-specific) disturbance term, w_t is the linear time control that is constant across all countries, and e_{it} is the disturbance term unique to each country at each point in time. I calculate and employ dummy variables to control for u_i, which controls for potential unobserved heterogeneity that is temporally invariant within countries (unit-specific intercepts). The unit-specific intercepts approach is

Table 1. Countries included in the study

Africa	*Asia*	*Europe, North America, and Oceania*
Algeria	Bangladesh	Australia
Benin	China	Austria
Burkina Faso	India	Belgium
Burundi	Indoesia	Canada
Cameroon	Iran	Denmark
Central African Republic	Israel	Finland
Chad	Japan	France
Congo, Dem. Rep.	Korea, Rep.	Georgia
Congo, Rep.	Malaysia	Greece
Cote d'Ivoire	Nepal	Hungary
Egypt	Pakistan	Ireland
Ghana	Phillippines	Italy
Kenya	Sri Lanka	Latvia
Liberia	Syrian Arab Republic	Mexico
Madagascar	Thailand	Netherlands
Malawi		New Zealand
Mauritania	*Latin America*	Norway
Morocco	Argentina	Papua New Guinea
Niger	Bolivia	Portugal
Rwanda	Brazil	Spain
Senegal	Chile	Sweden
Sierra Leone	Colombia	Switzerland
South Africa	Costa Rica	United Kingdom
Sudan	Dominican Republic	United States
Togo	Ecuador	
Tunisia	El Salvador	
Zambia	Guatemala	
Zimbabwe	Haiti	
	Honduras	
	Nicaragua	
	Panama	
	Paraguay	
	Peru	
	Uruguay	
	Venezuela	

analogous to the dummy variable fixed effects model. Including the linear time control lessens the likelihood of biased model estimates resulting from outcomes and predictors with relatively similar time trends. Overall, the employed modeling approach is robust against potentially omitted control variables and more closely approximates experimental conditions than other panel model approaches. The panel analyses are conducted with the "xtpcse" suite of commands in Stata (version 11) software.

The dependent variable for this preliminary study is total anthropogenic carbon dioxide emissions, measured in metric tons. I obtain the carbon dioxide emissions data from the World Resources Institute (2007). These data represent the mass of carbon dioxide produced during the combustion of solid, liquid, and gaseous fuels, as well as from gas flaring and the manufacture of cement. They do not include emissions from land use change or emissions from bunker fuels used in international transportation. More specifically, the emissions data come from the World Resources Institute's Climate Analysis Indicators Tool (CAIT), which is an information and analysis tool on global climate change.[1]

I employ total population measured in thousands as a key predictor (World Bank 2012). The measures of total population are based on the de facto definition of population, which counts all residents regardless of legal status or citizenship. Refugees (and temporary international migrants) not permanently settled in the country of asylum are generally considered to be part of the population of their country of origin.

I include gross domestic product per capita (GDP per capita) as a measure of a nation's level of economic development. These data are measured in 2000 constant U.S. dollars and obtained from the World Bank (2012).

I also control for urban population, which quantifies the percent of a country's population residing in urban areas. This is a commonly used measure of urbanization. These data are gathered from the World Bank (2012). Prior research consistently shows that urbanization in this form increases energy consumption, carbon emissions, and other forms of greenhouse emissions and air pollutants (e.g., Jorgenson, Rice, and Clark 2010; Rosa et al. 2004).

I include trade as percent GDP, which controls for the extent to which a country is integrated in the world economy. These data are also obtained from the World Bank (2012). Much research in various international political economy orientations indicates that forms of world economic integration, including this particular form, increase carbon emissions and especially so in developing nations (e.g., Jorgenson 2012; Roberts and Parks 2007).

I employ interactions between population size and each macro-region, where Europe, North America, and Oceania combined are the reference group. I also employ interactions between the macro-region dummy variables and gross domestic product per capita. These two sets of interactions allow for assessing the extent to which the estimated effects of population size and level of economic development on carbon emissions differ between the macro-regions.

In the final series of reported models I employ interactions between time as a linear measure and (1) population size and (2) GDP per capita to assess if the estimated effects of population and affluence (i.e., GDP per capita) on emissions change in value through time. These interactions are used in models estimated for the overall sample as well as models estimated for the samples restricted to nations in each of the macro-regions. Interactions between predictors and time are becoming increasingly common in research on the human dimensions of global and regional environmental change (e.g., Jorgenson 2011, 2012; Jorgenson and Clark 2009, 2010, 2011, 2012; Jorgenson and Kuykendall 2008; York 2012).

The Results

Table 2 reports two models. Model 1 includes all four independent variables. Model 2 also includes the interactions between population size and macroregion. Models 1 and 2 are as follows:

Model 1 in Table 2 of *Total Carbon Dioxide Emissions$_{it}$* =
$$B_1 \textit{Population}_{it} + B_2 \textit{GDP per capita}_{it} + B_3 \textit{GUrban Population}_{it} + B_4 \textit{Trade}_{it} + W_t + u_i + e_{it}$$

Model 2 in Table 2 of *Total Carbon Dioxide Emissions$_{it}$* =
$$B_1 \textit{Population}_{it} + B_2 \textit{Population}_{it} * \textit{Africa}_i + B_3 \textit{Population}_{it} * \textit{Asia}_i + B_4 \textit{Population}_{it} * \textit{Latin America}_i + B_5 \textit{GDP per capita}_{it} + B_6 \textit{Urban Population}_{it} + B_7 \textit{Trade}_{it} + W_t + u_i + e_{it}$$

The results of Model 1 indicate that all four predictors increase carbon emissions. A one percent increase in population size leads to a 1.48 percent increase in emissions, while a one percent increase in GDP per capita leads to a .76 percent increase in emissions. A one percent increase in urban population leads to a .74 percent increase in emissions, while a one percent increase in trade as percent total GDP leads to a .15 percent increase in emissions. These findings are consistent with most published research. Turning to Model 2, the interaction between population size and Africa is negative and statistically significant, while all other interactions in the model

Table 2. Unstandardized Coefficients for the Regression of Total Carbon
Dioxide Emissions in 85 Nations, 1960-2005

	Model 1	Model 2
Total Population	1.48***	1.95***
Total Population * Africa		-.71***
Total Population * Asia		-.18
Total Population * Latin America		-.19
Gross Domestic Product Per Capita	.76***	.68***
Urban Population as Percent of Total Population	.74***	.88***
Trade as Percent of Total Gross Domestic Product	.15***	.12**
R-sq overall	.99	.99
N	850	850
estimated coefficients	90	93

Notes: ***p<.001, **p<.01 *p<.05 #p<.10 (two-tailed);
all models include unreported unit-specific intercepts and linear year controls

are nonsignificant. Overall, this suggests that the estimated coefficient for
population size is 1.95 for nations in all macro-regions except for those in
Africa, where the estimated effect of population size is 1.24 (i.e. 1.95–.71).
Thus, there appears to be at least some regional differences in the relationship between carbon emissions and population size.

Table 3 presents two estimated models, where Model 1 is simply a replica-
tion of Model 1 in Table 2. Model 2 in Table 3 includes interactions between
GDP per capita and the macro-regions, and is as follows:

Model 2 in Table 3 of *Total Carbon Dioxide Emissions$_{it}$* =
   $B_1 GDP$ *per capita$_{it}$* + $B_2 GDP$ *per capita$_{it}$* * *Africa$_i$* + $B_3 GDP$ *per capita$_{it}$*
   * *Asia$_i$* + $B_4 GDP$ *per capita$_{it}$* * *Latin America$_i$* + $B_5 Population_{it}$* +
   B_6 *Urban Population$_{it}$* + $B_7 Trade_{it}$* + W_t + u_i + e_{it}

All interactions in this second model are nonsignificant, indicating that
in general, the estimated effect of level of development on total carbon emissions does not appear to differ between nations in the four macro-regions.
However, all analyses up to this point have not accounted for the possibility
that the estimated effects of population and affluence might change in value
through time.

Table 3. Unstandardized Coefficients for the Regression of Total Carbon Dioxide Emissions in 85 Nations, 1960-2005

	Model 1	Model 2
Gross Domestic Product Per Capita	.76***	.78***
Gross Domestic Product Per Capita * Africa		-.04
Gross Domestic Product Per Capita * Asia		-.01
Gross Domestic Product Per Capita * Latin America		-.02
Total Population	1.48***	1.49***
Urban Population as Percent of Total Population	.74***	.74***
Trade as Percent of Total Gross Domestic Product	.15***	.15**
R-sq overall	.99	.99
N	850	850
estimated coefficients	90	93

Notes: ***p<.001 **p<.01 *p<.05 #p<.10 (two-tailed);
all models include unreported unit-specific intercepts and linear year controls

Table 4 reports two models estimated for the overall sample as well as for the samples restricted to each of the macro-regions. Model 1 includes the four independent variables as well as the interaction between population size and year (the linear time control). Model 2 includes the four predictors as well as the interaction between GDP per capita and year. The two models are as follows:

Model 1 in Table 4 of *Total Carbon Dioxide Emissions$_{it}$* =
$$B_1 Population_{it} + B_2 Population * W_t + B_3 GDP\ per\ capita_{it} + B_4 Urban\ Population_{it} + B_5 Trade_{it} + W_t + u_i + e_{it}$$

Model 2 in Table 4 of *Total Carbon Dioxide Emissions$_{it}$* =
$$B_1 Population_{it} + B_2 GDP\ per\ capita_{it} + B_3 GDP\ per\ capita_{it} * W_t + B_4 Urban\ Populaiton_{it} + B_5 Trade_{it} + W_t + u_i + e_{it}$$

The focus here is on the interactions between time and the two drivers of interest: population and affluence. However, I note that the estimated effect of urban population is positive and significant in all estimated models, while the effect of trade as percent GDP is positive and significant in the models

Table 4. Unstardardized Coefficients for the Regression of Total Carbon Dioxide Emissions in 85 Nations, 1960–2005

	All Countries		Africa		Asia		Latin America		Europe, North America, & Oceania	
	Model 1	Model 2	Model 1	Model 2	Model 1	Model 2	Model 1	Model 2	Model 1	Model 2
Total Population	1.53***	1.52***	.55*	.52#	1.55***	1.84***	1.62***	1.50***	2.06***	2.01***
Total Population * Year	-.01**		-.02#		-.02***		-.01		-.01	
Gross Domestic Product Per Capita	.78***	.72***	.83***	.42*	.63***	.63***	.50***	.65***	.84***	.87***
Gross Domestic Product Per Capita * Year		.01		.04**		.01		-.02*		-.01
Urban Population as Percent of Total Population	.72***	.78***	.48**	.90***	.81***	.73***	1.42***	1.08***	1.25***	1.23***
Trade as Percent of Total Gross Domestic Product	.16***	.15***	.28**	.26*	.03	-.01	.19***	.17***	.08	.07
R-sq overall	.99	.99	.96	.96	.99	.99	.99	.99	.99	.99
N	850	850	280	280	150	150	180	180	240	240
estimated coefficients	91	91	34	34	21	21	24	24	30	30
number countries	85	85	28	28	15	15	18	18	24	24
estimated effect of Total Population in 1960	1.53		.55		1.55		1.62		2.06	
estimated effect of Total Population in 2005	1.44		.37		1.37		1.62		2.06	
estimated effect of GDP Per Capita in 1960		.72		.42		.63		.65		.87
estimated effect of GDP Per Capita in 2005		.72		.78		.63		.44		.87

Notes: ***p<.01 **p<.01 *p<.05 #p<.10 (two-tailed);
all models include unreported unit-specific intercepts and linear year controls

estimated for the entire sample as well as those estimated for the samples of nations in only Africa and Latin America. Conversely, the estimated effect of trade is nonsignificant in the models for the samples of nations in Asia and the sample of nations in Europe, North America, and Oceania.

For the overall sample, the results indicate that, with a significant negative interaction between population and year (-.01), the effect of population size on carbon emissions decreased from an estimated coefficient of 1.53 in 1960 to 1.44 in 2005. The interaction between GDP per capita and year is nonsignificant for the overall sample. Thus, based on these results, the estimated effect of affluence is .72 for each time point.

For the sample restricted to Africa, results of Model 1 indicate that the estimated coefficient for population size decreased from .55 in 1960 to .37 in 2005. Conversely, Model 2 indicates that for the Africa sample the estimated effect of GDP per capita increased from .42 in 1960 to .78 in 2005. Thus, we observe a moderate decoupling between population size and carbon emissions but a moderate intensification of the relationship between emissions and affluence in this macro-region. Turning to the analyses of nations in Asia, the interaction between population and time is negative and statistically significant, while the interaction between GDP per capita and time is nonsignificant. More specifically, the estimated coefficient for population size decreased from 1.55 in 1960 to 1.37 in 2005, while the estimated coefficient for GDP per capita remained a value of .63 for each time point in the study.

The results of the analyses of the sample of nations in Latin America indicate that the estimated effect of population size on total emissions is relatively time-invariant, with a value of 1.62 in 1960 as well as in 2005. However, the estimated effect of GDP per capita decreased moderately from a value of .65 in 1960 to .44 in 2005. For the sample of nations in Europe, North America, and Oceania, the estimated effect of both population size and level of economic development remained stable through time. The coefficient for population size is 2.06 in the beginning and end points of the study, while the estimated effect of GDP per capita is .87 at each time point.

In summary, and consistent with the foundational propositions of structural human ecology, I find that population and affluence are key drivers of total carbon dioxide emissions. The estimated effect of population size differs for nations in Africa relative to those nations in other regions of the world. The estimated effect of GDP per capita does not appear to differ between regions. However, these effects are observed when the effects of population size and GDP per capita are modeled as time-invariant. Employing the interactions between time and both population and affluence yield some notable findings that differ across regions. For the entire sample we observe a modest decrease in the estimated effect of population size, while the effect of development remains the same. For nations in Africa, the effect of population size decreases while the effect of GDP per capita increases. For nations in Asia, the effect of population size decreases, but the effect of level of development remains stable through time. For nations in Latin America, the effect of population size remains stable through time, while the effect of level of development decreases moderately. For the sample of mostly developed nations in Europe, North America, and Oceania, the effects of both population and affluence remain stable through time. While we see that population and affluence are key drivers of anthropogenic emissions as suggested by SHE, their effects of total emissions differ somewhat by region and also in some contexts increase or decrease in value through time in certain macro-regions, while they remain quite constant through time in other regions. Thus, future STIRPAT research in the SHE tradition would do well to consider such regional and temporal differences in the effects of the human drivers of greenhouse gas emissions and other environmental outcomes.

Conclusion

Structural human ecology is a central multidisciplinary orientation that focuses on the study of society / nature relationships, and STIRPAT has quickly become a well-established approach to evaluating the foundational propositions of SHE in disciplined research on the human drivers of environmental change. In this chapter I provided a brief overview of the origins of SHE and STIRPAT, and reviewed some of the foundational and benchmark studies that focus on the environmental impacts of population and affluence. A clear take-away message from this summary and focused literature review is that SHE and STIRPAT have come a great distance in a relatively short period of time, and their influence is evident in various disciplines. Further, multiple generations of scholars are actively conducting research using STIRPAT to test SHE-derived hypotheses, with many scholars broadening the application of SHE and STIRPAT in meaningful and creative ways. The new STIRPAT analyses reported in this chapter highlight the regional and temporal dynamics of the relationships between national-level carbon emissions and population size and affluence. While both regional and temporal variations appear to exist, population and affluence remain key drivers of carbon emissions for all nations throughout the world, which further underscores the validity and relevance of structural human ecology and the utility in employing the STIRPAT approach in comparative research on the human drivers of environmental change. Given the growing sustainability challenges facing the world today, SHE and STIRPAT should continue to be central in relevant areas of research and policy discussions.

Note

1. CAIT provides a comprehensive and comparable database of greenhouse gas emissions data (including all major sources and sinks) and other climate-relevant indicators. In order to provide the most complete and accurate dataset, CAIT compiles data from three sources—the Carbon Dioxide Information Analysis Center, the International Energy Agency, and the Energy Information Administration.

References

Burns, Thomas, Byron Davis, and Edward Kick. 1997. "Position in the World-System and National Emissions of Greenhouse Gases." *Journal of World-Systems Research* 3: 432-466.

Clark, Brett, Andrew K. Jorgenson, and Daniel Auerbach. 2012. "Up in Smoke: The Human Ecology and Political Economy of Coal Consumption." *Organization & Environment* 25: 452-469.

Clement, Matthew, and Jessica Schultz. 2012. "Political Economy, Ecological Modernization, and Energy Use: A Panel Analysis of State-Level Energy Use in the United States, 1960–1990." *Sociological Forum* 26(3): 581-600.

Dietz, Thomas, and Eugene A. Rosa. 1994. "Rethinking the Environmental Impacts of Population, Affluence and Technology." *Human Ecology Review* 1(2): 277-300.

———. 1997. "Effects of Population and Affluence on CO_2 Emissions." *Proceedings of the National Academy of Sciences, USA.* 94: 175-179.

Dietz, Thomas, Eugene A. Rosa, and Richard York. 2007. "Driving the Human Ecological Footprint." *Frontiers of Human Ecology* 5: 13-18.

Duncan, Otis Dudley. 1964. "Social Organization and the Ecosystem." In *Handbook of Modern Sociology*, edited by Robert E. L. Faris, 36-82. Chicago: Rand McNally.

Dunlap, Riley E., and William R. Catton Jr. 1979. "Environmental Sociology." *Annual Review of Sociology* 5: 243-273.

Intergovernmental Panel on Climate Change (IPCC). 2007a. *Climate Change 2007: The Physical Science Basis*. Cambridge: Cambridge University Press.

———. 2007b. *Climate Change 2007: Mitigation of Climate Change*. www.ipcc.ch.

Jorgenson, Andrew K. 2011. "Carbon Dioxide Emissions in Central and Eastern European Nations, 1992-2005: A Test of Ecologically Unequal Exchange Theory." *Human Ecology Review* 18: 105-114.

———. 2012. "The Sociology of Ecologically Unequal Exchange and Carbon Dioxide Emissions, 1960-2005." *Social Science Research* 41: 242-252.

Jorgenson, Andrew K., and Ryan Birkholz. 2010. "Assessing the Causes of Anthropogenic Methane Emissions in Comparative Perspective, 1990-2005." *Ecological Economics* 69: 2634-264.

Jorgenson, Andrew K., and Brett Clark. 2009. "The Economy, Military, and Ecologically Unequal Relationships in Comparative Perspective: A Panel Study of the Ecological Footprints of Nations, 1975-2000." *Social Problems* 56: 621-646.

—————. 2010. "Assessing the Temporal Stability of the Population / Environment Relationship: A Cross-National Panel Study of Carbon Dioxide Emissions, 1960-2005." *Population & Environment* 32: 27-41.

—————. 2011. "Societies Consuming Nature: A Panel Study of the Ecological Footprints of Nations, 1960-2003." *Social Science Research* 40: 226-244.

—————. 2012. "Are the Economy and the Environment Decoupling? A Comparative International Study, 1960-2005." *American Journal of Sociology* 118: 1-44.

Jorgenson, Andrew K., Brett Clark, and Vincent R. Giedraitis. 2012. "The Temporal (In)Stability of the Carbon Dioxide Emissions / Economic Development Relationship in Central and Eastern European Nations." *Society & Natural Resources* 25: 1182-1192.

Jorgenson, Andrew K., and Kennon Kuykendall. 2008. "Globalization, Foreign Investment Dependence, and Agriculture Production: A Cross-National Study of Pesticide and Fertilizer Use Intensity in Less-Developed Countries, 1990-2000." *Social Forces* 87: 529-560.

Jorgenson, Andrew K., James Rice, and Brett Clark. 2010. "Cities, Slums, and Energy Consumption in Less-Developed Countries, 1990-2005." *Organization & Environment* 23: 189-204.

Knight, Kyle. 2009. "Structural Human Ecology and STIRPAT: Theory and Method." Paper Presented as part of the Population-Environment Research Network (PERN) Cyberseminars (http://www.populationenvironmentresearch.org/seminars.jsp).

Liu, Jianguo, Thomas Dietz, Stephen R. Carpenter, Carl Folke, Marina Alberti, Charles L. Redman, Stephen H. Schneider, Elinor Ostrom, Alice N. Pell, Jane Lubchenco, William W. Taylor, Zhiyun Ouyang, Peter Deadman, Timothy Kratz, and William Provencher. 2007. "Coupled Human and Natural Systems." *AMBIO: A Journal of the Human Environment* 36: 639-649.

Marquart-Pyatt, Sandy. 2013. "The Implications of Structural Human Ecology for Environmental Concern's Global Reach." Chapter 9, this volume.

McKinney, Laura, Gregory Fulkerson, and Edward Kick. 2009. "Investigating the Correlates of Biodiversity Loss: A Cross-National Quantitative Analysis of Threatened Bird Species." *Human Ecology Review* 16: 103-113.

Roberts, Timmons, and Bradley Parks. 2007. *A Climate of Injustice: Global Inequality, North-South Politics, and Climate Policy.* Cambridge: MIT Press.

Rosa, Eugene A., Andreas Diekmann, Thomas Dietz, and Carlos C, Jaeger (eds.). 2010. *Human Footprints on the Global Environment: Threats to Sustainability.* Cambridge: MIT Press.

Rosa, Eugene A., and Thomas Dietz. 1998. "Climate Change and Society: Speculation, Construction and Scientific Investigation." *International Sociology.* 13: 421-455.

—————. 2012. "Human Drivers of National Greenhouse-gas Emissions." *Nature Climate Change* doi:10.1038/nclimate1506.

Rosa, Eugene A., Richard York, and Thomas Dietz. 2004. "Tracking the Anthropogenic Drivers of Ecological Impacts." *AMBIO: A Journal of the Human Environment* 33(8): 509-512.

Shandra, John M., Bruce London, Owen P. Whooley, John B. Williamson. 2004. "International Nongovernmental Organizations and Carbon Dioxide Emissions in the Developing World: A Quantitative, Cross-National Analysis." *Sociological Inquiry* 74(4): 520-545.

Shi, Anqing. 2003. "The Impact of Population Pressure on Global Carbon Dioxide Emissions: Evidence from Pooled Cross-Country Data." *Ecological Economics* 44: 24-42.

United States (U.S.) National Research Council. 2010. *Advancing the Science of Climate Change*. Washington, DC: National Academies Press.

World Bank. 2012. World Development Indicators. http://databank.worldbank.org/ddp/home.do. Accessed April 11, 2012.

World Resources Institute. 2007. *Earth Trends Data CD-ROM*. Washington, DC: World Resources Institute.,

York, Richard. 2006. "Demographic Trends and Energy Consumption in European Union Nations, 1960–2025." *Social Science Research* 36: 855–87.

————. 2007. "Structural Influences on Energy Production in South and East Asia, 1971–2002." *Sociological Forum* 22(4): 532-554.

————. 2012. "Do Alternative Energy Sources Displace Fossil Fuels?" *Nature Climate Change* 2: 441-443.

York, Richard, and Eugene A. Rosa. 2012. "Choking on Modernity: A Human Ecology of Air Pollution." *Social Problems* 59: 282-300.

York, Richard, Eugene A. Rosa, and Thomas Dietz. 2003a. "Footprints on the Earth: The Environmental Consequences of Modernity." *American Sociological Review* 68: 279-300.

————. 2003b. "A Rift in Modernity? Assessing the Anthropogenic Sources of Global Climate Change with the STIRPAT Model." *International Journal of Sociology and Social Policy* 23(10): 31-51.

CHAPTER 9

The Implications of Structural Human Ecology for Environmental Concern's Global Reach

Sandra T. Marquart-Pyatt, Michigan State University

Introduction

Environmental conditions like pollution and access to clean water are recognized as some of the most important problems facing the world (UNDP 2010; World Bank 2010). So it is no surprise that social scientists have sought to convey the emergence and salience of environmental concerns for more than four decades. Yet scholars have only recently embarked on cross-national investigations of concern for the environment across more than a handful of countries. Such investigations are vital for scholarship seeking to elucidate the interdependence of societies and the biophysical environment, as environmental issues are central to interstate relations and global initiatives, and have in recent decades continued to gain international prominence. Although scholars assert the importance of contexts for explaining the global reach of environmental concern, less is known about how these contextual factors affect its expression.

A growing literature seeks to reveal the contextual factors that underlie the expression of environmental concerns cross-nationally. Previous research is mixed, however, as some research asserts that environmental concerns are global (Brechin 1999; Dunlap, Gallup, and Gallup 1993; Dunlap and Mertig 1995, 1997; Dunlap and York 2008; Marquart-Pyatt 2007, 2008, 2012), while other studies contend that greater environmental concern tends to be expressed by citizens in wealthier or industrialized countries (Inglehart 1995; Kidd and Lee 1997; Diekmann and Franzen 1999; Franzen 2003). Previous research has examined the social bases of environmental concern across countries including individual characteristics like age, gender, education, income, and knowledge with mixed results. At the aggregate level, research examines effects of national affluence, economic development, political factors, and environmental conditions.

Recent research combines these approaches and investigates individual-level and aggregate-level characteristics as influences on environmental concerns (Franzen and Meyer 2010; Gelissen 2007; Givens and Jorgenson 2011, 2013; Haller and Hadler 2008; Marquart-Pyatt 2012). This line of inquiry shows that national wealth, political factors, and environmental conditions have mixed relations with concern for the environment. These inconclusive findings provide a baseline for this research, as none of these studies integrates expectations from structural human ecology as a set of aggregate factors affecting the expression of environmental concern. To address this gap in the literature, I examine individual and contextual factors affecting two measures of environmental concern—environmental threat awareness and environmental efficacy—to comprehensively examine how context affects concern for the environment across nations. Particular emphasis is placed on links between education, age, and environmental concerns across the two measures.

I examine concern for the environment using a multi-level, cross-national study. In this chapter, I begin by reviewing cross-national research on environmental concern, articulating the importance of individual-level and contextual-level factors. The International Social Survey Program (ISSP) Environment (2000) dataset, which provides information from more than 30,000 individuals in 25 countries, is used to examine a multilevel model including individual-level and country-level variables to predict two distinct dimensions of environmental concerns: environmental threat awareness and environmental efficacy. A series of cross-level interactions examine whether the strength of the association between education, age, and environmental concerns are similar across contexts, and the extent to which demographic, economic, political, and environmental conditions shape these relations.

Cross-National Research on Environmental Concern

Environmental concern is theorized to be comprised of a number of attitudes, beliefs, behavioral intentions, and behaviors. Although scholars have tracked public opinion on environmental issues and concerns for decades and have considered many explanations regarding the social factors influencing environmental concern, it is only in the last two decades that this research explored cross-national dynamics of opinion formation on environmental concern. From an initial emphasis that environmental concern should be present only in wealthy or advanced industrial countries, research has expanded to show its world-wide dispersion and multifaceted nature (for an excellent discussion, see Dunlap and York 2008).

Research seeking to explain the global reach of environmental concern argues for a prominent role of "context," providing two primary arguments. First, national affluence or prosperity has been advanced as a primary influence where citizens in some countries express greater levels of environmental concern given a certain baseline level of economic and material security (Franzen 2003; Inglehart 1995). Second, the objective problems-subjective values (OPSV) thesis advances contextual explanations linked with economic development to explain that environmental concerns exist across the globe, yet are driven by different factors rooted in contexts (Brechin 1999; Inglehart 1995).

The Affluence Thesis

National wealth and level of economic development are contextual factors postulated to influence individual-level expressions of environmental concern. Regarding national wealth or prosperity, initial formulations argue that more affluent countries with higher GDP were more likely to have a citizenry that expressed concern for the environment, as a baseline of material wealth or security afforded such opportunities (Inglehart 1995). These assertions followed largely from Inglehart's (1990, 1997) theory of postmaterialism, which sought to articulate how material conditions affect the expression of higher-order constructs like postmaterialist values, which in turn served as a basis for environmental concerns. In essence, experiencing economic prosperity rather than scarcity, particularly during one's formative years, leads to greater likelihood of expressing values related to subjective concerns including protecting free speech instead of concern with maintaining order and rising prices. Inglehart's explanatory framework also includes a socialization component to account for generational replacement, whereby what appears to be an effect of age may be a cohort effect. In support of the affluence thesis, research demonstrated country differences in support for environmental protection linked with economic development (Kemmelmeier et al. 2002; Kidd and Lee 1997). Other studies showed positive and negative relations between national wealth and pro-environmental attitudes, with researchers arguing for the globalization of environmental concern (Brechin 1999; Brechin and Kempton 1994, 1997; Dunlap and Mertig 1995, 1997).

To date, empirical examinations of proposed relations are largely incon-clusive. Although a positive association cross-nationally between environmen-tal concern and national wealth was confirmed for some measures (Dunlap and York 2008; Franzen 2003), negative and no associations were also shown between affluence and multiple measures of environmental concern (Dunlap and York 2008). More recent work demonstrates support for an effect of affluence on concern for the environment, showing positive, negative, and no relationships that depend on its measurement (Franzen and Meyer 2010; Gelissen 2007; Givens and Jorgenson 2011, 2013; Haller and Hadler 2008; Marquart-Pyatt 2012).

The Role of Environmental Conditions

A second, related contextual argument articulates a slightly different explana-tory mechanism related to industrial development. The objective problems-subjective values (OPSV) thesis advances contextual explanations linked with economic development to account for the existence of environmental concerns world-wide (Brechin 1999; Inglehart 1995). It proposes differences in factors affecting concern for the environment linked with a country's level of economic development (Inglehart 1995). Simply stated, citizens' subjective values influence environmental concern in advanced industrial countries (e.g. those in Europe and North America), while, in contrast, in industrializing/developing countries the roots of environmental concern were harsh, objective environmental conditions such as serious water and air pollution. This formulation served to explain why environmental concerns were expressed by citizens across the globe irrespective of level of national economic development (Inglehart 1995). Briefly, citizens express concern about the environment because they see the deleterious environmental effects of industrialization, urbanization, and economic development in their surrounding biophysical environment. Environmental concern arises from experience living in areas with high levels of water and/or air pollution and other physical manifestations of environmental degradation.

The objective problems explanation, as one aspect of the OPSV thesis, has been only partially confirmed in previous research. Brechin (1999) demonstrates higher levels of environmental concern related to perceived environmental threats for citizens in poorer nations, compared with those in richer countries. Greater expressed concern for the environment was shown for multiple measures of local environmental conditions related to environ-mental quality, health, and pollution (Brechin 1999). The OPSV perspec-tive has been critiqued on many fronts. For instance, research challenges its universal applicability and theoretical underpinnings, pointing to conflating of individual-level phenomena like value change as aggregate or national-level processes (Brechin 1999; Kidd and Lee 1997). Dunlap and York (2008) provide a comprehensive critique, arguing that the OPSV thesis is overly simplistic, empirically non-falsifiable, and providing an essentially "post hoc explanation." Results from empirical studies are also mixed for environmental conditions. Three studies show positive effects: Gelissen (2007) finds a positive effect for water quality on support for environmental protection, Givens and Jorgenson (2011) find that increases in carbon dioxide emissions relate positively to environmental concern, and Marquart-Pyatt (2012) finds a positive relation between ecosystem well-being and environmental attitudes. However, other research shows negative effects for ecological footprints (Haller and Hadler 2008; Marquart-Pyatt 2012), and no effect for a measure of environmental quality (Franzen and Meyer 2010).

Individual-Level Determinants of Environmental Concern

An individual's surrounding socio-economic context, including social characteristics and personal experiences, is believed to affect environmental concern. Key predictors from previous research examining the social bases of environmental concern include position in the social structure (i.e., education and income), knowledge, and socio-demographic variables. Education is believed to influence environmental concern through exposure to educational systems instilling norms and values or through psychological effects, either of which can include exposure to environmental awareness (Dietz, Stern, and Guagnano 1998; Dunlap, Xiao, and McCright 2002; Klineberg, McKeever, and Rothenbach 1998). Environmental concern is believed to be more likely among those with higher levels of income (Jones and Dunlap 1992; Klineberg et al. 1998). Greater knowledge is related to higher levels of environmental concern (Blocker and Eckberg 1997). Socio-demographic factors like age, gender, and place of residence are also purported to affect environmental concern. Younger individuals are more likely to express pro-environmental attitudes (Dunlap et al. 2000; Jones and Dunlap 1992; Klineberg et al. 1998), differences between men and women have been shown regarding environmental concern (Dietz, Kalof, and Stern 2002), and urban residents tend to exhibit higher levels of environmental concern (Jones and Dunlap 1992).

Many of these relations have been confirmed cross-nationally, particularly for education, age, gender, income, and knowledge. For instance, more highly educated and younger respondents demonstrate greater degrees of environmental concern across nations (Gelissen 2007; Haller and Hadler 2008; Kemmelmeier et al. 2002; Marquart-Pyatt 2007, 2008, 2012; Xiao and Dunlap 2007), and females have higher concern for the environment compared with males in some nations (Kemmelmeier et al. 2002; Xiao and Dunlap 2007). Income and knowledge have been shown to affect environmental concerns cross-nationally (Gelissen 2007; Haller and Hadler 2008; Marquart-Pyatt 2008).

Aggregate-Level Determinants of Environmental Concern

Cross-national research investigating the global reach of environmental concern typically specifies economic and environmental contexts. As described earlier, cross-national research on environmental concern's global reach argues for a prominent role of "context," providing two primary arguments: national affluence or prosperity and the environmental conditions component of the objective problems-subjective values (OPSV).

Briefly, the prosperity explanation postulates that more affluent countries with higher gross domestic product (GDP) are more likely to have a citizenry that expressed concern for the environment, as a baseline of material wealth or security afforded such opportunities to focus on such values, in line with a postmaterialist value explanation (Inglehart 1990, 1997). The OPSV thesis (Brechin 1999; Inglehart 1995) articulates environmental concern in somewhat parallel fashion, stressing how it relates to economic development and the role of context in shaping these views. Briefly, citizens' values are related to the expression of environmental concern in advanced industrial contexts like Europe and North America, while in industrializing/developing contexts environmental concern resulted from living with harsh, objective environmental conditions like a variety of forms of pollution. However, given that countries differ on a number of additional structural and institutional dimensions such as political systems and social organizational features related to population, for instance, this emphasis requires some expansion.

According to world society and world polity frameworks, the rapid rise in the expansion of an international system of environmental organizations, actors, and treaties has ideological roots that expanded over the twentieth century to account for increased emphasis on recognizing interdependencies among human societies and the physical environment (Frank 1997; Frank, Hironaka, and Schofer 2000; Schofer and Hironaka 2005). Political structures including democratic governments and international environmental memberships illustrate institutional structures supportive of these features and interrelationships. Country chapters of international environmental nongovernmental (INGO) associations embody citizen concern about specific environmental issues that are linked toward environmental protection through their focus on particular, localized actions (Frank et al. 2000). By extension, citizens of nations more integrated into the world polity may have differing degrees of environmental concern due to exposure to particular national political features like liberal democracy and national memberships in international environmental organizations. Some prior research offers mixed support, showing relations of differing signs for Green party presence in government and the political importance of environmental issues for different measures of environmental attitudes (Haller and Hadler 2008). More recent work reveals a role for international environmental organizations and democracy affecting environmental concerns (Givens and Jorgenson 2013; Marquart-Pyatt 2012). Previous research thus articulates economic, environmental, and political contextual-level measures as factors affecting environmental concern.

Structural Human Ecology

Structural human ecology (SHE), like other environmental impact theories, articulates anthropogenic forces as drivers of environmental change and ultimately seeks to examine coupled human and natural systems. Barring the effect of affluence, many of these factors are largely overlooked in cross-national research seeking to identify the social bases of environmental concerns. Incorporating these expectations refocuses the discussion about contextual factors to societal attributes like social institutions and social structure, social organization, technology, and demographic factors, in addition to the economic and environmental dimensions covered in previous studies. Essential to SHE are theoretical and empirical assessments of relations among population, affluence, technology, and the environment, with environmental impacts comprising the outcome variable as in the STIRPAT model (Dietz and Rosa 1994, 1997).

Research utilizing the STIRPAT frame has examined a wide range of environmental variables approximating the impacts of human societies on the environment. For instance, research has explored ecological footprints, total greenhouse gas emissions, and carbon dioxide emissions (Dietz and Rosa 1997; Dietz, Rosa, and York 2007, 2009; Rosa, York, and Dietz 2004; York, Rosa, and Dietz 2003). Findings from this research tradition on a variety of environmental impacts demonstrate that population and affluence are key factors affecting environmental degradation. (See the chapters in this volume by Mazur and Jorgenson that examine energy and greenhouse gas emissions, respectively. Both show complexities in how SHE helps shape our expectations regarding population-environment connections.)

Demographic factors feature prominently in this research. York et al. (2003) articulated expectations regarding the role of population structure in influencing environmental change through the population age structure, specifically the size of a country's adult population, and a country's urbanization. Subsequent studies further attest to the importance of model specification in relation particularly to the manner in which population measures are incorporated in empirical analyses, as stressed throughout STIRPAT research. In recent work, York and Rosa (2012) explore nuances of population in examining how social structures and air pollution are related. Findings reveal that in addition to population size and growth, the distribution of population across households is important for understanding how population affects environmental impacts (York and Rosa 2012).

Applications of structural human ecology and STIRPAT have thus far examined aggregate-level phenomena, using the nation-state as the unit of analysis. This research extends this to a multilevel framework that examines the extent to which aggregate-level processes affect the expression of individuals' environmental concerns. A major benefit of the SHE framework is that it recasts the focus on institutional aspects that may be important factors influencing citizens' expressions of environmental concerns. In doing so, it expands previous research and includes demographic attributes of nations in addition to their economic and environmental contexts.

Research examining individual- and aggregate-level explanations regarding environmental concerns cross-nationally using multilevel modeling finds factors at both levels are important to take into account, yet also provides inconclusive results that inform this empirical investigation. Studies demonstrate some support for aggregate and subjective values hypotheses, yet differences are also evident regarding the precise nature of the relationships given that different country-level indicators are included. For instance, national affluence has been shown to have positive, negative, and no effects on different measures of environmental concern; results are similarly mixed regarding environmental conditions (Franzen and Meyer 2010; Gelissen 2007; Givens and Jorgenson 2011, 2013; Haller and Hadler 2008; Marquart-Pyatt 2012). These studies vary with regard to datasets used, measures of environmental concern examined (and analytical techniques used in their creation), and the empirical models investigated including their specification and the variables included at both the individual and aggregate levels.[1] This variability has consequences for knowledge accumulation for society-environment relations, specifically with regard to how contexts shape environmental concerns.

To fill an important gap in the cross-national literature, this research examines a series of multilevel models incorporating individual and contextual factors affecting country mean values of two measures of environmental concerns—environmental threat awareness and environmental efficacy. Expectations from structural human ecology related to influences of population structure and density are examined in addition to national-level economic, environmental, and political factors. Following that, this study describes how aggregate-level factors interact with the effects of education and age, two conceptually important explanatory mechanisms according to previous research, on the two measures of environmental concern.

Data and Methods

Individual-level data are from the *International Social Survey Programme (ISSP) 2000: Environment* (ISSP 2003). Data from 31,039 individuals in 25 countries are used in analyses presented here: Austria, Bulgaria, Canada, Chile, Czech Republic, Denmark, Finland, Germany, Ireland, Israel, Japan, Latvia, Mexico, Netherlands, New Zealand, Norway, Philippines, Portugal, Russia, Slovenia, Spain, Sweden, Switzerland, United Kingdom, and the United States. The sample of countries is largely composed of industrialized, higher-income European nations. External weights are used in the analyses to equalize sample sizes ranging from 958 in Spain to 1,717 in the United Kingdom. Multilevel structural equation modeling is used for the analyses. In this section, the measurement of all variables and methodological approach are discussed.[2]

Dependent Variables: Environmental Threat Awareness and Environmental Efficacy

The 2000 ISSP Environment survey asks a broad array of questions on environmental attitudes, beliefs, and behaviors. The measures of environmental concern are created using confirmatory factor analysis (CFA), a technique from structural equation modeling (Bollen 1989; Kline 2010). A CFA is theoretically driven, given that the model and the relationships between indicators and the latent construct(s) are specified in advance, shifting the focus to latent variables, which is crucial for research on an abstract construct like environmental concern. Few cross-national studies of environmental concern use CFA (Marquart-Pyatt 2007, 2008, 2012; Xiao and Dunlap 2007). Both latent variables—environmental threat awareness and environmental efficacy—exemplify multiple-topic/multiple-expression measures of environmental concern that capture the substantive content of environmental concern (Dunlap and Jones 2002; Milfont and Duckitt 2010). Further, both measures are based on the broad scope of environmental concerns and are grounded in previous research (Marquart-Pyatt 2008, 2012).

Environmental threat awareness contains five items showing an awareness of the environmental consequences of societies' modern, industrial activities. Respondents were asked: "In general, do you think [Air pollution caused by cars; Air pollution caused by industry; Pollution of country's rivers, lakes, and streams; Pesticides and chemicals used in farming; The rise in the world's temperature caused by the 'greenhouse effect'] is extremely dangerous for the environment, very dangerous, somewhat dangerous, not very dangerous, or not dangerous at all for the environment." CFA results indicate excellent fit of environmental threat awareness.[3] The second latent construct, *environmental efficacy*, contains six items that, combined, convey the importance of addressing environmental problems and of collective effort for resolving environmental issues, and how environmental issues intersect with economic issues, science, and progress. The individual measures include statements like "People worry too much about human progress harming the environment," "We worry too much about the future of the environment and not enough about prices and jobs today," and "Modern science will solve our environmental problems with little change to our way of life." CFA results indicate very good fit of the latent construct environmental efficacy.[4]

Individual-Level Independent Variables

Two measures capture position in the social structure. *Education* is measured as the number of years of schooling completed. *Income* is standardized as a z-score for comparison across contexts, created individually for each country. The *knowledge* scale sums responses to five items designed to measure an individual's general level of scientific knowledge (Hayes 2001; Marquart-Pyatt 2008; Smith 1996). Three final variables are socio-demographic controls. *Age* is measured in years.[5] Respondent's *sex* is a dummy variable (female=1). Respondents living in towns with populations over 50,000 people are coded as residing in an *urban* area (urban=1).

Country-Level Independent Variables

At the country level, there are seven variables. Given predictions of structural human ecology frameworks, three aggregate demographic measures are included in the model (World Bank 2008). Population size is the total number of individuals in the nation (logged). Population density is the number of people per square kilometer of land (logged). The population age structure or age dependency ratio is the ratio of individuals younger than 15 and older than 64 (i.e. dependents) to individuals aged 15 to 64 years (i.e. the working age population) (logged). To gauge urbanization, a logged measure of urban population as a percent of the total population of a country is included (World Bank 2008). To measure national wealth or affluence, *gross domestic product* (GDP) in purchasing power parity, averaged from 1990 to 1999, converted to 1999 international dollars and logged, is included (World Bank 2008). The liberal *democracy* score from 1995 is an index ranging from 0 to 100 that measures national political structure (i.e., a country's political rights, legislative effectiveness, process of legislative selection, suffrage, and whether groups are excluded from the political process) (Bollen 2001). The *Ecosystem Wellbeing Index* averages indices gauging land use, water use, and biodiversity (Prescott-Allen 2001). Higher scores on the index indicate greater levels of ecosystem well-being. The measure approximates the state of the nation's ecosystems regarding its diversity and quality related to the adaptability to support human societies and other communities.

The Multilevel Model

To examine expectations from previous research, a multilevel model is used that estimates individual and country-level effects simultaneously (Raudenbush and Bryk 2002; Snijders and Bosker 2012). The data are organized hierarchically, with individuals nested in countries. Central to a multilevel approach is that there is variation at more than one level of aggregation to take into account, and that it is important to include predictors at each of these levels to account for these nested relations. The hierarchical multilevel model thus improves the classic linear regression model by properly allocating variability to each level of aggregation specified in the model. In this way, there are conceptual links with ANOVA regarding within- and between-group elements. The innovation of the multilevel approach is in its joint consideration of within- and between-group relations that correctly accounts for clustering (Snijders and Bosker 2012). In this analysis, to account for clustering, the models use countries as the group and seek to explain 1) how country-level variables affect the individual-level expression of environmental threat awareness and environmental efficacy through random intercept models and 2) how country-level variables affect the individual-level within-country slopes or why there are differences between countries in the effects of education and age on levels of environmental awareness and efficacy through random slope models.

Table 1 contains descriptive information for the individual and country-level variables included in the multilevel model, including bivariate correlations among environmental threat awareness and environmental efficacy and the country-level independent variables. Given prior research expectations articulated earlier, information is used at the individual level and country level to determine concern for the environment. HLM 6.08 is used to complete the analyses (Raudenbush, Bryk, and Congdon 2009).

The level one model of the multi-level model for environmental concern is:

$$Y_{ij} = \beta_{0j} + \beta_{1j} \text{ EDUCATION} + \beta_{2j} \text{ INCOME} + \beta_{3j} \text{ KNOWLEDGE} + \beta_{4j} \text{ AGE} + \beta_{5j} \text{ FEMALE} + \beta_{6j} \text{ URBAN} + r_{ij}$$

where Y_{ij} is the environmental threat awareness (or environmental efficacy) score for person i in country j. As an important step in modeling building in multilevel analysis, random coefficient models were completed as preliminary analyses (not shown). These analyses indicate which effects of individual-level variables vary across countries for both measures of environmental concern. The effects of four level-one individual variables vary across countries for *environmental threat awareness* and are therefore estimated as random (i.e. allowed to vary across countries). For *environmental efficacy*, the effects of five level-one individual variables vary across countries and are estimated as random. Specifications of the country-level models for the intercepts and two slopes (education and age), respectively, are:

$$\beta_{0j} = \gamma_{00} + \gamma_{01} \text{ TOTAL POPULATION} + \gamma_{02} \text{ POP AGE STRUCTURE} + \gamma_{03} \text{ POP DENSITY} + \gamma_{04} \text{ GDP} + \gamma_{05} \text{ DEMOCRACY} + \gamma_{06} \text{ URBAN POPULATION} + \gamma_{07} \text{ ECOSYSTEM WELLBEING} + u_{0j}$$

$$\beta_{1j} = \gamma_{10} + \gamma_{11} \text{ TOTAL POPULATION} + \gamma_{12} \text{ POP AGE STRUCTURE} + \gamma_{13} \text{ POP DENSITY} + \gamma_{14} \text{ GDP} + \gamma_{15} \text{ DEMOCRACY} + \gamma_{16} \text{ URBAN POPULATION} + \gamma_{17} \text{ ECOSYSTEM WELLBEING} + u_{1j}$$

$$\beta_{2j} = \gamma_{20}$$

$$\beta_{6j} = \gamma_{60} + u_{6j}$$

Where $i = 1,2,3,\ldots N_{ij}$ ($N_{ij} = 31039$) and $j = 1,2,3,\ldots J$ ($J = 25$).[6]

The individual-level independent variables education, age, income, and knowledge are grand mean centered (averaged across all respondents in all countries).[7]

Table 1. Descriptive Statistics for Country-Level Variables

Environmental Concerns	Mean	Std Dev	Range			1	2	3	4	5	6	7	8	9
Threat Awareness	3.19	0.62	2.56	3.86	1	1.00								
Envtal. Efficacy	2.09	0.79	1.00	3.02	2	0.02	1.00							
Aggregate Variables			Min	Max										
Total pop. (logged)	16.56	1.41	14.50	19.40	3	0.39	0.29	1.00						
Pop. age structure (logged)	3.97	0.13	3.80	4.32	4	-0.22	0.31	0.12	1.00					
Pop. density (logged)	4.18	1.24	1.39	6.13	5	-0.02	0.65*	0.08	-0.07	1.00				
GDP (logged)	9.77	0.66	7.79	10.54	6	-0.41*	0.48*	-0.09	-0.51*	0.01	1.00			
Democracy	93.53	9.11	70.83	100	7	-0.31	-0.45	-0.41*	-0.57*	-0.09	0.66*	1.00		
Urban Population	72.21	11.24	50.60	90.90	8	-0.01	0.33	0.13	0.15	-0.15	0.31	-0.05	1.00	
Ecosys. Well-Being	3.53	0.24	3.04	3.91	9	-0.12	0.68*	-0.35	-0.11	-0.55*	0.07	0.37	-0.06	1.00

Notes: * p < .05 or greater, two-tailed.

Results

Analyses reveal statistically significant country-level variance in both latent variable grand means, showing that these two measures of environmental concern vary a significant amount across the countries in this sample. Calculations of the intraclass correlation coefficient (ICC) indicate that 27 percent of the total variance in environmental risk perception and 53 percent of the total variance for environmental efficacy can be attributed to between-country differences. Therefore, a substantial amount of variation occurs across countries for both measures of environmental concern. If we are to have a sound understanding of environmental concern, then it is important to explain this between-country variation as well as variation across individuals within countries.

Table 2 includes coefficients and standard errors for the empirical models of environmental concerns. These random intercept models highlight how countries vary in mean levels of environmental threat awareness and efficacy and introduce country characteristics to explain between-country differences in means, net of effects of individual-level variables. These models answer the question of why some countries have higher mean levels of environmental threat awareness and environmental efficacy than others, taking into account expectations from structural human ecology and predictions regarding economic, political, and environmental factors affecting each of the intercepts. For the individual-level variables included in the models that capture the within-country relations anticipated from the literature (e.g. Franzen and Meyer 2010; Gelissen 2007; Givens and Jorgenson 2011, 2012; Haller and Hadler 2008; Marquart-Pyatt 2008, 2012; Xiao and Dunlap 2007), expected relations are largely confirmed. For instance, inverse relations between age and both environmental threat awareness and environmental efficacy are revealed, and gender differences are revealed for both measures. Education has the anticipated positive effect only on efficacy, and urban residence has a positive effect on threat awareness.

Results show important effects for structural human ecology, and economic and political features, in explaining differing mean levels of environmental concerns for both measures. Population factors have positive and negative effects. Total population has a positive relation with environmental threat awareness. The population age structure is a measure of the working age population relative to those groups below 15 and above 64, the latter of which are primary groups defined as dependent. In this regard, it is one way to show how population can be linked with economic growth. This measure of age

Table 2. Predicting Environmental Concerns with Individual-level and
        Country-level Variables

	Threat Awareness	Environmental Efficacy
Country-level Variables		
Total Population	0.068**	-0.003
	(0.026)	(0.042)
Age Structure	-1.115**	-0.816
	(0.344)	(0.561)
Population Density	-0.092*	-0.127**
	(0.036)	(0.046)
GDP	-0.209*	0.065
	(0.103)	(0.139)
Democracy	-0.001	-0.035**
	(0.008)	(0.008)
Urban Population	0.001	-0.014**
	(0.004)	(0.005)
Ecosystem Well-Being	-0.162	0.139
	(0.214)	(0.262)
Individual-level Variables		
Intercept	3.146**	2.013**
	(0.046)	(0.152)
Education	0.003	0.025**
	(0.004)	(0.003)
Income	0.000	0.033**
	(0.013)	(0.008)
Knowledge	-0.003	0.039**
	(0.006)	(0.007)
Age	-0.002**	-0.003**
	(0.001)	(0.001)
Gender	0.070**	0.055**
	(0.012)	(0.014)
Urban	0.056**	0.015
	(0.019)	(0.014)
Variance Components		
Individual-level variance	0.294	0.215
Country-level variance	0.065	0.626

Notes: Table includes coefficients and standard errors in parentheses.
* $p < .05$, **$p < .01$ or above. All are two-tailed tests. $N_i = 31,039$ $N_j = 25$.

dependency that gauges the relative size of adults active in economic sectors is negatively related to awareness of environmental threats, as is population density. National affluence (logged GDP) is negatively related to awareness of environmental threats. Awareness of environmental threats is substantially lower in countries with higher levels of national affluence. Awareness is also substantially lower in countries with higher levels of working-age population and greater population density. Combined, these institutional factors account for 35 percent of variability in countries' mean levels of awareness of environmental threats, controlling for compositional differences of countries.

Results in the second column of Table 2 reveal that demographic and political factors also affect environmental efficacy, yet uncover a different pattern. The three significant aggregate level variables—population density, democracy, and urban population—have negative relations with environmental efficacy. Environmental efficacy is higher in countries with lower population density. Environmental efficacy is lower in more democratic countries and in countries with a greater proportion of the population living in urban areas. These factors combined account for 44 percent of between-country variance in mean levels of environmental attitudes, net of compositional differences.

As specified in structural human ecology, these findings demonstrate important demographic factors that have been largely condoned in previous research (Franzen and Meyer 2010; Gelissen 2007; Givens and Jorgenson 2011; Haller and Hadler 2008; Marquart-Pyatt 2012). These measures reflect aspects of society's organization structure, introducing complexities of population for elucidating society-environment relations at aggregate and individual-level scales. Findings reveal that population measures affect environmental concerns in a nuanced fashion—positive and negative effects on threat awareness and negative effects on efficacy. Results also partially confirm expectations from previous research regarding affluence and political structures. Associations between affluence and awareness of environmental threats are negative. Results for political factors offer some support for previous research (Haller and Hadler 2008; Marquart-Pyatt 2012). In summary, results differ for aggregate factors depending on the measure or dimension of environmental concern being examined.

Given results of random coefficient regression models and previous cross-national research, random slope models were assessed for the individual-level effects of education and age for the two measures of environmental concern. These models investigate which country characteristics predict why some countries have greater educational (and age) effects on levels of environmental awareness and efficacy, respectively, than others, using the same country-level predictors. They examine why in some countries the association between education and environmental concerns, and age and environmental concerns, is stronger than in others, revealing whether the aggregate level variables predict the individual-level within-country slopes. That is, the approach assumes that the way individual education and age affects environmental concern will vary depending on characteristics of the country in which an individual lives. For instance, incorporating expectations from SHE, these models enable the exploration of whether countries with higher population density differ from countries with lower population density in terms of the strength of the association between the education slope and environmental threat awareness and efficacy. The same applies for the age slope.

Results in the first column in Table 3 reveal only one significant relation—that there is a tendency for countries with a greater proportion of age-dependent population to have weaker or smaller slopes for education's effect on *threat awareness*. Put differently, countries with larger age dependent populations have an enhanced negative effect of education on awareness, suggesting the effects of education on awareness are dampened in countries with a larger age dependent population. This segment of the population is less directly engaged in activities of the labor force relative to other groups, thus the link between education and environmental concern may differ accordingly. For instance, there may be some groups of individuals who in a potentially burgeoning economy may be less attuned to economy-environment trade-offs or have either not yet been enrolled in educational institutions or completed their education some time ago under a different educational regime. Country-level characteristics explain 9 percent of the variation in the education slope across countries. Results in the second column in Table 3 reveal effects for four aggregate measures on *environmental efficacy*: population age structure, population density, urban population, and democracy, all of which are positive. For instance, results indicate that there is a tendency for countries with a greater proportion of age-dependent population to have a larger education slope on environmental efficacy than countries with a smaller proportion of age-dependent population, suggesting that the effects of education on efficacy are even more pronounced in countries with a greater age dependent population. Other significant variables reveal that the effects of education on efficacy are even more pronounced in countries with a greater population density, in countries that are more democratic, and in countries with larger urban populations. Combined, these country-level factors explain 12 percent of the variation in the education slope across countries for environmental efficacy.

Table 3. Random Slope: Education and Environmental Concern

	Threat Awareness	Environmental Efficacy
Education Slope	0.0029	0.0249**
	(0.0034)	(0.0032)
Country-level Variables		
Total Population	0.0013	0.0013
	(0.0011)	(0.0010)
Age Structure	-0.0312*	0.0415**
	(0.0134)	(0.0120)
Population Density	0.0012	0.0049**
	(0.0012)	(0.0015)
GDP	-0.0003	0.0035
	(0.0027)	(0.0032)
Democracy	-0.0001	0.0018*
	(0.0002)	(0.0003)
Urban Population	0.0000	0.0004*
	(.0001)	(0.0002)
Ecosystem Well-Being	-0.0008	0.0020
	(.0059)	(0.0066)
Individual-level Variables		
Intercept	3.1463**	2.0121**
	(0.0608)	(0.1227)
Age	-0.0015*	-0.0032**
	(0.0005)	(0.0006)
Gender	0.0669**	0.0551**
	(0.0191)	(0.0141)
Urban	0.0559**	0.0155
	(0.0183)	(0.0139)
Income	0.0000	0.0328**
	(0.0127)	(0.0076)
Knowledge	-0.0029	0.0391**
	(0.0062)	(0.0066)

Notes: Table includes coefficients and standard errors in parentheses.
* $p < .05$, **$p < .01$ or above. All are two-tailed tests. $N_i = 31,039$ $N_j = 25$.

Results in Table 4 indicate that the population age structure in a country enhances the effect of age on *awareness*, suggesting the effects of age on awareness are more pronounced in countries with a larger age-dependent population. Effects of age on awareness are also more pronounced in more democratic countries. Combined, however, effects on the age slope are negligible. Results in Table 4 also reveal that the population age structure in a country enhances the effect of age on environmental efficacy, such that the effect of age on efficacy is more pronounced in countries with a larger age-dependent population.

Results of random slope models shown in Tables 3 and 4 extend previous research by including cross-level effects and confirming integral roles for both education and age in influencing the individual-level expression of two dimensions of environmental concern across nations. Notably absent are effects for environmental conditions on either dimension. Instead, features of nations' social organization are influential. For instance, a country's population age structure dampens the effects of education on awareness of environmental threats, but the effects of age on environmental threat awareness and efficacy are enhanced in countries with larger proportions of age dependent populations. Demographic features have non-trivial effects on environmental efficacy, as population density and urban population also influence the education slope. That is, the effects of education on efficacy are even more pronounced in countries with a greater population density and in countries with larger urban populations. These findings overall demonstrate that aggregate-level factors shape environmental concerns cross-nationally, providing an important extension of previous research through the inclusion of not only economic, political, and environmental factors, but most notably of demographic factors. Yet they also lay out complexities for future research to consider, as elaborated in the final section.

Discussion and Conclusion

Findings from this research reveal that country-level factors influence individuals within countries, modifying mean levels of environmental threat awareness and environmental efficacy. Results reveal that demographic factors illuminating the SHE framework affect environmental concerns, societal features pertinent to investigations of society-environment relations that have not yet been incorporated into the empirical models investigated in previous public opinion scholarship. Most important, they point to the need for

Table 4. Random Slope: Age and Environmental Concern

	Threat Awareness	Environmental Efficacy
Age Slope	-0.0016**	-0.0032**
	(0.0005)	(0.0006)
Country-level Variables		
Total Population	0.0013	0.0002
	(0.0011)	(0.0003)
Age Structure	0.0066*	0.0078*
	(0.0033)	(0.0032)
Population Density	0.0002	0.0000
	(0.0003)	(0.0003)
GDP	-0.0005	-0.0001
	(0.0005)	(0.0007)
Democracy	0.0001t	0.0001
	(0.0000)	(0.0001)
Urban Population	0.0000	-0.0001
	(0.0000)	(0.0000)
Ecosystem Well-Being	-0.0013	0.0003
	(0.0015)	(0.0018)
Individual-level Variables		
Intercept	3.1463**	2.0130**
	(0.0608)	(0.1226)
Education	0.0029	0.0249**
	(0.0036)	(0.0034)
Gender	0.0667**	0.0554**
	(0.0123)	(0.0142)
Urban	0.0560**	0.0154
	(0.0192)	(0.0139)
Income	0.0002	0.0332**
	(0.0127)	(0.0077)
Knowledge	-0.0031	0.0391**
	(0.0062)	(0.0065)

Notes: Table includes coefficients and standard errors in parentheses.
* $p < .05$, **$p < .01$ or above. All are two-tailed tests. N_i = 31,039 N_j = 25.

further analysis of population measures, as they do not have uniform effects on environmental concerns. In other words, although demographic measures affect environmental concerns, more nuanced analyses should be undertaken as the relations are both positive and negative. We cannot assume that increasing population pressures or attributes have uniform effects on environmental views, and we are challenged to develop hypotheses about these complexities. Relations between population density and environmental concern illustrate this at a basic level: environmental threat awareness is lower in countries with a greater population density, and environmental efficacy is higher in countries with lower population density. A similarly nuanced picture is provided for the effects of age dependency, which is negatively related to mean levels of awareness of environmental threats but not environmental efficacy. Further models, described below, add to this narrative of degrees and complexity for future scholars to explore.

The findings also reveal partial support for affluence and political structures in shaping environmental threat awareness and efficacy as anticipated from previous research (Franzen and Meyer 2010; Gelissen 2007; Givens and Jorgenson 2011; Haller and Hadler 2008; Marquart-Pyatt 2012). There are nuances to these findings, however. For instance, affluence negatively affects environmental awareness but not efficacy, in line with prior research articulating that national wealth does not always translate into greater expressed environmental concern (Dunlap and York 2008). Limited effects are revealed for a country's political structure, as democracy affects the expression of environmental efficacy but not threat awareness (Haller and Hadler 2008; Marquart-Pyatt 2012). And no effects were revealed for environmental conditions, counter to expectations from the OPSV thesis.

Findings from random slope models in some respects provide more information gradients regarding the presumed link between exposure to norms and values promoting general environmental awareness from contact with educational institutions and the expression of environmental concern, and for conceptual arguments about the manner in which age and concern for the environment relate. These findings show that a country's population age structure both enhances and dampens effects on the relations between education and these two dimensions of environmental concerns, and it also enhances the relations between age and both environmental concern measures. Notably absent are effects for economic or environmental conditions on either dimension. Complex relations are once again shown between measures of population and individual-level slopes for education and age, and uniformity of effects should not be assumed. For instance, although a country's population age structure dampens the effects of education on awareness of environmental threats, in contrast the effects of education on efficacy are even more pronounced in countries with a greater population density and in countries with larger urban populations. And the effects of age on environmental threat awareness and efficacy are enhanced in countries with larger proportions of age dependent populations. Overall, these findings demonstrate that aggregate-level factors, particularly measures of countries' demographic attributes, shape environmental concerns cross-nationally. They provide an important extension of expectations from previous research by incorporating expectations from the structural human ecology framework.

This research demonstrates important relationships between individual and country-level variables on two dimensions of environmental concerns across twenty-five nations, using a multilevel modeling strategy to test key insights from prior cross-national research. Like previous research, this research demonstrates important individual-level factors as influences on environmental concerns cross-nationally (Marquart-Pyatt 2007, 2008, 2012; Xiao and Dunlap 2007). At the individual level, age and being female influence environmental concerns, whereas education, living in an urban area, income, and knowledge have influences that differ to some degree as a result of the dimensionality of environmental concern.

Country-level results reveal important effects of demographic features including the population age structure and population density. These national features, as well as economic and political attributes, to some degree shape concern about the environment, and have positive and negative influences. Ultimately, effects of contextual variables depend on how environmental concern is measured (Marquart-Pyatt 2012). These factors are important not only for explaining country differences in mean levels of dimensions of environmental concerns, but also why in some countries the association between education and environmental concern, and age and environmental concern, measured as two distinct attitudinal dimensions of environmental threat awareness and environmental efficacy, are stronger than in others.

Yet the presumed links between demographic attributes of a country and the environmental concerns of citizens within its national boundaries need to be more clearly outlined in future research. Here, SHE requires scholars to revisit our assumptions about presumed demographic-environment links. Previous cross-national work on country-level factors affecting the expression of individual-level environmental concerns has not examined an exhaustive suite of societal institutions that may be influential in shaping the expression of such a complex array of attitudes, beliefs, and concerns. Demographic forces may play different roles depending on the national economic structure, much the same way that institutional legacies shape the expression of political attitudes like trust cross-nationally (Mishler and Rose 2001). For instance, the presence of a large working-age population (i.e. a large age dependency value) could signal the presence of potential large-scale economic changes like economic growth where individuals may have certain outlooks on economy-environment trade-offs. Yet they may also signal differences in population segments regarding expressed environmental concerns, complexities that are not attributable necessarily to individual differences but instead speak to cohort effects or experiential differences that depend on labor force activity. Such differences may speak to group-based processes linked with a particular stage in the life course, developments that introduce nuances for individuals. These processes have potentially parallel dynamics operating at the national or aggregate level. These demographic, institutional features may interact with economic or political attributes of a nation, may be fundamentally driven by them, or may be tapping into different facets of industrial development when nations are also categorized as developing, industrial, or post-industrial societies. To tease out such complexities, future research will require multiple levels of data (i.e. for individuals and for nations) gathered at multiple points of time to comprehensively examine such interrelations.

SHE refocuses our attention on forms of social organization as key processes involved in shaping the intersection between structural conditions and individual-level environmental concerns. As such, it offers an important contribution to cross-national research on environmental concern, which previously emphasized economic and environmental features of countries as important contextual level factors to take into account. By outlining multiple demographic features, future research is challenged to articulate how these organizational attributes intersect with the industrialization/economic development arguments that dominate past scholarship.

For the cross-national literature on environmental concern to move forward, scholars are challenged to further examine the society-environment interface with emphasis on the effect of the environment on humans (Dietz, Rosa, and York 2009). Continuing to build models that investigate relations among individual-level and institutional-level attributes regarding the sources and consequences of individuals' environmental concerns are fruitful extensions of this research. Further, extensions to larger samples of countries with varying contexts and integrating additional spatial and temporal scales are important theoretical and empirical extensions for subsequent cross-national, comparative research.

Notes

1. Franzen and Meyer (2010), Haller and Hadler (2008), Gelissen (2007), Givens and Jorgenson (2011), and Marquart-Pyatt (2012) use different datasets and different individual-level measures of environmental concern. Franzen and Meyer (2010) measure environmental concern with a nine-item scale using the 1993 and 2000 ISSP Environment data with samples of 18 and 26 countries, respectively (with zero and three industrializing nations). Haller and Hadler (2008) include two attitudinal measures of environmental concern with a sample of 23 countries from 2000 ISSP Environment data (three industrializing nations). Gelissen (2007) measures environmental concern as support for environmental protection using the World Values Survey (WVS) with a sample of 50 geographically dispersed, industrialized and industrializing nations. Givens and Jorgenson (2011) use a single attitudinal measure of the importance of caring for nature across 38 developed and developing countries from the WVS. Marquart-Pyatt (2012) examines three multi-item measures of environmental concern using 27 countries from the 2000 ISSP Environment data that includes three developing countries. The country-level indicators in these studies differ as well, as although all include economic measures (i.e. GDP), indicators of environmental conditions differ. Only two studies incorporate political factors (Haller and Hadler 2008; Marquart-Pyatt 2012). Pointedly, none include expectations from structural human ecology.

2. To preserve sample sizes, missing data were accounted for using multiple imputation procedures, specifically the EM algorithm (Allison 2002). SAS 9.2 was used to complete the structural equation modeling analyses (i.e., confirmatory factor analyses). Imputed data were analyzed using HLM 6.08. Results are similar across alternate specifications (i.e. analyses using listwise deletion completed as a robustness check). To retain the full sample of cases, results using the imputed data are reported here.

3. CFAs were completed in a number of stages for each latent variable. Latent constructs were first tested in the pooled sample of 30,139 individuals, as described in the text. CFAs were also conducted for each of the 25 countries individually. These results indicate very good to excellent fit for all 25 countries individually for environmental threat awareness and environmental efficacy. In addition, multigroup CFAs demonstrate configural and metric invariance of both measures of environmental concerns (Bollen 1989; Cheung and Rensvold 2002). Theoretically-derived correlated errors are included for each latent measure as appropriate. More information is available upon request. Regarding component fit, standardized factor loadings for environmental threat awareness range from 0.633 to 0.815 and the unstandardized factor loadings from 0.857 to 1.000 (all significant, p<.001). Overall model fit statistics are excellent—the chi-square is non-significant, and values for the Incremental Fit Index (IFI), the Comparative Fit Index (CFI), and Adjusted Goodness of Fit Index (AGFI) are 1.00. Traditionally, values above .95 are recognized to suggest excellent fit (Hu and Bentler 1999; Kline 2010). The Root Mean Square Error of Approximation (RMSEA) is .003, with values closer to zero indicative of better fit.

4. For component fit, the standardized factor loadings range from 0.353 to 0.675 and the unstandardized factor loadings from 0.569 to 1.186 (all significant, p<.001).

Overall model fit statistics are very good—although the chi-square value is significant, the AGFI is 1.00, the IFI and CFI are .98, and the RMSEA is .03.

5. This study is cross-sectional, thus precluding the ability to distinguish between age and cohort effects. Including age as a linear measure is consistent with previous cross-national public opinion research.

6. Equations in the text are shown for environmental awareness, presenting the random intercept model and the random slope equation for education. For *awareness of environmental threats*, education, age, gender, and urban are estimated as random (i.e. allowed to vary across countries) whereas income and knowledge are estimated as fixed. For *environmental efficacy*, five level-one individual variables vary whereas urban residence is estimated as fixed.

7. Grand-mean centering is advised to hold compositional differences in individual characteristics constant. This strategy is appropriate when aggregate measures of the variables are not included in the models (Raudenbush and Bryk 2002).

References

Allison, Paul. 2002. *Missing Data*. Thousand Oaks: Sage Publications.

Blocker, T. Jean, and Douglas L. Eckberg. 1997. "Gender and Environmentalism: Results from the 1993 General Social Survey." *Social Science Quarterly* 78: 841-858.

Bollen, Kenneth. 1989. *Structural Equations with Latent Variables*. New York: Wiley.

Brechin, Steven. 1999. "Objective Problems, Subjective Values, and Global Environmentalism: Evaluating the Postmaterialist Argument and Challenging A New Explanation." *Social Science Quarterly* 84(4): 793-809.

Brechin, Steven, and Willet Kempton. 1994. "Global Environmentalism: A Challenge to the Postmaterialism Thesis?" *Social Science Quarterly* 75: 245-269.

————. 1997. "Beyond Postmaterialist Values: National Versus Individual Explanations of Global Environmentalism." *Social Science Quarterly* 78: 16-20.

Cheung, Gordon, and Roger Rensvold. 2002. "Evaluating Goodness-of-Fit Indexes for Testing Measurement Invariance." *Structural Equation Modeling* 9(2): 233-255.

Diekmann, Andreas, and Axel Franzen. 1999. "The Wealth of Nations and Environmental Concern." *Environment and Behavior* 31(4): 540-549.

Dietz, Thomas, Linda Kalof, and Paul C. Stern. 2002. "Gender, Values and Environmentalism." *Social Science Quarterly* 83(1): 353-364.

Dietz, Thomas, and Eugene A. Rosa. 1994. "Rethinking the Environmental Impacts of Population, Affluence and Technology." *Human Ecology Review* 1: 277-300.

————. 1997. "Effects of Population and Affluence on CO2 Emissions." *Proceedings of the National Academy of Sciences of the USA* 94: 175-179.

Dietz, Thomas, Eugene A. Rosa, and Richard York. 2007. "Driving the Human Ecological Footprint." *Frontiers in Ecological Environment* 5(1): 13-18.

————. 2009. "Environmentally Efficient Well-Being: Rethinking Sustainability as the Relationship between Human Well-being and Environmental Impacts." *Human Ecology Review* 16(1): 114-123.

Dietz, Thomas, Paul Stern, and Gregory Guagnano. 1998. "Social Structural and Social Psychological Bases of Environmental Concern." *Environment and Behavior* 30: 450-471.

Dunlap, Riley, George Gallup, and Alec Gallup. 1993. "Of Global Concern: Results of the Health of the Planet Survey." *Environment* 35(9): 7-40.

Dunlap, Riley, and Robert Jones. 2002. "Environmental Concern: Conceptual and Measurement Issues." In *Handbook of Environmental Sociology*, edited by Riley Dunlap and William Michelson, 482-524. Westport: Greenwood Press.

Dunlap, Riley, and Angela Mertig. 1995. "Global Concern for the Environment: Is Affluence a Prerequisite?" *Journal of Social Issues* 51: 121-137.

————. 1997. "Global Environmental Concern: An Anomaly for Postmaterialism." *Social Science Quarterly* 78(1): 24-29.

Dunlap, Riley, Chenyang Xiao, and Aaron McCright. 2002. "Politics and Environment in America: Partisan and Ideological Cleavages in Public Support for Environmentalism." *Environmental Politics* 10: 23-48.

Dunlap, Riley, and Richard York. 2008. "The Globalization of Environmental Concern and the Limits of the Postmaterialist Values Explanation: Evidence from Four Multinational Surveys." *The Sociological Quarterly* 49(3): 529-563.

Frank, David. 1997. "Science, Nature, and the Globalization of the Environment, 1870-1990." *Social Forces* 76(2): 409-435.

Frank, David, Ann Hironaka, and Evan Schofer. 2000. "The Nation State and the Natural Environment, 1900-1995." *American Sociological Review* 65: 96-116.

Franzen, Axel. 2003. "Environmental Attitudes in International Comparison: An Analysis of the ISSP Surveys 1993 and 2000." *Social Science Quarterly* 83: 297-308.

Franzen, Axel, and Reto Meyer. 2010. "Environmental Attitudes in Cross-National Perspective: A Multilevel Analysis of the ISSP 1993 and 2000." *European Sociological Review* 26(2): 219-234.

Gelissen, John. 2007. "Explaining Popular Support for Environmental Protection: A Multilevel Analysis of 50 Nations." *Environment and Behavior* 39 (3): 392-415.

Givens, Jennifer, and Andrew Jorgenson. 2011. "The Effects of Affluence, Economic Development, and Environmental Degradation on Environmental Concern: A Multilevel Analysis." *Organization and Environment* 24(1): 74-91.

————. 2012. "Individual Environmental Concern in the World Polity: A Multilevel Analysis." *Social Science Research* 42: 418-431.

Haller, Max, and Markus Hadler. 2008. "Dispositions to Act in Favor of the Environment: Fatalism and Readiness to Make Sacrifices in Cross-National Perspective." *Sociological Forum* 23(2): 281-311.

Hayes, Bernadette. 2001. "Gender, Scientific Knowledge and Attitudes Toward the Environment: A Cross-National Analysis." *Political Research Quarterly* 54: 657–671.

Hu, Li-Tze, and Peter Bentler. 1999. "Cutoff Criteria for Fit Indexes in Covariance Structure Analysis: Conventional Criteria versus New Alternatives." *Structural Equation Modeling* 6(1): 1-55.

Inglehart, Ronald. 1990. *Culture Shift in Advanced Industrial Society*. Princeton: Princeton University Press.

————. 1995. "Public Support for Environmental Protection: The Impact of Objective Problems and Subjective Values in 43 Societies." *PS: Political Science and Politics* (March): 57-71.

————. 1997. *Modernization and Postmodernization: Cultural, Economic, and Political Change in 43 Societies.* Princeton: Princeton University Press.

International Social Survey Program. 2003. International Social Survey Program [ISSP], 1985-2000 [CD-ROM]. Cologne, Germany: Zentralarchiv fuer Empirische Sozialforschung an der Universitaet zu Koeln [producer], 2003. Cologne, Germany: Zentralarchiv fuer Empirische Sozialforschung/Ann Arbor, MI: Inter-university Consortium for Political and Social Research [distributors].

Jones, Robert, and Riley Dunlap. 1992. "The Social Bases of Environmental Concern: Have They Changed Over Time?" *Rural Sociology* 57: 28-47.

Kemmelmeier, Markus, Grzegorz Krol, and Young Hun Kim. 2002. "Values, Economics, and Pro-Environmental Attitudes in 22 Societies." *Cross-Cultural Research* 36(3): 256-285.

Kidd, Quentin, and Aie-Rie Lee. 1997. "Post Materialist Values and the Environment: A Critique and Reappraisal." *Social Science Quarterly* 78(1): 1-15.

Kline, Rex. 2010. *Principles and Practice of Structural Equation Modeling.* New York: The Guilford Press.

Klineberg, Stephen, Matthew McKeever, and Bert Rothenbach. 1998. "Demographic Predictors of Environmental Concern: It Does Make a Difference How It's Measured." *Social Science Quarterly* 79(4): 734-753.

Marquart-Pyatt, Sandra T. 2007. "Concern for the Environment Among General Publics: A Cross-National Study." *Society and Natural Resources* 20(10): 883-898.

————. 2008. "Are There Similar Influences on Environmental Concern?: Comparing Industrialized Countries." *Social Science Quarterly* 89(5): 1-24.

————. 2012. "Contextual Influences on Environmental Concern Cross-Nationally: A Multilevel Investigation." *Social Science Research* 41(5): 1085-1099.

Mishler, William, and Richard Rose. 2001. "What Are the Origins of Political Trust? Testing Institutional and Cultural Theories in Post-Communist Societies." *Comparative Political Studies* 34(1): 30-62.

Raudenbush, Steven, and Anthony Bryk. 2002. *Hierarchical Linear Models: Applications and Data Analysis Methods*, Second edition. Thousand Oaks: SAGE.

Rosa, Eugene A., Richard York, and Thomas Dietz. 2004. "Tracking the Anthropogenic Drivers of Ecological Impacts." *AMBIO: A Journal of the Human Environment* 33(8): 509-512.

Stern, Paul, and Thomas Dietz. 1994. "The Value Basis of Environmental Concern." *Journal of Social Issues* 50: 65-84.

United Nations Development Programme (UNDP). 2010. *Human Development Report 2010: The Real Wealth of Nations: Pathways to Human Development.* New York: Palgrave Macmillan, UNDP.

World Bank. 2010. *World Development Report 2010: Development and Climate Change.* Washington, DC: World Bank Publishers.

Xiao, Chenyang, and Riley Dunlap. 2007. "Validating a Comprehensive Model of Environmental Concern Cross-Nationally: A U.S.-Canadian Comparison." *Social Science Quarterly* 88: 471-493.

York, Richard, and Eugene A. Rosa. 2012. "Choking on Modernity: A Human Ecology of Air Pollution." *Social Problems* 59(2): 282-300.

York, Richard, Eugene A. Rosa, and Thomas Dietz. 2003. "Footprints on the Earth: The Environmental Consequences of Modernity." *American Sociological Review* 68: 279-300.

IV. Directions for the Future

CHAPTER 10

Context Matters:
Eugene A. Rosa's Lessons for
Structural Human Ecology

Thomas Dietz, Michigan State University

I N LOOKING AT THE BODY OF GENE ROSA's contributions to scholarship, several major themes are evident. They cut across his writing and reflect how he thought about the conduct of research in environmental social science and human ecology. Perhaps the most central of them is the importance of context. As Richard York notes in Chapter 2 "context matters" was virtually Gene's definition of sociology. Understanding context was the motivation for the research program in structural human ecology (SHE) Gene pioneered. It is the common thread of the essays collected here.

This volume is based on a conference celebrating Gene's work on the event of his receiving the Boeing Professorship of Environmental Sociology at Washington State University.[1] The Thomas S. Foley Institute for Public Policy and Public Service and the Department of Sociology, Gene's academic homes for decades, were generous in sponsoring the event. Gene insisted that the papers presented not be about his work, but rather that they represent leading-edge scholarship in the emerging area of structural human ecology. Of course, Gene had made such immense contributions to so many aspects of structural human ecology that the papers collected here naturally reflect his thinking. Our original plan was for Gene to write the last chapter reflecting on where research should head in the future. Unfortunately, Gene's battle with cancer prevented him from completing that task.[2]

I cannot claim to offer the insights on the future of structural human ecology Gene would have. Instead, I review the areas in which Gene made foundational contributions. My goal is to extract lessons from his oeuvre that can guide our future work. Gene's scholarship had the rare quality of addressing large conceptual issues while examining in detail concrete empirical and policy matters. He felt it was essential to get the conceptual underpinnings to our work correct and to continually discipline theory with data. His work reflected long term programmatic efforts. Few of his writings were "one off"; rather they reflect ongoing engagement with major research and policy issues. The systematic nature of his work offers lessons at what Gene would call the "meta" level—lessons about how we should conduct our research—as well as more specific contributions to theory, methods, and substantive understanding. Indeed, one of the most important lessons we can learn from Gene is the value of patient pursuit of a systematic research program, one that produces linked work spanning decades and interjects new ideas on a regular basis. To put it succinctly: Progress comes from long conversations, not from short monologues.

Gene was a scientist and his central professional commitment was to advance fundamental knowledge. I think the essays in this volume demonstrate how much he achieved. But from early in his career, Gene also was engaged with matters of great practical importance to society, especially energy, nuclear power, and over the last two decades, global environmental change. Recently he was very active in the Millennium Alliance for Humanity and the Biosphere (MAHB, http://mahb.stanford.edu/welcome/). As Paul Ehrlich notes in the Preface, Gene helped that emergent network think about deploying the insights of both the social and the ecological sciences to help humanity face the difficult problems of the twenty-first century. Gene's work is solidly in what Donald Stokes labeled "Pasteur's Quadrant"—work that contributes to fundamental knowledge while also addressing critical practical problems (Stokes 1997).

I will review three major themes in Gene's work: the micro-foundations of structural human ecology, risk, and the STIRPAT and EIWB programs of macro-comparative analysis. His body of work is too large to cover in detail. My goal is more modest: to reflect on how Gene conducted his scholarship in order to identify the general lessons that can guide future work in structural human ecology. Gene has much to tell us about how to craft a research program in Pasteur's Quadrant—he was very successful at advancing science while engaging policy issues.

Micro-level Foundations of Structural Human Ecology

The best known work in structural human ecology has centered on macro-comparative analysis, especially cross-national comparisons. But the macro focus in this work should not eclipse the attention to micro-level theory that underpins SHE. Gene wanted to link the literature on coupled human and natural systems (CHANS) to the emerging literature in SHE in order to provide more robust understanding of how context matters. Most CHANS research has been based on analyses of individuals and households in local areas or relatively small regions (Rosa and Dietz 2010a, 2010b; Moran 2010; Entwistle and Stern 2005; Turner, Lambin, and Reenberg 2007). Powerful as those studies are, it is difficult to extract the effects of context in analyses that are local in scope. SHE was motivated by a desire to understand how context influences CHANS, bringing to human ecology consideration of large social factors and historical influences such as political institutions and culture.[3] In an ideal world, such investigations would begin with micro-level data on individuals and households and then examine the effects of context by comparing micro-level data across multiple countries and over decades of time (Dietz, Rosa, and York 2010). Sandra Marquart-Pyatt in Chapter 9 shows the power of multi-level analysis, linking the study of environmental attitudes to the STIRPAT research program. But the lack of investment in data suitable for human ecological research has led to a field largely bifurcated between micro and macro studies (Rosa and Dietz 2010b). Because culture and institutions vary little over time or across observational units in the locally focused studies, investigation of structural influences has, of necessity, mostly been done at the macro-level. We hope that new data sets and integration of existing data will move us beyond this split towards a more unified literature. When we have the data for more integrated analyses, we will need concepts and theories that span from the micro to the macro. Gene was attentive to those issues from the start of his career.

While he is known primarily for conceptual and empirical work on large scale structures and processes, Gene also engaged in micro-theory and empirical work at the individual level. His dissertation was an analysis of small group interaction that led him to what he termed "biosociology" (Rosa 1976). Rejecting the then-prevalent grand claims that human behavior could be reduced to the biological, Gene showed strong causal influence moving, not from biology to social interaction, but from social interaction to biology (Rosa 1979; Barchas et al. 1984; Mazur et al. 1980). While he did not pursue these lines of analysis after the mid-1980s, they laid the groundwork for his thinking about integrative theory.

In a statement that presaged what has become structural human ecology, Gene and I argued for progressive contextualization as a way to understand causation in human ecology (Dietz and Rosa 2002; Dietz, Rosa, and York

2010). Progressive contexualization had been advocated by ecological anthropologist Andrew P. Vayda as a logical extension of his earlier work with Bonnie McCay, but this literature was little known by environmental sociologists (Vayda 1988, 2009; McCay and Vayda 1975). The core idea is that the object of explanation for human ecology is human action that has consequences for the environment. We want to understand why the farmer swings the ax to cut a tree and why the suburbanite turns the car key to run an errand. Understanding those environmentally consequential behaviors requires understanding social psychological processes (Stern et al. 1999; Stern 2000). It also requires understanding the factors that shape and constrain those decision processes (Guagnano, Stern, and Dietz 1995). Progressive contextualization calls for moving up sequentially across levels of analysis from the action of an individual at a particular time and location to the various historical and geopolitical forces that have shaped the contexts in which the action takes place.[4]

Gene deployed a multi-level logic that reflects progressive contextualization in both his comparative studies of risk and in thinking through the STIRPAT models of human drivers of environmental stress (see below). In a series of papers, he and his collaborators compared risk perceptions across countries, and especially between Japan and the United States (Hinman et al. 1993; Kleinhesselink and Rosa 1991, 1994; Rosa, Matsuda, and Kleinhesselink 2000; Rosa and Matsuda 2005). Gene's comparative logic emphasized the contrast across major industrial nations that have similar technologies but important cultural and historical differences. This comparative insight shows very clearly in how nuclear technology is perceived. U.S. and Japanese respondents view most risks in much the same way despite a very different cultural heritage: "With similar life experiences, including the exposure to common risks, people in dissimilar cultures may be coming to have similar perceptions of risks" (Hinman et al. 1993, 453). Yet the striking difference between the two countries in perception of nuclear energy and weapons makes sense given the history of each: American respondents found nuclear risks to be newer, less well known, and more voluntary than did Japanese respondents. Of course, Japan is the only nation to have been attacked with nuclear weapons and is a nation heavily dependent on nuclear energy. Macro-historical forces impinge on micro-level perceptions. But those influences produce context-specific differences in the midst of large scale convergence. Context matters.

Gene's overall micro-theory stance was one that emphasized the decisions that underpin human actions. It was grounded in the complex cognitive architecture of human perceptions and decision making, rather than the formally tractable but empirically troubled rational actor paradigm (see next section). Gene insisted that solid micro-foundations have to be in place to build a theoretical structure at more aggregate levels. And indeed, he insisted not just on solid micro-foundations but a careful look at the theory of knowledge—epistemology and ontology—that is the bedrock on which we build. This led to his key contributions in risk theory.

Foundational Thinking on Risk

Risk became a topic in the environmental social sciences in the early 1980s. The Society for Risk Analysis was founded in 1980, providing a home for interdisciplinary discussions of risk analysis, including those grounded in the social sciences. Jim Short presented a Presidential Address on risk to the American Sociological Association in 1984 (Short 1984). The social science interest was spurred in part by the emergence of risk as a central theme in environmental and technology policy at about the same time (Dietz and Rycroft 1987; Dietz, Frey, and Rosa 2001; Dietz, Frey, and Rosa 2002; Rosa, McCormick, and Frey 2007). The contentious debate about nuclear power in the United States spawned interest in public perceptions of risk. Many saw risk analysis as a mechanism to "depoliticize" decision making about environmental and technological policy (Ruckelshaus 1985; Starr 1969). The convergence in 1986 of Chernobyl, the *Challenger* disaster, and the pollution of the Rhine River from a major chemical spill raised concerns about societal governance of risk and attracted the interest of a number of prominent social theorists (Rosa, McCright, and Renn 2013).

Gene's thinking about energy and especially nuclear power predisposed him to work on risk. At the invitation of Riley Dunlap, Gene, Scott Frey, and I formed a team to write the chapter on risk, technology. and society for the *Handbook of Environmental Sociology* (Dietz, Frey, and Rosa 2002). This was the starting point of my long collaboration with Gene.[5] While the *Handbook* did not appear until 2002, drafts of our chapter circulated for a number of years before that. The chapter launched Gene's central role in the emerging sociology of risk (Short 1984; Clarke and Short 1993).

Gene knew that solid underpinnings were essential for cumulative work that could both advance knowledge and inform policy. He respected theories of the middle range but was concerned that without meta-theoretical grounding, our efforts would be ad hoc rather than cumulative. This led him to a thoughtful examination of the ontology and epistemology of risk. Gene was unique among his generation of environmental sociologists for his broad and careful reading of the philosophy of science. He drew on this understanding in what came to be called the HERO (Hierarchical Epistemology applied with a Realist Ontology) model of risk. In a very influential essay, Gene argued that we should approach risk with a realist ontology—there is an objective world independent of our understanding of it (Rosa 1998b). But he also argued for a hierarchical epistemology—our knowledge of the world is never certain and is influenced by social forces. However, some things are much better known than others. There are contexts where social forces dominate and our understanding may not have much relationship to an underlying reality; in other cases the phenomena under scrutiny are ostensible and repeatable and thus social influences on our understanding can be minimized. The essay has generated an ongoing discussion in the literature (Rosa 1998a, 2010; Rosa and Clarke 2012; Aven and Renn 2010, 2009; Ravetz and Funtowicz 1998; Aven 2013), and is the theme of Chapters 2 and 3.[6]

Having laid meta-theoretical underpinnings for risk theory, Gene, in collaboration with Carlo Jaeger, Ortwin Renn, and Tom Webler, explored the relationship between the rational actor paradigm (RAP) and risk (Jaeger et al. 2001) in *Risk, Uncertainty and Rational Action*.[7] The RAP is the most influential micro-theory in the social sciences and dominates policy analysis as well. Many of us have offered arguments about why the RAP is not an adequate basis for describing either how we make decisions or how we should make decisions (Dietz 1994; Dietz and Stern 1995; Stern 2000; Stern 1986; Kahneman 2003). But Gene and his colleagues offered the most thorough analysis of the RAP I have read, delving into the philosophical underpinnings of RAP logic as well as its implications for policy. They argued that the RAP has such great influence because it is at the same time a worldview, a general theory, and a set of specific models. As a worldview, the RAP holds that humans are fundamentally rational and that the world can be seen as the interaction of atomistic entities. As a general theory, the RAP holds that the behavior of atomistic humans can be understood in terms of self-interested rational action. The RAP then entrains a utilitarian normative theory arguing that the actions of such agents in markets will yield socially desirable outcomes (Dietz 1994). Finally, the RAP manifests itself as several closely related models of behavior, including expected utility maximization, rational choice theory, and public choice theory. These formal theories dominate economics and are highly influential in all the other social sciences. Yet the RAP is a limited view of human decision making, with substantial flaws both as a description of how we actually make decisions and as a prescription for how we should make decisions. Gene and his collaborators argued persuasively that for problems of risk, the formalism of the RAP should be at least supplemented by, and perhaps entirely displaced by, deliberative processes.[8]

In his last book, *The Risk Society Revisited*, Gene and his collaborators expanded their critique of the RAP and offered a new view of risk by engaging the work of social theorists Ulrich Beck, Anthony Giddens, Niklas Luhmann, and Jürgen Habermas (Rosa, McCright, and Renn 2013). They synthesized the views of risk offered by these influential scholars and offered clear and practical suggestions about how to meld deliberative processes with scientific analysis. Their analysis is the most sophisticated statement to date in a tradition of using Dewey and Habermas as guides for environmental decision making (Dietz 2013, 1984, 1987, 1994; Dietz and Stern 1998; Stern 2005; U.S. National Research Council 2008, 1996). They also offered practical advice about "Who should deliberate when?" (Chess, Dietz, and Shannon 1998)—about what forms of deliberation are appropriate in what circumstances.

The move away from an overarching theory in the RAP and the argument that a single epistemological stance will not suffice for understanding environmental problems argue for context specific analyses. Gene's meta-theory encourages comparative work of the sort evident in his many cross-national analyses of risk perception. It especially encourages comparisons across forms of risk (Rosa and Clark 1999; Rosa et al. 2012; Stern et al. 2009). Such risk comparisons underpin the analyses in Chapter 4 by Ortwin Renn and collaborators, in Chapter 5 by Roger Kasperson, and in Chapter 6 by Paul Stern. These distinguished risk scholars were frequent collaborators with Gene and here take up his examination of the insights about technological risks that can be gained only by comparing technologies and contexts.

In addition to his theoretical and conceptual contributions to risk research, Gene was committed to engaging in policy discussions, "to integrate the lofty whiteness of risk society theory with the sooty details of risk decision-making" (Rosa, McCright, and Renn 2013, 9). The practical suggestions in the final chapters of *The Risk Society Revisited* demonstrated this commitment, but it was one that started near the beginning of Gene's career. As early as 1983, he spent time at Brookhaven National Laboratories working on processes for decision making under uncertainty, work he continued on a sabbatical at the London School of Economics and Political Science and during visits to the Akademie für Technikfolgenabschätzung in Stuttgart. His contributions included technical analyses of decision-making processes and the issue of "operator error" in nuclear power plants (Rosa and Humphreys

1988; O'Brien, Rosa, and Stengrevics 1983; Rosa et al. 1984). For over three decades he made regular and important contributions to discussions of nuclear power and nuclear waste, offering careful assessments of public opinion as it influenced both national policy and local siting controversies (Rosa 1978; Rosa and Freudenburg 1984; Rosa 1988; Rosa and Dunlap 1994; Rosa and Clark 1999; Rosa 2007; Whitfield et al. 2009; Freudenburg and Rosa 1984; Dunlap, Kraft, and Rosa 1993; Hinman et al. 1993). Perhaps his most prominent policy engagement was through a collaboration of scholars he helped organize to address nuclear waste policy (Rosa et al. 2010). They established that effective nuclear waste management must take account of insights from the social sciences as well as from the physical and ecological sciences and engineering. As a result of their arguments Gene and several other social scientists were asked to appear before President Obama's Blue Ribbon Commission on America's Nuclear Future (Rosa 2011). In his testimony, Gene noted that the American public views nuclear waste as a dread risk. Thus a lack of trust in the organizations that would govern waste management is a key issue (Rosa and Clark 1999; Whitfield et al. 2009; Rosa 1998a). He emphasized "an obdurate asymmetry where it is much easier to lose trust than to regain it, once lost" (Rosa 2011, 3) And of course, as an endlessly creative scholar, he also identified a series of research issues that could help resolve the waste problem.

One of Gene's last contributions on risk was intended to both open up a new line of research and to encourage policy dialogues that could facilitate effective social learning and better decision making (Rosa et al. 2012). Gene and his collaborators argued that risk analysis should be a central feature in our thinking about sustainability, thus drawing ideas of adaptive risk management into the sustainability discourse. At the same time, the paper challenged the risk community to move from narrow analyses of particular technologies or individual facilities to broad comparisons across the repertoire of risks facing global society. To demonstrate the approach called for, the paper compared risks from climate change with risks from terrorism and offered sixteen criteria for making broad risk comparisons. Such comparisons help society prioritize across categories of risk and at the same time enhance our understanding of each risk under consideration. Gene had planned further efforts along these lines and perhaps other scholars will take up his approach.

Gene's work on risk is so extensive and so influential that it is challenging to extract only a few lessons from it. Yet one meta-lesson is clear: serious work on an issue as complex as risk requires careful thinking about both epistemology and ontology. Too often scholars proceed with unexamined, taken-for-granted assumptions underpinning their theoretical and empirical work. That can lead to incoherent and even contradictory results. Gene enjoyed the vigorous and respectful discussion that followed his own formulation of hierarchical epistemology and realist ontology—defending his formulation while emphasizing that careful, critical discussion is how understanding advances.

STIRPAT and EIWB

Gene and his doctoral mentor Allan Mazur were pioneers in rethinking the relationship between energy use and societal development. They inspired what became the STIRPAT research program on anthropogenic drivers of environmental stress. Work examining the relationship between stress placed on the environment and human well-being, a research program labeled Ecological Intensity of Well-Being (EIWB), is a direct extension of their analyses. Before their work, the conventional wisdom in the social sciences and in most policy discussions was that increased energy use was virtually synonymous with societal development (Rosa, Machlis, and Keating 1988; Rosa 1983). Increases in per capita energy use were a hallmark of societal "evolution" from food foraging to horticultural and agricultural societies and ultimately to industrial societies. High levels of energy consumption were often viewed as essential for high quality of life and a modern lifestyle. But early in the first global energy crunch in the 1970s, Allan and Gene published an influential paper that led to a substantial reevaluation of the role of energy consumption in contemporary societies (Mazur and Rosa 1974; Rosa, Keating, and Staples 1981; Rosa 1997). They showed that once a modest threshold is passed, energy consumption is not tightly coupled to life style or human well-being. Allan's Chapter 7 in this volume and his recent book show that the relationship he and Gene identified persists—high levels of energy consumption are not necessary for improvements in human well-being (Mazur 2013).

The 1974 paper shows another theme in Gene's work that echoes throughout the STIRPAT and EIWB research program. Theory must be disciplined with data and data are most useful when deployed to test theory. When Allan and Gene published their analysis, arguments about energy and societal development were decades old. Reasonable if not perfect data to address the relationship between the two were readily available but had not been used to address questions about life-style and energy consumption. Using existing data they were able to show that long-standing, taken-for-granted assumptions were incorrect. In doing so, they began a major shift in both theoretical and policy debates and inspired a substantial body of current scholarship in the STIRPAT and EIWB research programs.

The STIRPAT approach emerged during the work leading up to *Global Environmental Change: Understanding the Human Dimensions*, one of the first reviews of global change social science (U.S. National Research Council 1992). I was on the U.S. National Research Council committee that wrote the report, and since I had a long-standing interest in population and the environment, I volunteered to review the literature in that area (Dietz 1996/1997; Dietz and Rosa 1994). I knew that there were a number of empirical and conceptual papers written as background to the report of the Rockefeller Commission on Population Growth and the American Future (U.S. Commission on Population Growth and the American Future 1972; Ridker 1972). These included the core papers in the debate between Paul Ehrlich and John Holdren on the one hand and Barry Commoner on the other (Holdren and Ehrlich 1974; Ehrlich and Holdren 1970, 1971, 1972b, 1972a; Commoner 1972b, 1972a; Commoner, Corr, and Stamler 1971). This exchange led to the formulation of the IPAT model. IPAT (Impacts = Population * Affluence * Technology) postulated that environmental impacts (I)[9] are the product of human population size (P), affluence (A), and the technology (T) used to produce goods and services.[10] The origins of IPAT have been described in several reviews (Dietz, Rosa, and York 2010; Chertow 2001; Holdren 1993) while Andrew Jorgenson in Chapter 8 examines the links between IPAT and STIRPAT and the development of comparative analysis using STIRPAT.

To my surprise, when I searched the literature, I found that other than some applications of the IPAT formulation, there had been essentially no empirical work in the nearly two decades since *Population and the American Future*. Applications of IPAT use values for I, P, and A to solve for T = (I / PA). In the hands of skilled analysts this approach has yielded some interesting results (Mazur 1994, 2013; Bongaarts 1992; Waggoner and Ausubel 2002; Soule and DeHart 1998; DeHart and Soule 2000). But it seemed to Gene and me that such efforts were ultimately limited because an accounting equation like IPAT cannot be used to test hypotheses. We endorsed the multiplicative relationship between human drivers and environmental stress that is at the heart of IPAT but recast it into a form that could bridge between the social and ecological sciences.[11] We posited a regression model that estimates an elasticity for each driver:

(1) $I = aP^{b}A^{c}T^{d}e$

In this approach a, b, c, and d become coefficients to be estimated using standard statistical procedures and e is an observation-specific error term. IPAT assumes that the values of a, b, c, and d are 1; we estimate and test hypotheses about them.

From the start we acknowledged that this basic model needed to be elaborated by disaggregating each driver (Dietz and Rosa 1994). Perhaps most important, the technology term in the equation is a stand-in not only for technology per se but for institutions, culture, and other aspects of social organization. In our first empirical work, Gene and I captured all these "technology" effects in the error terms in our regression model in order to examine the relative importance of population and affluence in a "reduced form" model (Dietz and Rosa 1997b; Dietz and Rosa 1997a). But it was always clear that unpacking technology would capture a variety of structural effects that vary across contexts.

Richard York saw the potential in the approach and led a collaboration where we greatly expanded our initial work into what became the STIRPAT model (York, Rosa, and Dietz 2002, 2003a, 2003c, 2003b, 2005; Rosa, York, and Dietz 2004; Knight 2009). STIRPAT was a term of Gene's invention and means both "stirp" (descendent) of IPAT and STochastic Impacts by Regression on Population, Affluence, and Technology. The goal of this enterprise was to establish a defensible methodology for testing hypotheses about the factors that generate anthropogenic stress on the environment and then to use that methodology to expand the scope of explanation from simply population and affluence to social structure, power relationships, culture, institutions, and aspects of the biophysical environment.

Scholars throughout the West and also in China have taken up the approach. Google Scholar finds hundreds of papers using the STIRPAT formulation and the original half dozen or so STIRPAT papers have garnered over 1,400 citations.[12] Perhaps most gratifying is the robust literature that is careful about functional form in estimating the effects of diverse driving forces on environmental change. Several recent publications summarize both the theories being tested and the empirical results that have accumulated to date so it would be redundant to review them here (Dietz, Rosa, and York 2010; Rosa and Dietz 2012; Levy and Morel 2012) But perhaps the most important result of the STIRPAT program is that it is being expanded in creative ways. While most initial STIRPAT work was based on cross-national comparisons, analyses based on sub-national units such as provinces, states, counties, and cities are now too common to enumerate here.

STIRPAT also is being expanded in a variety of ways. A growing literature uses it to determine what aspects of population shape the stress placed on the environment. There has been a useful examination of the relative importance of population size versus number of households (Cramer 1997; Cramer 1998; Liu et al. 2003; Knight and Rosa 2012; York and Rosa 2012). Other research looks at age structure (Liddle and Lung 2010; Liddle 2011; Wang et al. 2012), urbanization (Liddle 2013; Lankao, Tribbia, and Nychkla 2009; Wang et al. 2012; Zhang and Lin 2012; Clement and Schultz 2010; Jorgenson, Rice, and Clark 2010) and immigrant versus long-term resident populations (Squalli 2010, 2009). STIRPAT is flexible enough to be used in planning and policy analysis (Meng, Niu, and Shang 2012; Wang et al. 2011; Tallarico and Johnson 2010). Richard York recently used the approach to ask if alternative energy sources displace fossil fuels and found that they do to some degree, but the substitution is less than 100 percent (York 2012b; Jorgenson 2012). Both Andrew Jorgenson and Richard have probed the detailed effects of economic growth on the environment using modifications of STIRPAT (Jorgenson and Clark 2012; Jorgenson, Clark, and Giedratis 2012; York 2012a). Innovative recent analyses by Gene, Kyle Knight, and Juliet Schor showed that stress on the environment increases with longer working hours, suggesting that a social policy (reduced working hours) could provide an environmental side benefit (Knight, Rosa, and Schor 2013a, 2013b). A key theme of recent work, evident in Chapter 8 and other work by Andrew Jorgenson (Jorgenson, Clark, and Giedratis 2012; Jorgenson and Clark 2012), is to use STIRPAT to examine how the relation of drivers to environmental stress may change over time and across countries—contextual analysis.

One of the most interesting developments in the STIRPAT tradition is a return to the question that Allan Mazur and Gene Rosa asked four decades ago: what is the relationship between the stress we place on the environment and human well-being? Gene, Richard York, Kyle White, and I have begun examining the "Ecological Intensity of Human Well-Being (EIWB) (Dietz, Rosa, and York 2009, 2012; Knight and Rosa 2011; Dietz, York, and Rosa 2001). The core idea is that humans make use of the environment in order to generate human well-being. But nations and other units of social organization may differ massively in their efficiency at doing so and there may be systematic structural reasons for those differences.[13]

As with STIRPAT, the EIWB research program is intended to apply social science theories, concepts, and methods to ideas that are influential in the ecological and sustainability sciences. At least since the Millennium

Ecosystem Assessment, considerable attention has been given to the role of ecosystem services in generating human well-being (Alcalmo et al. 2003; Reid et al. 2005; Daily 1997). Most work on ecosystems services has been done at a local to regional level. The EIWB program is intended to provide a macro-level complement that allows for examination of structural influences, including those of institutions, political economy, culture, and the macroscopic features of the biophysical environment. This is yet another problem where data that would allow for hierarchical analysis and progressive contextualization would be ideal. But following one of Gene's basic insights, we should take the advice of Voltaire and remember that "the best is the enemy of the good." There are many flaws to any micro-level or macro-level analysis. We will learn more by conversations across studies that use alternative approaches than we will from any one approach used in isolation. If we have data, we should deploy it to test theory, even as we work towards better data.

The STIRPAT and EIWB research programs emphasize the importance of moving outside disciplinary boundaries. From its inception, STIRPAT was designed to foster discussion between the ecological and social sciences. Now STIRPAT and EIWB publications are appearing in journals across the disciplines, including of course sociology, but also economics, geography, and planning as well as journals in ecology, ecological economics, industrial ecology, and many other environmental sciences. Thus we see another general lesson from Gene's work: If our field has something to say, we shouldn't be talking to ourselves.

Extracting the Lessons

I have suggested five general lessons I have learned from working with Gene. I would add a sixth, what Gene called "the functional delusion."[14] He argued that we are always deluded about how hard it will be to do a project, how much time it will take, how messy the results will be. But this delusion is functional because if we weren't deluded we wouldn't take on the project and as a result, much interesting work would be displaced by trivial tasks. Gene's embrace of the functional delusion—taking on hard problems and persisting to wrestle with them over decades—has certainly been functional for all of us who have learned from the long conversation of scholarship we've had with him.

Table 1 summarizes the general lessons about building a research program that Gene's work offers us. The most fundamental insight, one that

Table 1. Lessons on scholarship from Rosa's work

• Context matters.

• Progress comes from long conversations, not short monologues.

• Get the ontology and the epistemology right.

• The purpose of theory is to be tested; the purpose of data is to test theory.

• If our field has something to say, we shouldn't be talking to ourselves.

• The functional delusion: Everything takes longer than you think it will but being deluded about that helps us take on important work.

---

motivated all of his work, is that context matters. It matters if one is trying to decide on what epistemological stance to apply to a given body of knowledge. It matters in understanding how technologies are perceived. It matters in understanding what factors drive human pressure on the environment. Context—the variation across observations in the effects of structure—is what drives our science.

The complexity of what we study leads to the second lesson I have learned from Gene: that progress comes not so much from the single brilliant analysis but from the ongoing, often decades-long conversation composed of multiple research projects and theoretical conversations. Gene wrote individual papers that have been highly influential—the most visible STIRPAT papers and "Metatheoretical Foundations for Post-Normal Risk" each have over 300 citations. But his largest impact has come from his patient persistence rather than from any single analysis. He would take on important problems, think deeply about them, and continue to develop new ideas and perspectives in scholarly conversation with his colleagues over years and even decades. Because context matters, because we are dealing with great complexity, our understanding evolves by the social learning that is the outcome of scientific discourse. The process requires humility, patience, persistence, and an openness to change.

However, for the long conversation to yield cumulative understanding it has to be grounded in careful thinking about the bedrock on which we build, including the meta-theoretical stance we take with regard to ontology and epistemology. That is the third lesson Gene offers. But while Gene engaged in meta-theory, he was also impatient with too many "words about words." Theory is important if and only if it is disciplined with data. Data is useful if and only if we can use it to refine our theoretical understandings. Gene's body of work involved formal experiments, surveys, macro-comparative statistical analyses, case studies, and virtually every other methodology used by social scientists. He was a methodological pluralist but insistent on a constant interplay between theory and data. So the fourth lesson I take from Gene's writings is that we must constantly be using data to test theory.

Pursuing a long-term research program requires patience and enough self-confidence to believe that the research matters. From this follows a fifth lesson from Gene's work: if our field, our research program, has something of value to offer, we should be offering it in multiple venues and expanding the conversation across disciplines. While Gene's primary academic home was in sociology, he was confident that sociology had much to offer other approaches to the study of the environment and technology. In turn sociology had much to gain from interdisciplinary engagement. So he was often a missionary, taking sociological insights into diverse journals and into workshops and meetings throughout North America, Europe, and Japan. He was always engaged not only with other social scientists, but also with physical scientists, ecological scientists, and engineers. He learned a great deal from these interactions, and as his pattern of citations show, he has had great influence beyond his home discipline.

Gene was an artist as well as a scholar.[15] As an artist, Gene was attentive to the importance of patient craft—for some of his pieces he took years to assemble the right components. So too with his scholarship—it involved patient assembly of multiple pieces of the large puzzle, always in conversation with colleagues around the globe. As a friend I will miss deeply my conversations with him. We are fortunate that as scholars, we can continue to hold those conversations, if not with Gene directly, at least with his many ideas.

Notes

1. Gene was also the Edward R. Meyer Distinguished Professor of Natural Resource and Environmental Policy in the Foley Institute and in 2013 was named Regents Professor at Washington State University.

2. He remained intellectually engaged throughout his struggle with cancer up to his death on 21 February 2013. We discussed this book only shortly before his death, and he remained as insightful and as full of good humor as ever. Thanks to the timely work of the contributors and the diligent efforts of Rachel Kelly, who served

as a research assistant for the project, just before he died Gene was given a copy of the volume formatted as a book and including all but this last chapter.

3. My work with Gene on these issues presaged some ideas that are now emerging in the telecoupling approach to CHANS (Liu et al. 2013).

4. Of course, contexts may not be strictly embedded in one another, a point emphasized by notions of polycentric governance (Ostrom 2010b, 2009, 2010a), networks (Frank 2011; Frank et al. 2011; Henry and Dietz 2011) and telecoupling (Liu et al. 2013).

5. After Sue Stern met Gene and me at the 1980 American Sociological Association meeting in New York, she suggested that Gene, Paul Stern, and I should talk. The three of us finally met in fall 1982 at the International Conference on Consumer Behaviour and Energy Policy in Noordwijkerhout, The Netherlands.

6. Gene's grace and intellectual openness is evident in the fact that a major component of the literature on HERO is a cordial debate between Gene and his good friend and collaborator Ortwin Renn and Ortwin's collaborator Terje Aven. After exchanging ideas in print, the three co-authored a synthetic paper (Aven, Renn, and Rosa 2011).

7. *Risk, Uncertainty and Rational Action* (Jaeger et al. 2001) won the Outstanding Publication Award of the American Sociological Association's Section on Environment and Technology in 2002. Gene won the award again in 2004 for STIRPAT work. He and his student Richard York are the only people to have won the award twice.

8. Part of their critique is based on the absence of an evolutionary or Darwinian logic in the RAP (Rosa, McCright, and Renn 2013, 89): "Norm evolution and the genesis of values are explicitly excluded from the body of knowledge within RAP. For RAP, they are simply 'givens' or 'out there'—exogenous to any particular context of choice." While Gene seldom wrote about evolutionary thinking, he was quite familiar with it, and his views, including his thinking on the importance of ostensibility and repeatability in epistemology, always struck me as entirely consistent with evolutionary approaches to social theory (McLaughlin 2012a, 2012b; Dietz, Burns, and Buttel 1990; Burns and Dietz 1992; Dietz and Burns 1992; Campbell 1960, 1987).

9. The same formulation was developed by Kaya and colleagues and has been influential in projections of future greenhouse gas emissions (Kaya 1990; Kaya and Yokobori 1997; Yamaji et al. 1991; Kaya et al. 1993; Intergovernmental Panel on Climate Change 2000).

10. While I is called "Impact" in the equations, most STIRPAT and EIWB studies do not model impact but rather stress or pressure placed on the environment. Impact is the result of how ecosystems and the biosphere respond to human action. The terms stress or pressure capture what humans do rather than how ecosystems respond. Ideally we would model both the stress we place on the environment and the way the environment responds. But the state of the science does not allow us to do this in a robust way, so while I is the abbreviation for impact, what is modeled in the STIRPAT and EIWB literatures so far is stress or pressure.

11. In our earliest discussions of what would become STIRPAT, we considered a planetary level analysis, using total human population for P, world economic activity for A, and either global greenhouse gas emissions or globe ecological footprint as I. Paul

Stern and R. Scott Frey were involved in those early discussions. Once again, data limitations precluded progress. P, A, and I at the global level exhibit strong trends (non-stationarity) and high colinearity. That makes the problems of estimating their relationship in a relatively short time series formidable. After the global analysis turned out to not be fruitful, Gene and I later moved on to cross-sectional analyses (Dietz and Rosa 1997b; Dietz and Rosa 1997a).

12. Google Scholar 12 May 2013.

13. This idea of EIWB was inspired in part by the insights of one of my undergraduate mentors, Tom Lough, a pioneer of environmental sociology. In the aftermath of the killings at Kent State, Tom was indicted by an Ohio Grand Jury as one of the Kent 25. That slowed his scholarly productivity. But even in the late 1960s he was making coherent arguments about structural influences on energy use and environmental impact that were not published until many years later (Lough 1996, 1999).

14. Robert Heinlein used the idea of a functional delusion in one of his late novels *Time Enough for Love*. And of course the idea of a functional delusion is used in psychiatry. I am not sure if Gene read the novel or if this is one of many examples of his ability to find acronyms or phrases to capture the essence of a concept. Among the others are HERO, STIRPAT, and PaSSAGE (Rosa and Dietz 2010a).

15. This essay neglects Gene's work as an artist. From 2001 Gene held the position of Affiliated Professor in the Department of Fine Arts at Washington State University (WSU). His artistic work, which he called "Ecolage," was featured frequently in faculty shows at WSU and in other venues. One of his images graces the cover of this book. Photos of his work and his program statement "Toward Ecolage: Art and Environment" (Rosa 1998c) can be found at http://cooley.libarts.wsu.edu/ROSA/artistry.html. Aside from his magnificent wine cellar, one of the joys of visiting Gene in Moscow, Idaho, was the professional-caliber gallery he had constructed on the third floor of his home.

References

Alcalmo, Joseph, Neville J. Ash, Colin D. Butler, J. Baird Callicot, Doris Capistrano, Stephen R. Carpenter, Juan Carlos Castilla, Robert Chambers, Kanchan Chopra, Angela Cropper, Gretchen C. Daily, Partha Dasgupta, Rudolf de Groot, Thomas Dietz, Anantha Kumar Duraiappah, Madhav Gadgil, Kirk Hamiltion, Rashid Hassan, Eric F Lambin, Louis Lebel, Rik Leemans, Liu Jiyuan, Jean-Paul Malingreau, Robert M. May, Alex F. McCalla, A. J. McMichael, Bedrich Moldan, Harold Mooney, Shahid Naseem, Gerald C. Nelson, Niu Wen-Yuan, Ian Noble, Ouyang Zhiyun, Stefano Pagiola, Daniel Pauly, Steve Percy, Prabhu Pingali, Robert Prescott-Allen, Walter V. Reid, Taylor H. Rickets, Cristian Samper, Robert Scholes, Henk Simons, Ferenc L. Toth, Jane K. Turpie, Robert Tony Watson, Thomas J. Wilbanks, Meryl Williams, Stanley Wood, Zhao Shidong, and Monika B. Zurek. 2003. *Ecosystems and Human Well-being: A Framework for Analysis*. Washington, DC: Island Press.

Aven, Terje. 2013. "On Funtowicz and Ravetz's 'Decision Stake–System Uncertainties' Structure and Recently Developed Risk Perspectives." *Risk Analysis* 33 (2):270-280.

Aven, Terje, and Ortwin Renn. 2009. "On Risk Defined as an Event Where the Outcome is Uncertain." *Journal of Risk Research* 12 (1):1-11.

———. 2010. "Response to Professor Eugene Rosa's Viewpoint to Our Paper." *Journal of Risk Research* 13 (3):255-259.

Aven, Terje, Ortwin Renn, and Eugene A. Rosa. 2011. "On the Ontological Status of the Concept of Risk." *Safety Science* 49 (8):1074-1079.

Barchas, Patricia R., William A. Harris, William S. Jose II, and Eugene A. Rosa. 1984. "Social Interaction and Hemispheric Laterality." In *Social Cohesion: Essays Toward A Sociophysiological Perspective*, edited by Patricia R. Barchas and Sally P. Mendoza, 139-150. New York: Greenwood Press.

Bongaarts, John. 1992. "Population Growth and Global Warming." *Population and Development Review* 18:299-319.

Burns, Tom R., and Thomas Dietz. 1992. "Socio-cultural Evolution: Social Rule Systems, Selection and Agency." *International Sociology* 7:259-283.

Campbell, Donald T. 1960. "Blind Variation and Selective Retention in Creative Thought as in Other Knowledge Processes." *Psychological Review* 67:380-400.

———. 1987. "Evolutionary Epistemology." In *Evolutionary Epistemology, Rationality and the Sociology of Knowledge*, edited by Gerard Radnitzky and W.W. Bartley III, 47-89. La Salle, Illinois: Open Court.

Chertow, Marion. 2001. "The IPAT Equation and Its Variants: Changing Views of Technology and Environmental Impact." *Journal of Industrial Ecology* 4 (4):13-29.

Chess, Caron, Thomas Dietz, and Margaret Shannon. 1998. "Who Should Deliberate When?" *Human Ecology Review* 5:45-48.

Clarke, Lee, and James F. Short Jr. 1993. "Social Organization and Risk: Some Current Controversies." *Annual Review of Sociology* 19:375-399.

Clement, Mathew, and Jessica Schultz. 2010. "Political Economy, Ecological Modernization, and Energy Use: A Panel Analysis of State-Level Energy Use in the United States, 1960–1990." *Sociological Forum* 26 (3):581-600.

Commoner, Barry. 1972a. "A Bulletin Dialogue on 'The Closing Circle': Response." *Bulletin of the Atomic Scientists* 28 (5):17, 42-56.

———. 1972b. "The Environmental Cost of Economic Growth." In *Population, Resources and the Environment*, edited by Ronald G. Ridker, 339-363. Washington, DC: Government Printing Office.

Commoner, Barry, Michael Corr, and Paul J. Stamler. 1971. "The Causes of Pollution." *Environment* 13 (3):2-19.

Cramer, James C. 1997. "A Demographic Perspective on Air Quality: Conceptual Issues Surrounding Environmental Impacts of Population Growth." *Human Ecology Review* 3:191-196.

———. 1998. "Population Growth and Air Quality in California." *Demography* 35:45-56.

Daily, Gretchen C. 1997. *Nature's Services: Societal Dependence on Natural Ecosystems*. Washington, DC: Island Press.

DeHart, Jennifer L., and Peter T. Soule. 2000. "Does I=PAT Work in Local Places?" *Professional Geographer* 52 (1):1-10.

Dietz, Thomas. 1984. "Social Impact Assessment as a Tool for Rangelands Management." In *Developing Strategies for Rangelands Management*, edited by National Research Council, 1613-1634. Boulder, Colorado: Westview.

————. 1987. "Theory and Method in Social Impact Assessment." *Sociological Inquiry* 57:54-69.

————. 1994. "'What Should We Do?' Human Ecology and Collective Decision Making." *Human Ecology Review* 1 (2):301-309.

————. 1996/1997. "The Human Ecology of Population and Environment: From Utopia to Topia." *Human Ecology Review* 3:168-171.

————. 2013. "Bringing Values and Deliberation to Science Communication." *Proceedings of the National Academy of Sciences* 110:14081-14087.

Dietz, Thomas, and Tom R. Burns. 1992. "Human Agency and the Evolutionary Dynamics of Culture." *Acta Sociologica* 35:187-200.

Dietz, Thomas, Tom R. Burns, and Frederick H. Buttel. 1990. "Evolutionary Theory in Sociology: An Examination of Current Thinking." *Sociological Forum* 5:155-171.

Dietz, Thomas, R. Scott Frey, and Eugene A. Rosa. 2002. "Risk, Technology and Society." In *Handbook of Environmental Sociology*, edited by Riley E. Dunlap and William Michelson, 562-629. Westport, Connecticut: Greenwood Press.

————. 2001. "Risk Assessment and Management." In *The Environment and Society Reader*, edited by R. Scott Frey, 272-299. New York: Allyn and Bacon.

Dietz, Thomas, and Eugene A. Rosa. 1997a. "Environmental Impacts of Population and Consumption." In *Environmentally Significant Consumption: Research Directions*, edited by Paul C. Stern, Thomas Dietz, Vernon Ruttan, Robert H. Socolow, and James Sweeney, 92-99. Washington, DC: National Academy Press.

————. 2002. "Human Dimensions of Global Change." In *Handbook of Environmental Sociology*, edited by Riley E. Dunlap and William Michelson, 370-406. Westport, Connecticut: Greenwood Press.

Dietz, Thomas, Eugene A. Rosa, and Richard York. 2009. "Environmentally Efficient Well-Being: Rethinking Sustainability as the Relationship between Human Well-being and Environmental Impacts." *Human Ecology Review* 16 (1):113-122.

————. 2010. "Human Driving Forces of Global Change: Examining Current Theories." In *Human Footprints on the Global Environment: Threats to Sustainability*, edited by Eugene A. Rosa, Andreas Diekmann, Thomas Dietz, and Carlo Jaeger, 83-132. Cambridge, Massachusetts: MIT Press.

————. 2012. "Environmentally Efficient Well-Being: Is There a Kuznets Curve?" *Journal of Applied Geography* 32:21-28.

Dietz, Thomas, and Eugene A. Rosa. 1994. "Rethinking the Environmental Impacts of Population, Affluence and Technology." *Human Ecology Review* 1:277-300.

————. 1997b. "Effects of Population and Affluence on CO2 Emissions." *Proceedings of the National Academy of Sciences, USA* 94:175-179.

Dietz, Thomas, and Robert W. Rycroft. 1987. *The Risk Professionals*. New York: Russell Sage Foundation.

Dietz, Thomas, and Paul C Stern. 1998. "Science, Values and Biodiversity." *BioScience* 48 (5):441-444.

————. 1995. "Toward a Theory of Choice: Socially Embedded Preference Construction." *Journal of Socio-Economics* 24 (2):261-279.

Dietz, Thomas, Richard York, and Eugene Rosa. 2001. "Ecological Democracy and Sustainable Development." Rio de Janeiro, Brazil: 2001 Open Meeting of the International Human Dimensions of Global Change Community.

Dunlap, Riley E., Michael E. Kraft, and Eugene A. Rosa. 1993. *The Public and Nuclear Waste: Citizen's Views of Repository Siting.* Durham, North Carolina: Duke University Press.

Ehrlich, Paul R., and John P. Holdren. 1970. "Hidden Effects of Overpopulation." *Saturday Review* 53(31):52.

———. 1971. "Impact of Population Growth." *Science* 171:1212-1217.

———. 1972a. "A Bulletin Dialogue on 'The Closing Circle': Critique." *Bulletin of the Atomic Scientists* 28(5):16, 18-27.

———. 1972b. "Impact of Population Growth." In *Population, Resources and the Environment*, edited by Ronald G. Ridker, 365-377. Washington, DC: U.S. Government Printing Office.

Entwistle, Barbara, and Paul C. Stern. 2005. *Population, Land Use and Environment: Research Directions.* Washington, DC: National Academy Press.

Frank, Kenneth A. 2011. "Social Network Models for Natural Resource Use and Extraction." In *Social Networks and Natural Resource Management: Uncovering the Social Fabric of Environmental Governance*, edited by Örjan Bodin and Christina Prell, 180-205. Cambridge, UK: Cambridge University Press.

Frank, Kenneth A., S. Maroulis, D. Belman, and Michael D. Kaplowitz. 2011. "The Social Embeddedness of Natural Resource Extraction and Use in Small Fishing Communities." In *Sustainable Fisheries: Multi-level Approaches to a Global Problem*, edited by William W. Taylor, Amy J. Lynch and M. G. Schechtler, 302-332. Bethesda, Maryland: American Fisheries Society.

Freudenburg, William F., and Eugene A. Rosa. 1984. *Public Reactions to Nuclear Power: Are There Critical Masses?* Boulder, Colorado: Westview Press/ American Association for the Advancement of Science.

Guagnano, Gregory A., Paul C. Stern, and Thomas Dietz. 1995. "Influences on Attitude-Behavior Relationships: A Natural Experiment with Curbside Recycling." *Environment and Behavior* 27:699-718.

Henry, Adam D., and Thomas Dietz. 2011. "Information, Networks, and the Complexity of Trust in Commons Governance." *International Journal of the Commons* 5 (2):188-212.

Hinman, George W., Eugene A. Rosa, Randall R. Kleinhesselink, and Thomas C. Lowinger. 1993. "Perceptions of Nuclear and Other Risks in the U.S. and Japan." *Risk Analysis* 13:449-455.

Holdren, John P. 1993. *A Brief History of 'IPAT' (Impact= Population x Affluence x Technology).* Cambridge, Massachusetts: Harvard University.

Holdren, John P., and Paul R. Ehrlich. 1974. "Human Population and the Global Environment." *American Scientist* 62:282-292.

Intergovernmental Panel on Climate Change. 2000. *Emissions Scenarios.* Cambridge, England: Cambridge University Press.

Jaeger, Carlo, Ortwin Renn, Eugene A. Rosa, and Thomas Webler. 2001. *Risk, Uncertainly and Rational Action.* London: Earthscan.

Jorgenson, Andrew K. 2012. "Energy: Analyzing Fossil Fuel Displacement." *Nature Climate Change* 2:398-399.

Jorgenson, Andrew K., and Brett Clark. 2012. "Are the Economy and the Environment Decoupling? A Comparative International Study, 1960-2005." *American Journal of Sociology* 118 (1):1-44.

Jorgenson, Andrew K., Brett Clark, and Vincent R. Giedratis. 2012. "The Temporal (In) Stability of the Carbon Dioxide Emissions / Economic Development Relationship in Central and Eastern European Nations." *Society and Natural Resources* 25:1182-1192.

Jorgenson, Andrew K., James Rice, and Brett Clark. 2010. "Cities, Slums, and Energy Consumption in Less-Developed Countries, 1990-2005." *Organization & Environment* 23:189-204.

Kahneman, Daniel. 2003. "A Perspective on Judgment and Choice." *American Psychologist* 58 (9):697-720.

Kaya, Yoichi. 1990. *Impact of Carbon Dioxide Emission Control on GNP Growth: Interpretation of Proposed Scenarios*. Paris: IPCC Energy and Industry Subgroup, Response Strategies Working Group.

Kaya, Y., Y. Fujii, R. Matsuhashi, I. Furugaki, K. Yamaji, O. Kobayaski, Y. Shindo, and H. Saiki. 1993. *Assessment of Technologies for Reducing CO_2 Emission*. Laxenburg, Austria: International Instiute for Applied Systems Analysis.

Kaya, Yoichi, and Keiichi Yokobori. 1997. *Environment, Energy, and Economy: Strategies for Sustainability*. Tokyo & New York: United Nations University Press.

Kleinhesselink, Randall R., and Eugene A. Rosa. 1991. "Cognitive Representation of Risk Perceptions: A Comparision of Japan and the United States." *Journal of Cross-Cultural Psychology* 22:11-28.

———. 1994. "Nuclear Trees in a Forest of Hazards: A Comparison of Risk Perceptions Between American and Japanese University Students." In *Nuclear Power at the Crossroads*, edited by George W. Hinman, S. Kondo, T. C. Lowinger, and K. Matsui, 109-119. Boulder, Colorado: International Research Center for Energy and Economic Development.

Knight, Kyle, and Eugene A. Rosa. 2011. "The Environmental Efficiency of Well-Being: A Cross-National Analysis." *Social Science Research* 40:931-949.

———. 2012. "Household Dynamics and Fuelwood Consumption in Developing Countries: A Cross-National Analysis." *Population and Environment* 33 (4):365-378.

Knight, Kyle W. 2009. "Structural Human Ecology and STIRPAT: Theory and Method." In *Panel Contribution to the Population-Environment Research Network's Cyberseminar on Theoretical and Methodological Issues in the Analysis of Population Dynamics and the Environment*. New York: Population-Environment Research Network.

Knight, Kyle W., Eugene A. Rosa, and Juliet B. Schor. 2013a. "Could Working Less Reduce Pressures on the Environment? A Cross-National Panel analysis of OECD Countries, 1970–2007." *Global Environmental Change*. Forthcoming.

———. 2013b. "Reducing Growth to Achieve Environmental Sustainability: The Role of Work Hours." In *Capitalism on Trial: Explorations in the Tradition of Thomas Weisskopf*, edited by Jeannette Wicks-Lin and Robert Pollin, 187-204. Cheltenham, United Kingdom: Edward Elgar Publishing.

Lankao, Patricia Romero, John L. Tribbia, and Doug Nychkla. 2009. "Testing Theories to Explore the Drivers of Cities' Atmospheric Emissions." *Ambio* 38 (4):236-244.

Levy, Marc A., and Alexandra C. Morel. 2012. "Drivers." In *Global Environmental Outlook 5*, edited by United Nations Environment Programme, 3-30. Nairobi, Kenya: United Nations Environment Programme.

Liddle, Brantley. 2011. "Consumption-driven Environmental Impact and Age Structure Change in OECD Countries: A Cointegration-STIRPAT Analysis." *Demographic Research* 24:749-770.

———. 2013. "Urban Density and Climate Change: A STIRPAT Analysis Using City-level Data." *Journal of Transport Geography* 28:22-29. doi: http://dx.doi.org/10.1016/j.jtrangeo.2012.10.010.

Liddle, Brantley, and Sidney Lung. 2010. "Age-structure, Urbanization, and Climate Change in Developed countries: Revisiting STIRPAT for Disaggregated Population and Consumption-related Environmental Impacts." *Population and Environment* 31:317-343.

Liu, Jianguo, Gretchen C. Daily, Paul R. Ehrlich, and Gary W. Luck. 2003. "Effects of Household Dynamics on Resource Consumption and Biodiversity." *Nature* 421:530-533.

Liu, Jianguo, Vanessa Hull, Mateus Batistella, Ruth DeFries, Thomas Dietz, Feng Fu, Thomas W. Hertel, Roberto Cesar Izaurralde, Eric F. Lambin, Shuxin Li, Luiz A. Martinelli, William McConnell, Emilio F. Moran, Rosamond Naylor, Zhiyun Ouyang, Karen R. Polenske, Anette Reenberg, Gilberto de Miranda Rocha, Cynthia A. Simmons, Peter H. Verburg, Peter Vitousek, Fusuo Zhang, and Chunquan Zhu. 2013. "Framing Sustainability in a Telecoupled World." *Ecology and Society* 18(2).

Lough, Thomas S. 1996. "Energy Analysis of the Structures of Industrial Organizations." *Energy* 21 (2):131-139.

———. 1999. "Energy, Agriculture, Patriarchy and Ecocide." *Human Ecology Review* 6 (2):100-111.

Mazur, Allan. 1994. "How Does Population Growth Contribute to Rising Energy Consumption in America?" *Population and Environment* 15:371-378.

———. 2013. *Energy and Electricity in Industrial Nations: The Sociology and Technology of Energy*. Oxford: Earthscan.

Mazur, Allan, and Eugene Rosa. 1974. "Energy and Life-Style: Massive Energy Consumption May Not Be Neccessary to Maintain Current Living Standards in America." *Science* 186:607-610.

Mazur, Allan, Eugene A. Rosa, Mark Faupel, Joshua Heller, Russell Lean, and Blake Thurman. 1980. "Physiological Aspects of Communication via Mutual Gaze." *American Journal of Sociology* 86 (51-74).

McCay, Bonnie J., and Andrew P. Vayda. 1975. "New Directions in Ecology and Ecological Anthropology." *Annual Review of Anthropology* 4:293-306.

McLaughlin, Paul. 2012a. "Climate Change, Adaptation, and Vulnerability: Reconceptualizing Societal–Environment Interaction Within a Socially Constructed Adaptive Landscape." *Organization & Environment* 24 (3):269-291.

———. 2012b. "Ecological Modernization in Evolutionary Perspective." *Organization & Environment* 25 (2):178-196.

Meng, Ming, Dongxiao Niu, and Wei Shang. 2012. "CO_2 Emissions and Economic Development: China's 12th Five-year Plan." *Energy Policy* 42 (0):468-475. doi: http://dx.doi.org/10.1016/j.enpol.2011.12.013.

Moran, Emilio. 2010. "Progress in the Last Ten Years in the Study of Land Use/Cover Change and the Outlook for the Next Decade." In *Human Footprints on the Global Environment: Threats to Sustainability*, edited by Eugene A. Rosa, Andreas Diekmann, Thomas Dietz, and Carlo C. Jaeger, 135-164. Cambridge, Massachusetts: MIT Press.

O'Brien, John, Eugene A. Rosa, and John M. Stengrevics. 1983. *A Feasibility Assessment Utilizing Organizational and Sociological Research in Understanding, Assessing, and Improving Control Room Operations*. Upton, New York: Brookhaven National Laboratory.

Ostrom, Elinor. 2009. "A General Framework for Analyzing Sustainability of Social-Ecological Systems." *Science* 325:419-422.

———. 2010a. "A Long Polycentric Journey." *Annual Review of Political Science* 13:1-23.

———. 2010b. "Polycentric Systems for Coping with Collective Action and Global Environmental Change." *Global Environmental Change* 20:550-557.

Ravetz, Jerry, and Silvio Funtowicz. 1998. "Commentary." *Journal of Risk Research* 1 (1):45-48.

Reid, Walter V., Harold A. Mooney, Angela Cropper, Doris Capistrano, Stephen R. Carpenter, Kanchan Chopra, Partha Dasgupta, Thomas Dietz, Anantha Kumar Duraiappah, Rashid Hassan, Roger Kasperson, Rik Leemans, Robert M. May, Tony (A.J.) McMichael, Prabhu Pingali, Cristián Samper, Robert Sholes, Robert T. Watson, A. H. Zakri, Zhao Shidong, Neville J. Ash, Elena Bennett, Pushpam Kumar, Marcus J. Lee, Ciara Raudsepp-Hearne, Henk Simons, Jillian Thonell, and Monica B. Zurek. 2005. *Ecosystems and Human Well-Being: Synthesis*. Washington, DC: Island Press.

Ridker, Ronald G. 1972. *Population, Resources and the Environment*. Washington, DC: U.S. Government Printing Office.

Rosa, Eugene A. 1976. *Initial Eye Glance and Status Emergence in Small Groups*, Maxwell School of Citizenship and Public Affairs, Syracuse University, Syracuse, New York.

———. 1978. "Public Concern Over the Energy Problem." *The Bulletin of the Atomic Scientists* 34:5-7.

———. 1979. "Sociobiology, Biosociology, or Vulgar Biologizing?" *Sociological Symposium* 27 (Summer):28-49.

———. 1983. "Energetic Theories of Society: An Evaluative Review." *Sociological Inquiry* 53 (2):152-178.

———. 1988. ""NAMBY PAMBY and NIMBY PIMBY: Public Issues in the Siting of Hazardous Waste Facilities." *Forum for Applied Research and Public Policy* 3:114-123.

———. 1997. "Cross National Trends in Fossil Fuel Consumption, Societal Well-Being and Carbon Releases." In *Environmentally Significant Consumption: Research Directions*, edited by Paul C. Stern, Thomas Dietz, Vernon W. Ruttan, Robert H. Socolow, and James L. Sweeney, 100-109. Washington, DC: National Academy Press.

———. 1998a. "Comments on Commentary by Ravetz and Funtowicz: 'Old Fashioned Hypertext'." *Journal of Risk Research* 1 (2):111-115.

———. 1998b. "Metatheoretical Foundations for Post-Normal Risk." *Journal of Risk Research* 1:15-44.

———. 1998c. Toward Ecolage©: Art and the Environment.

———. 2007. "Long-Term Stewardship and Risk Management: Analytic and Policy Challenges." In *Long-Term Management of Contaminated Sites*, edited by Thomas Leschine, 227-255. Amsterdam: Elsevier.

————. 2010. "The Logical Status of Risk – to Burnish or to Dull." *Journal of Risk Research* 13 (3):239-253.

————. 2011. "Background Comments to the Blue Ribbon Commission on America's Nuclear Future." In *Blue Ribbon Commisssion on America's Nuclear Future*. Washington, DC: Blue Ribbon Commisssion on America's Nuclear Future.

Rosa, Eugene A., and Donald L. Clark Jr. 1999. "Historical Routes to Technological Gridlock: Nuclear Technology as Prototypical Vehicle." *Research in Social Problems and Public Policy* 7:21-57.

Rosa, Eugene A., and Lee Clarke. 2012. "Collective Hunch?: Risk as the Real and the Elusive." *Journal of Environmental Studies and Science* 2:39-52.

Rosa, Eugene A., and Thomas Dietz. 2010a. "Global Transformations: PaSSAGE to a New Ecological Era." In *Human Footprints on the Global Environment: Threats to Sustainability*, edited by Eugene A. Rosa, Andreas Diekmann, Thomas Dietz, and Carlo C. Jaeger, 1-45. Cambridge, Massachusetts: MIT Press.

————. 2010b. "Human Dimensions of Coupled Human-Natural Systems: A Look Backward and Forward." In *Human Footprints on the Global Environment: Threats to Sustainability*, edited by Eugene A. Rosa, Andreas Diekmann, Thomas Dietz, and Carlo C. Jaeger, 295-314. Cambridge, Massachusetts: MIT Press.

————. 2012. "Human Drivers of National Greenhouse Gas Emissions." *Nature Climate Change* 2:581-586.

Rosa, Eugene A., Thomas Dietz, Richard H. Moss, Scott Atran, and Susanne Moser. 2012. "Risk and Sustainability: A Look at Two Global Threats." *Solutions* 3 (2):59-65.

Rosa, Eugene A., and Riley E. Dunlap. 1994. "The Polls-Poll Trends: Nuclear Energy: Three Decades of Public Opinion." *Public Opinion Quarterly* 58:295-325.

Rosa, Eugene A., and William R. Freudenburg. 1984. "Nuclear Power at the Crossroads." In *Public Reactions to Nuclear Power: Are There Critical Masses?*, edited by William R. Freudenburg and Eugene A. Rosa, 3-37. Boulder, Colorado: Westview/AAAS.

Rosa, Eugene A., and Patrick Humphreys. 1988. "A Decomposition Approach to Measuring Human Error Probabilities in Nuclear Power Plants: A Case Example of the SLIM-MAUD Methodology." In *Strategic Decision Support: Frames and Case Studies*, edited by Patrick Humphreys, O. Larichev, A. Vari, and J. Vecsenyi. Amsterdam: North Holland.

Rosa, Eugene A., Patrick C. Humphreys, C. M. Spettell, and D. E. Embrey. 1984. *Application of Slim-Maud: A Test of an Interactive Computer-Based Method for Organizing Expert Assessment of Human Performance and Reliability*. Upton, Long Island: Brookhaven National Laboratory.

Rosa, Eugene A., Kenneth M. Keating, and Clifford L. Staples. 1981. "Energy, Economic Growth and Quality of Life: A Cross-National Trend Analysis." In *International Congress on Applied Systems Research and Cybernetics*, edited by G.E. Lasker. New York: Pergamon.

Rosa, Eugene A., Gary E. Machlis, and Kenneth M. Keating. 1988. "Energy and Society." *Annual Review of Sociology* 14:149-172.

Rosa, Eugene A., and Noriyuki Matsuda. 2005. "Risk Perceptions in the Risk Society: The Cognitive Architecture of Risk Between Americans and Japanese." In *Peace, Security, and Kyosei*, edited by Yoichiro Murakami, Noriko Kawamura and Shin Chiba, 113-130. Pullman, Washington: Washington State University Press.

Rosa, Eugene A., Noriyuki Matsuda, and Randall R. Kleinhesselink. 2000. "The Cognitive Architecture of Risk: Pancultural Unity or Cultural Shaping?" In *Comparative Risk Perception*, edited by Ortwin Renn and Bernd Rohrmann, 185-210. Dordrecth, The Netherlands: Kluwer.

Rosa, Eugene A., Sabrina McCormick, and R. Scott Frey. 2007. "The Sociology of Risk." In *21st Century Sociology: A Reference Handbook*, edited by Clifton D. Bryant and Dennis L. Peck, 81-87. Thousand Oak, California: Sage.

Rosa, Eugene A., Aaron McCright, and Ortwin Renn. 2013. *The Risk Society Revisited: Social Theory and Governance*. Philadelphia: Temple University Press.

Rosa, Eugene A., Seth P. Tuler, Baruch Fischhoff, Thomas Webler, Sharon M. Friedman, Richard E. Sclove, Kristin Shrader-Frachette, Mary R. English, Roger E. Kasperson, Robert L. Goble, Thomas M. Leschine, William Freudenburg, Caron Chess, Charles Perrow, Kai Erikson, and James F. Short. 2010. "Nuclear Waste: Knowledge Waste?" *Science* 329:762-763.

Rosa, Eugene, Richard York, and Thomas Dietz. 2004. "Tracking the Anthropogenic Drivers of Ecological Impacts." *AMBIO: A Journal of the Human Environment* 33 (8):509-512.

Ruckelshaus, William W. 1985. "Risk, Science and Democracy." *Issues in Science and Technology* 1:19-38.

Short, James A. 1984. "The Social Fabric at Risk: Toward the Social Transformation of Risk Analysis." *American Sociological Review* 49:711-725.

Soule, Peter T., and Jennifer L. DeHart. 1998. "Assessing IPAT Using Production- and Consumption-based Measures of I." *Social Science Quarterly* 79 (4):754-765.

Squalli, Jay. 2009. "Immigration and Environmental Emissions: A U.S. County-level Analysis." *Population and Environment* 30:247-260.

———. 2010. "An Empirical Assessment of U.S. State-level Immigration and Environmental Emissions." *Ecological Economics* 59 (5):1170-1175.

Starr, Chauncey. 1969. "Societal Benefit Versus Technological Risk." *Science* 236:280-285.

Stern, Paul C. 1986. "Blind Spots in Policy Analysis: What Economics Doesn't Say about Energy Use." *Journal of Policy Analysis and Management* 5:200-227.

———. 2000. "Toward a Coherent Theory of Environmentally Significant Behavior." *Journal of Social Issues* 56 (3):407-424.

———. 2005. "Deliberative Methods for Understanding Environmental Systems." *BioScience* 55:976-982.

Stern, Paul C., Thomas Dietz, Troy Abel, Gregory A. Guagnano, and Linda Kalof. 1999. "A Social Psychological Theory of Support for Social Movements: The Case of Environmentalism." *Human Ecology Review* 6:81-97.

Stern, Paul C., Thomas J. Wilbanks, Susan Cozzens, and Eugene Rosa. 2009. *Generic Lessons Learned about Societal Responoses to Emerging Technologies Perceived as Involving Risks*. Oak Ridge, Tennessee: Oak Ridge National Laboratory.

Stokes, Donald E. 1997. *Pasteur's Quadrant: Basic Science and Technological Innovation*. Washington, DC: Brookings Institution.

Tallarico, Carol D., and Arvid C. Johnson. 2010. "The Implications of Global Ecological Elasticities for Carbon Control: A STIRPAT Formulation." *Journal of Management Policy and Practice* 11 (4):86-94.

Turner, B. L. III, Eric F. Lambin, and Annette Reenberg. 2007. "The Emergence of Land Change Science for Global Environmental Change and Sustainability." *Proceedings of the National Academy of Sciences, USA* 104 (52):20666-20671.

U.S. Commission on Population Growth and the American Future. 1972. *Population and the American Future*. New York: Signet.

U.S. National Research Council. 1992. *Global Environmental Change: Understanding the Human Dimensions*. Washington, DC: National Academy Press.

———. 1996. *Understanding Risk: Informing Decisions in a Democratic Society*. Edited by Paul C. Stern and Harvey Fineberg. Washington, DC: National Academy Press.

———. 2008. *Public Participation in Environmental Assessment and Decision Making*. Edited by Thomas Dietz and Paul C. Stern. Washington, DC: National Academy Press.

Vayda, Andrew P. 1988. "Actions and Consequences as Objects of Explanation in Human Ecology." In *Human Ecology: Research and Applications*, edited by Richard J. Borden, Jamien Jacobs, and Gerald L. Young, 9-18. College Park, Maryland: Society for Human Ecology.

———. 2009. *Explaining Human Actions and Environmental Change*. Lanham, Maryland: Altamira Press.

Waggoner, Paul E., and Jesse H. Ausubel. 2002. "A Framework for Sustainability Science: A Renovated IPAT Identity." *Proceedings of the National Academy of Sciences, USA* 99 (12):7860-7865.

Wang, Mingquan, Yanyu Song, Jingshuang Liu, and Jinda Wang. 2012. "Exploring the Anthropogenic Driving Forces of China's Provincial Environmental Impacts." *International Journal of Sustainable Development & World Ecology* 19 (5):442-450. doi: 10.1080/13504509.2012.712924.

Wang, Mingwei, Yue Che, Kai Yang, Min Wang, Lijun Xiong, and Yuchi Huang. 2011. "A Local-scale Low-carbon Plan Based on the STIRPAT Model and the Scenario Method: The Case of Minhang District, Shanghai, China." *Energy Policy* 39 (11):6981-6990.

Whitfield, Stephen, Eugene A. Rosa, Thomas Dietz, and Amy Dan. 2009. "The Future of Nuclear Power: Value Orientations and Risk Perceptions." *Risk Analysis* 29 (3):425-437.

Yamaji, K., R. Matsuhashi, Y. Nagata, and Y. Kaya. 1991. "An Integrated System for CO_2/Energy/GNP Analysis: Case Studies on Economic Measures for CO_2 Reduction in Japan." Paper read at Workshop on CO2 Reduction and Removal: Measures for the Next Century, 19-21 March 1991, at Laxenburg, Austria.

York, Richard. 2012a. "Asymmetric Effects of Economic Growth and Decline on CO_2 Emissions." *Nature Climate Change* 2(11):762-764.

———. 2012b. "Do Alternative Energy Sources Displace Fossil Fuels?" *Nature Climate Change* 2:441-443.

York, Richard, and Eugene A. Rosa. 2012. "Choking on Modernity: A Human Ecology of Air Pollution." *Social Problems* 59 (2):282-300.

York, Richard, Eugene A. Rosa, and Thomas Dietz. 2002. "Bridging Environmental Science with Environmental Policy: Plasticity of Population, Affluence and Technology." *Social Science Quarterly* 83 (1):18-34.

———. 2003a. "Footprints on the Earth: The Environmental Consequences of Modernity." *American Sociological Review* 68 (2):279-300.

————. 2003b. "A Rift in Modernity? Assessing the Anthropogenic Sources of Global Climate Change with the STIRPAT Model." *International Journal of Sociology and Social Policy* 23 (10):31-51.

————. 2003c. "STIRPAT, IPAT and ImPACT: Analytic Tools for Unpacking the Driving Forces of Environmental Impact." *Ecological Economics* 46:351-365.

————. 2005. "The Ecological Footprint Intensity of National Economies." *Journal of Industrial Ecology* 8 (4):139-145.

Zhang, Chuanguo, and Yan Lin. 2012. "Panel Estimation for Urbanization, Energy Consumption and CO_2 Emissions: A regional analysis in China." *Energy Policy* 49 (0):488-498. doi: http://dx.doi.org/10.1016/j.enpol.2012.06.048.

Contributors

Thomas Dietz

Thomas Dietz is a professor of sociology, environmental science and policy, and animal studies, and assistant vice president for environmental research at Michigan State University.

He holds a doctorate in ecology from the University of California, Davis, and a bachelor of general studies from Kent State University. At MSU he was founding director of the Environmental Science and Policy Program and associate dean in the Colleges of Social Science, Agriculture and Natural Resources and Natural Science. Dr. Dietz is a fellow of the American Association for the Advancement of Science.

At the National Research Council he has served as chair of the U.S. National Research Council Committee on Human Dimensions of Global Change and the Panel on Public Participation in Environmental Assessment and Decision Making, and as vice chair of the Panel on Advancing the Science of Climate Change of the America's Climate Choices study. He has coauthored or coedited twelve books and more than 100 papers and book chapters. His current research examines structural human ecology, environmental values, and the interplay between science and democracy in environmental issues.

Sylvia Hiller

Sylvia Hiller, sociologist and economist, is a research associate in the Interdisciplinary Research Unit for Risk Governance and Sustainable Technology Development (ZIRN) at the University of Stuttgart and the nonprofit company DIALOGIK, a research institute for the investigation of communication and participation processes in environmental policy making. Her research interests include sociology of technology as well as risk participation and risk communication involving aspects of the public perception of climate engineering and ways of involving the public in the discourse on climate engineering.

Andrew K. Jorgenson

Andrew K. Jorgenson, Ph.D., conducts comparative-international research on the political-economy and human ecology of environmental change and public health.

His research on such topics is published in dozens of scholarly journals, including the *American Journal of Sociology, Social Forces, Social Problems, Social Science Research, Global Environmental Politics, International Sociology, Ecological Economics, Organization & Environment,* and *Human Ecology Review.*

He is professor and director of graduate studies in sociology at the University of Utah, as well as a faculty affiliate of the Environmental and Sustainability Studies Program and an affiliate investigator for the Institute for Policy and International Affairs. He is also a lead contributing member of the American Sociological Association's Task Force on Sociology and Global Climate Change.

Roger E. Kasperson

Roger E. Kasperson is research professor and distinguished scientist at the George Perkins Marsh Institute at Clark University. He received his doctorate from the University of Chicago. His expertise is in risk analysis, global environmental change, and environmental policy.

Dr. Kasperson is a fellow of the American Association for the Advancement of Science and the Society for Risk Analysis. He has served on numerous committees of the U.S. National Research Council. He chaired the International Geographical Commission on Critical Situations/Regions in Global Environmental Change and has served on EPA's Science Advisory Board.

He is an elected member of the National Academy of Sciences and the American Academy of Arts and Sciences, and has authored or coedited 22 books and monographs and more than 146 articles or chapters in scholarly journals or books. From 2000 to 2004, Kasperson was executive director of the Stockholm Environment Institute in Sweden.

Kasperson has been honored by the Association of American Geographers for his hazards research and in 2006 he was the recipient of the Distinguished Achievement Award of the Society for Risk Analysis. In 2007, he was appointed as associate scientist at the National Center for Atmospheric Research in the United States. His current research involves disaster reduction, funded by the Chinese government.

Sandra T. Marquart-Pyatt

Sandra T. Marquart-Pyatt (Ph.D. Ohio State University) is an associate professor in sociology and the Environmental Science and Policy Program. Her research and teaching areas of expertise are in comparative social change, environmental sociology, political sociology, and quantitative methods. Her current work focuses on identifying cross-national patterns in environmental attitudes, beliefs, behavioral intentions, and behaviors that include climate change, general concern for the environment, and sustainability. Other current projects examine democratic attitudes, views of welfare state institutions, and political participation comparatively.

Dr. Marquart-Pyatt's work has been published in such journals as *Environment, Society and Natural Resources, Social Science Quarterly, Social Science Research, Political Behavior, Rural Sociology*, and *International Journal of Sociology*. She is coauthor of the monograph *Nonrecursive Models: Endogeneity, Reciprocal Relationships and Feedback Loops* in the SAGE series on Quantitative Applications in the Social Sciences (QASS). She has also been an instructor in the InterUniversity Consortium for Political and Social Research's (ICPSR) Summer Program in Quantitative Methods at the University of Michigan for a graduate seminar on simultaneous equation models.

Allan Mazur

Allan Mazur, a sociologist and engineer, is professor of public affairs in the Maxwell School at Syracuse University, and a fellow of the American Association for the Advancement of Science. He is author or coauthor of over 150 academic articles and nine books, most recently *Energy and Electricity in Industrial Nations: The Sociology and Technology of Energy* (Routledge 2013).

Mazur does research on social aspects of science, technology and environment, and on biological aspects of sociology.

Ortwin Renn

Ortwin Renn serves as full professor and chair of environmental sociology and technology assessment at the University of Stuttgart (Germany). He directs the Stuttgart Research Center for Interdisciplinary Risk and Innovation Studies at the University of Stuttgart (ZIRIUS) and the nonprofit company DIALOGIK, a research institute for the investigation of communication and participation processes in environmental policy making. Renn also serves as adjunct professor for integrated risk analysis at Stavanger University (Norway) and as affiliate professor for risk governance at Beijing Normal University.

Ortwin Renn has a doctoral degree in social psychology from the University of Cologne. His career has included teaching and research positions at the Juelich Nuclear Research Center, Clark University (Worcester, USA), the Swiss Institute of Technology (Zurich), and the Center of Technology Assessment (Stuttgart). He is a member of the Scientific Advisory Board of EU President Barroso, the Scientific and Technical Council of the International Risk Governance Council (IRGC) in Lausanne, the National Academy of Disaster Reduction and Emergency Management of the People's Republic of China, and the Risk Communication Advisory Committee of the European Food Safety Authority in Parma (Italy), among others. In 2012 he was elected president of the Society for Risk Analysis (SRA).

His honors include an honorary doctorate from the Swiss Institute of Technology (ETH Zurich), an honorary affiliate professorship at the Technical University Munich, and the Distinguished Achievement Award of the Society for Risk Analysis (SRA), and several best publication awards. Renn has published more than 30 books and 250 articles, most prominently the monograph, *Risk Governance* (Earthscan: London 2008).

Dirk Scheer

Dirk Scheer studied political science and romance literature at the University of Heidelberg (Germany) and the University of Seville (Spain). He holds a doctorate in sociology from the University of Stuttgart. Since 2008 he has been a researcher in the Department for Sociology of Technologies and Environment, University of Stuttgart. From 2001 until 2008, Scheer was project leader at the Institute for Ecological Economy Research (IÖW), where he carried out research projects on topics such as environmental governance, product related environmental policy, sustainability impact assessment, and risk communication. His main emphasis while working for the Stuttgart Research Center for Interdisciplinary Risk and Innovation Studies (ZIRIUS) has been on potentials of simulation technologies at the science-policy interface, technology assessment studies, and risk governance for emerging technologies. He is editor or author of several books, including *The Governance of Integrated Product Policy* (Greenleaf Publishing 2006), and *Computersimulationen in politischen Entscheidungsprozessen* (Springer 2013), as well as several peer-reviewed articles and scientific reports.

Paul C. Stern

Paul C. Stern is a senior scholar at the National Research Council/National Academy of Sciences, where for over 20 years he was director of its Standing Committee on the Human Dimensions of Global Change. He is also president of the Social and Environmental Research Institute, Greenfield, Massachusetts.

His research interests include the determinants of environmentally significant behavior, particularly at the individual level; participatory processes for informing environmental decision making; and the governance of environmental resources and risks. He is coauthor of the textbook *Environmental Problems and Human Behavior* (second edition, 2002); and coeditor of numerous National Research Council publications, including *Public Participation in Environmental Assessment and Decision Making* (2008), *Decision Making for the Environment: Social and Behavioral Science Priorities* (2005), *The Drama of the Commons* (2002), *Making Climate Forecasts Matter* (1999), and *Understanding Risk: Informing Decisions in a Democratic Society* (1996). He coauthored the article "The Struggle to Govern the Commons," which was published in *Science* in 2003 and won the 2005 Sustainability Science Award from the Ecological Society of America.

He is a fellow of the American Association for the Advancement of Science and the American Psychological Association. He holds a bachelor's degree from Amherst College and master's and doctorate degrees from Clark University, all in psychology.

Richard York

Richard York is professor of sociology and environmental studies at the University of Oregon, the Friends of the Institute member of the School of Social Science for 2013-14 at the Institute for Advanced Study, and chair of the Environment and Technology Section of the American Sociological Association.

His research examines the anthropogenic forces driving environmental degradation and the philosophy, history, and sociology of science. He has published over fifty articles, including ones in *American Sociological Review, Conservation Biology, Sociological Theory*, and *Theory and Society*. He has published three books with Monthly Review Press: *The Critique of Intelligent Design* and *The Ecological Rift*, both with John Bellamy Foster and Brett Clark, and *The Science and Humanism of Stephen Jay Gould* with Brett Clark.

He has twice (2004 and 2007) received the Outstanding Publication Award and once (2011) the honorable mention for the same award from the Environment and Technology Section (ETS) of the American Sociological Association (ASA). He has also received the Teaching and Mentorship Award (2011) from the ETS of the ASA.

Index